Maruta Herding
Inventing the Muslim Cool

global local Islam

Maruta Herding (Dr.) is a sociologist at the German Youth Institute (Deutsches Jugendinstitut e.V.) in Halle, Germany. The book »Inventing the Muslim Cool« is the publication of her doctoral research, which she conducted at the University of Cambridge. Her research interests include the study of young people, subcultures and Muslims in Europe.

MARUTA HERDING

Inventing the Muslim Cool
Islamic Youth Culture in Western Europe

[transcript]

Bibliographic information published by the Deutsche Nationalbibliothek
The Deutsche Nationalbibliothek lists this publication in the Deutsche Natio-
nalbibliografie; detailed bibliographic data are available on the Internet at
http://dnb.d-nb.de

© 2013 transcript Verlag, Bielefeld

Cover concept: Kordula Röckenhaus, Bielefeld
Cover illustration: Sarah Elenany: »Throw yo' hands«, London, 2008.
Printed by Majuskel Medienproduktion GmbH, Wetzlar
ISBN 978-3-8376-2511-0

Table of Contents

Acknowledgements

This book is based on my PhD dissertation, which I completed at the University of Cambridge in 2012. In preparing and writing it, I was privileged to work with and enjoy the support of a vast amount of people who have contributed to this project in one way or other, and I am much indebted to them.

First of all, I would like to thank all the interviewees who participated in this study and granted me very personal insights into their lives and the members of Muslim organisations who welcomed me at their events. I equally owe thanks to my PhD supervisor Göran Therborn, whose continued enthusiasm for my topic was a constant motivation and whose academic sagacity provided me with the best support I could have wished for. My examiners Monika Wohlrab-Sahr and David Lehmann deserve many thanks for their insightful comments and for making the viva voce an inspiring discussion in an unconstrained setting. On an institutional level I thank the Department of Sociology and Girton College for many ways of personal support, and the latter also for a generous fieldwork studentship. The Economic and Social Research Council (ESRC) has equipped me with a full fees scholarship and research training, and the Kurt Hahn Trust with a maintenance bursary.

The transcript Verlag has provided me with excellent support in turning my PhD dissertation into a book. Among others of her colleagues I would especially like to thank Stefanie Hanneken for her assistance and for the prompt communication at all times. I am grateful to the copyright owners of the images used in Chapter III and I confirm that copyright permission has been obtained for all figures in this book.

I am thankful to Amina Yaqin and Peter Morey of the *Framing Muslims* research network for a paper invitation and their continued interest in my research and to Gordon Lynch for inviting me to present my project at his workshops within the *Religion and Youth Programme*. Jane Nolan has helped me with qualitative data analysis and typologies and Jan Kruse through his methodological expertise and advice. I also thank Gary Alan Fine for profound discussions about the choice of fieldwork places, Jørgen Nielsen for his comments on my papers at conferences, and Jocelyne Cesari for the time I spent in her research team of the *Euro-Islam* website project. During my fieldwork in Frankfurt I have enjoyed the support of Ursula Apitzsch in her biography research colloquium and in Marseille that of the researchers at the EHESS institute *Sociologie, Histoire, Anthropologie des Dynamiques Culturelles (SHADyC)*.

Academically as well as personally, I am much obliged to Lois Lee and Shirin Shahrokni for their comments on single chapters, for mutual "supervisions", encouragement and friendship. I owe thanks to Martin Langebach for our collaboration in the analysis of our interviews and in fighting methodological struggles. Everyone working in the Attic of the Department of Sociology at Cambridge deserves a round of thanks for contributing to a great community and work setting. I am also thankful to the students who helped transcribing the interviews and to Paula Francis and Margaret Hiley for proofreading.

Finally, I would like to express a very personal thanks. I am grateful to my parents for cheering along all throughout my PhD. Last but very certainly not least, I deeply thank Georg for appearing in my life at the outset of this project and our yet unborn child who waited just long enough to let me finalise the manuscript of this book.

I. Introduction

Clothing to believe in
URBAN UMMAH

Qui a dit que les musulmans n'avaient pas
d'humour?
A PART ÇA TOUT VA BIEN

15 Jahre MJD... und kein bisschen leise!
MUSLIMISCHE JUGEND IN DEUTSCHLAND

Put your tawheeds up, ones in the air
And praise Allah
POETIC PILGRIMAGE

This isn't your ordinary Friday talk. This is the
iCircle. We have games, workshops, football,
and fun-tastic stuff that will make you shout Al-
lahuakbar out loud without being perceived as
some sort of terrorist.
YOUNG MUSLIMS UK

Read Quran, charge your iman
STYLEISLAM

Du kannst mir Millionen bieten
doch eine Sache ist klar
Das beste Angebot
kommt immer noch von Allah
AMMAR114

Comedy, 200% halal
SAMIA, ORIENTAL COMIC

Mach mit beim Muslim Comedy Contest!
WAYMO & STYLEISLAM

Waymo salamt dich
WAYMO JUGENDPLATTFORM

These slogans, brand mottos and lyrics encapsulate the spirit of a young, European Islam. They are found on T-shirts, in rap songs, youth magazines, online platforms, video clips, comedy shows and at youth meetings that have been developed by and for young Muslims in France, Germany and the United Kingdom. Having mainly emerged in the first decade of the twenty-first century, this phenomenon is rather young itself and is still a largely unfamiliar sight.[1]

This study is an exploration of the recent development of Islamic youth culture in Western Europe, which is a combination of religion and youth culture and which manifests itself in explicitly religious rap, Islamic comedy, young urban fashion with pious slogans or media products catering for young European Muslims. In this book, I aim to present a well-rounded picture of this youth culture and to shed light on its character and the details of its cultural components. Its emergence gives rise to many questions about contemporary Islam, the significance of youth cultures in society and in Islam, and about the context in which it takes place – Western Europe as a non-Muslim place with a significant Muslim presence. I have therefore researched into why Islamic youth culture has become established and what motivates people to create it, either individually or as part of a perceived movement.

My approach is an ethnographic one, providing a close description of Islamic youth culture in its diverse dimensions, and at the same time giving a thorough analysis of the reasons for its development. This takes into account a vast array of artefacts, my own observations among the participants and in-depth interviews with the producers of this youth culture, all of which I collected during extensive field research. To conceptualise this, I have drawn on youth culture theory and on concepts of hybridity, as well as previous research in the field of Islam in Europe. This combination should illuminate the study of the empirical phenomenon, which in turn reveals some of the limitations of these theoretic approaches.

The label "Muslim" can never be a given category, as it raises questions of self-identification and ascriptions by others. Thus, when I claim to research young Muslims, this requires some clarification. One definition that comes to mind is that of family background. Theologically, a child born into a Muslim family is automatically a Muslim, but this only applies to clear-cut cases and simplifies multifaceted issues. For instance, it homogenises people of various convictions, ranging from pious devotion to belief without practice, to agnosticism or indifference. All of these people could have a Muslim family background, but to label them "Muslim" would essentialise a very diverse population and take part of their identity as a whole – not to mention the exclusion of con-

---

1   Arabic expressions are explained in the Glossary in Appendix F.

verts to Islam. Another basis for a definition would be self-attribution, regarding only those as Muslim who identify themselves as such, clearing the term of its predetermined ethnic dimension. But at times research practicality requires a slightly more pragmatic approach. For example, the following section presents data on the Muslim populations of Western Europe as background information. The figures correspond to people with family ties to Islamic countries rather than taking individual self-identification into account, since the large numbers are based on estimates. In this study, however, I look at "practising Muslims" with a high religiosity, who attend events with a strong religious focus or express their faith in public – often in the form of Islamic youth cultural artefacts. The population under study is therefore only a fraction of the larger category of all those who are Muslim by background.

Islam and Muslims in Germany

Muslims have been present in Germany since the seventeenth century, when during several wars the Ottomans came to Germany, either as prisoners of war or as military officials (Abdullah 1981). After World War I, students, intellectuals and converts made up the small but growing Muslim community that was mainly active in Berlin and opened the first mosque in Berlin-Wilmersdorf, which still exists today, in 1924 (Deutsche Islam Konferenz 2008). The first major wave of immigration from Islamic countries, however, came as a result of bilateral agreements between West Germany and several Mediterranean countries in the 1950s and 1960s, recruiting "guest workers" for the German economy, including contracts with Turkey in 1961, but also with Morocco (1963), Tunisia (1965) and Yugoslavia (1968) (ibid.). When Germany ended the agreements in 1973, many of the immigrant workers remained in their new home country and were often joined by their families. However, Germany denied their long-term presence and insisted on their status as temporary migrants (Penn/Lambert 2009: 35–36). Until 2000, this was reflected in the German citizenship rules, which were traditionally based on descent rather than place of birth. As Ruud Koopmans et al. (2005) show, Germany's naturalisation rate is still the lowest in Western Europe, which explains the high percentage of foreigners among Muslims living in Germany. Roger Penn and Paul Lambert point out, however, that a "partial incorporation" took place, since although full political and citizenship rights were largely denied, immigrants were granted inclusion into the state welfare system, including social security and public housing, the latter preventing ghettoised residential patterns from emerging (Penn/Lambert 2009: 37).

A report by the Federal Office for Migration and Refugees (Bundesamt für Migration und Flüchtlinge, BAMF) estimated the number of Muslims living in

Germany to be 3.8 to 4.3 million, or 4.6% to 5.2% of the general population, which is more than previous estimates have suggested (Haug et al. 2009). Around 45% have German nationality, while 55% own a foreign passport; German converts, of whom no reliable numbers exist, are not counted in this study (ibid.: 74–75). The estimate relies on a thorough analysis of nearly 50 Islamic countries of origin from which people have migrated into Germany. The most important regions from where foreign Muslims and naturalised German Muslims originate are Turkey (2,600,000), Southeast Europe (550,000), the Middle East (330,000), North Africa (280,000), South/Southeast Asia (187,000), then Iran, Central Asia and other parts of Africa (ibid.: 61–74). The vast majority are Sunni Muslims (72%), followed by Alevis (14%), Shiites (7%) and other smaller denominations (ibid.: 128–131).

The BAMF study reveals that the average age of Muslims living in Germany is rather young (just over 30), compared with the average age of the overall German population and of those with a non-Islamic migratory background. The proportion of children under 16 years (around 25% of German Muslims) is more than 10% higher than that of the general population, while the 16- to 24-year-olds (nearly 17%) make up 6% more than their corresponding age group among non-Muslims (Haug et al. 2009: 97–99). If the total Muslim population amounts to around 4 million, the share of young Muslims under 25 thus adds up to 42% or approximately 1.7 million.

Because Islam is not institutionalised like the Church, the religion has not acquired the legal status of a religious community in Germany, which would, for instance, be a prerequisite for providing Islamic education in schools. Religious organisations usually take the form of associations (*Vereine, e.V.*) that are recognised under general association law, and some of these have been acknowledged as religious communities on a local level (Robbers 2009: 141–142; Bodenstein 2010: 57–59). Owing to the lack of a formalised dialogue partner, the Interior Minister at the time, Wolfgang Schäuble, initiated the German Islam Conference (*Deutsche Islam Konferenz*) in 2006, which has become the most important committee for the state to interact with a broad variety of Muslim organisations and individuals shaping Islam in Germany (Robbers 2009: 142; Rohe 2010: 218–219). Committed to improving integration, it provides policy recommendations on topics including imam training, mosque construction or Islamic education in schools. Apart from an annual plenary meeting, several project groups meet frequently to develop more practical initiatives such as improved integration into the labour market or the prevention of radicalisation of young people.[2] Although it is obvious on the one hand, and highly contested by parts of the

---

2   Deutsche Islam Konferenz: http://www.deutsche-islam-konferenz.de.

population on the other hand, it was an important affirmation by the former German President Christian Wulff to underline that Islam is a part of Germany, which he stated in a speech on the occasion of 20 years of German reunification (Der Tagesspiegel 03/10/2010).

There have been several attempts by Muslim representatives to create umbrella organisations for the many associations, in order to speak with one voice. Around 150,000 Turkish Muslims are represented by the Turkish Islamic Union of the Institution for Religion (*Türkisch-Islamische Union der Anstalt für Religion e.V., DITIB*), which is supervised by the Turkish Presidency for Religious Affairs. The Central Council of Muslims in Germany (*Zentralrat der Muslime in Deutschland e.V., ZMD*) represents numerous mosque associations with a total of 12,000 members of chiefly non-Turkish background. The Islam Council for the Federal Republic of Germany (*Islamrat für die Bundesrepublik Deutschland*) has 136,000 members and hosts the Islamic Community Milli Görüş (*Islamische Gemeinschaft Milli Görüş, IGMG*), an international Turkish movement that has been strongly criticised for anti-democratic tendencies, but which has also been described as "post-Islamist" (Schiffauer 2010). Finally, the Union of Islamic Cultural Centres (*Verband der Islamischen Kulturzentren e.V., VIKZ*) represents 20,000 Sunni Muslims (Robbers 2009: 143). In 2007, these four umbrella organisations (DITIB, ZMD, Islamrat, VIKZ) established the Coordination Council of Muslims in Germany (*Koordinierungsrat der Muslime in Deutschland, KRM*) to facilitate cooperation in matters of common interest (ibid.; Bodenstein 2010: 60). There are several other organisations, including the Federation of European Alevites (*Föderation der europäischen Aleviten, AABF*), representing at least 20,000 German Alevites. The problem is, however, that the majority of German Muslims are not part of these large organisations, whose representatives therefore cannot claim to speak on behalf of the entire Muslim population, since only 10 to 15% seem to be represented by the umbrella organisations (Robbers 2009: 143). Five organisations have been banned for not acting in line with the constitution (ibid.: 142).

The largest youth organisation is the Muslim Youth in Germany (*Muslimische Jugend in Deutschland, MJD*), founded in 1994 in Berlin, which has several hundred members according to its own website.[3] Local groups meet regularly, and an annual gathering with up to 1,500 young people takes place at Easter every year. While the MJD attracts most young Muslims, not least by being ethnically mixed as well as highly organised and present all over Germany, other organisations also have a youth branch, including the Milli Görüş and smaller mosque associations.

---

3 Muslimische Jugend in Deutschland: http://www.mjd-net.de.

Around 2,600 buildings serve as mosques, many of which are not purpose-built, as only about 180 of them have been erected as a traditional mosque, with another 150 currently under construction. There have been a few conflicts with sections of the general population regarding the construction of some of the mosques, but the establishment of prayer houses is recognised and protected as a matter of religious freedom by the law (Rohe 2010: 221). Islamic education is usually provided by mosque associations, but as part of the school curriculum it remains a matter of debate. A number of German states have introduced such classes, but this is far from providing a general model on the federal level (ibid.: 223; Robbers 2009: 144–146). In 2010, the German Council of Science and Humanities (*Wissenschaftsrat*) recommended that universities should take over the training of Islamic schoolteachers and imams (Wissenschaftsrat 2010: 35–44, 69–80), which is currently being put into practice at the universities of Erlangen-Nürnberg, Frankfurt, Münster and Osnabrück. The degree of advice that Islamic organisations should provide in this process is still under debate (Euro-Islam 30/01/2010).

Wearing the headscarf, *hijab*, is permitted in public spaces, schools and offices, but in many German states it is banned for schoolteachers. Federal law requires an equal treatment of religions – either allowing or banning all religious symbols – but it is up to the individual states to implement laws based on this. Court appeals and public debate are likely to continue (Rohe 2010: 228–229).

Recent public debates on Islam in Germany have included a variety of topics and voices. In 2010, Muslims and non-Muslims alike discussed the question whether it were possible and legitimate to criticise Islam, making use of the full spectrum of opinions from Islamophobic statements to rational, weighted arguments, to apologetic declarations (Euro-Islam 05/02/2010); in the same year, a small anti-Islamic party *(Die Freiheit)* was founded. Following the recommendation for universities to train imams and Islamic teachers, discussions began about the role of state institutions in religious affairs and the influence of religious institutions on state curricula. The ongoing discourse about security issues and radicalisation was fuelled once more by the attack of a radical Islamist, who killed two American soldiers at Frankfurt airport in March 2011. Debates emphasised the possibly growing influence of extreme Salafist thought among German Muslims (Der Spiegel 14/03/2011). Islamophobia is addressed once in a while, though tentatively, but it was discussed profoundly after a supremacist stabbed and killed Egyptian Marwa el-Sherbini in a Dresden courtroom during a trial in which he was charged with previous racist remarks against the woman (Die Zeit 14/07/2009). Highly emotional disputes were fought after the 2010 publication of Thilo Sarrazin's book, which depicts Germany's alleged "down-

fall" caused by the country's many Muslims who did not contribute to the economy and instead took advantage of the welfare system or were criminals (Sarrazin 2010). Although the author enjoyed significant popularity from sections of
the population, he faced massive criticism from the majority of politicians and
members of the public, who largely stood by their Muslim fellow citizens. Even
if similar debates take place in other European countries, the German case is
often marked by a certain indecisiveness about how to deal with Islam, which
has not been recognised as playing a significant role in public life for a long
time, and – for better or worse – all varieties of opinions are present in public
debate.

Islam and Muslims in France

Historically, the relationship of France and Islam stretches back a long time, for
as early as 716 a group of soldiers from North Africa arrived and later built a
mosque in Narbonne near the Mediterranean. Similar appearances continued
until the nineteenth century, but with the colonisation of Algeria in 1830, France
was exposed to more intense contact with Muslim populations (Fetzer/Soper
2005: 63). The first wave of immigration took place during World War I, when
North Africans, but also West Africans and Comorians came to serve in the ar-
my and work in factories, whose contributions were rewarded with the construction of the large Mosque of Paris in 1926 (ibid.). The second and much larger
immigration wave was due to economic recruitment after World War II, and by
1975 over a million workers from Islamic countries, mainly Algeria, Morocco
and Tunisia, but also Senegal, Mauritania and Mali had arrived in France, and in
fact in possession of full French citizenship (ibid.; Penn/Lambert 2009). After
1974 recruitment stopped, but as in Germany, family reunification continued and
turned temporary migration into a permanent settlement. Despite a few attempts
to cap immigration, France has become a multi-ethnic society, and the liberal
citizenship law has been widely upheld, granting French nationality to anyone
born in France, irrespective of their parents' origin (Fetzer/Soper 2005: 65).

Providing reliable numbers with regard to France's Muslim population is a
challenge: an 1872 law continues to disallow any state census to identify people
by their religion, and any data collection in this respect is carried out by commercial companies on behalf of news agencies, who widely differ in their methodological approach, focus and agenda (Zwilling 2010: 183). The High Council
for Immigration estimated the Muslim population to be over 4 million in 2000
(Haut Conseil à l'Intégration 2000: 26). Other estimates ranged from 3.7 up to 7
million, with the National Institute of Statistics claiming in 2007 that Muslims
made up 7.1% or 4.5 million of the total population (Zwilling 2010: 184). Data

on self-definition and religiosity vary no less. One survey found that 3% of the total population identified themselves as being Muslim (ibid.), while another showed a result of 5.8% (IFOP 2009: 4), with one third of people with a Muslim family background claiming to be believing and practising, over a third to be believing but not practising, and one fourth to be of Muslim origin only (ibid.: 7). The majority originate from North Africa, in particular from Algeria (1,500,000), Morocco (1,000,000) and Tunisia (350,000), but also Turkey (315,000), sub-Saharan Africa (250,000), the Middle East (100,000) and a few other regions (Haut Conseil à l'Intégration 2000: 26).[4] With these countries of origin, French Islam is to a large extent Sunni. On average, the Muslim population is very young, as 35% are 15 to 24 years old, compared with 16% of the general population (IFOP 2009: 5).

The most relevant principle defining the relationship of any religion with the French state is *laïcité*, keeping religious and state affairs separate. While this means that the state does not generally recognise or support any denominations – and, above all, religious authorities have no influence on public affairs – there are a few exceptions to the rule. Religions that were recognised before this law was established in 1905 enjoy concessions such as tax exemptions, permission to found religious associations or subsidies to maintain places of worship, only some of which are available to Islam, and usually every issue, for instance the introduction of Islamic finance, is subject to debate (Zwilling 2010: 188). The principle itself continues to be passionately discussed, and especially left-wing defenders of multiculturalism, some Christian and Jewish representatives, along with most French Muslims and human rights advocates propose a "soft *laïcité*", urging the state not only to respect all religions, but also to actively further their practice (Fetzer/Soper 2005: 74).

Like in Germany, many French Muslims are organised into small mosque associations, but there are several umbrella organisations on the national level. The main one is the Union of Islamic Organisations in France (*Union des Organisations Islamiques de France, UOIF*), founded in 1983 and representing a variety of ethnicities. Predominantly Algerian Muslims are organised into the *Grande Mosquée de Paris (GMP)*, while Muslims of Moroccan origin are represented by the National Federation of Muslims of France (*Fédération Nationale des Musulmans de France, FNMF*) or the Assembly of Muslims of France (*Rassemblement des Musulmans de France, RMF*). The Coordination Committee of Turkish Muslims of France (*Comité de Coordination des Musulmans Turcs de France*) and the Milli Görüş (*CIMG France*) represent Turkish Islam. There is also the French Federation of Islamic Associations of Africa, the Comoros and

---

4   Numbers are minima, based on a total of 4.2 million Muslims in the year 2000.

the Antilles (*Fédération française des associations islamiques d'Afrique, des Comores et des Antilles, FFAIACA*). These organisations send representatives to the French Council of the Muslim Religion (*Conseil Français du Culte Musulman, CFCM*), which was founded in 2002 at the request of the French state in order to be able to communicate with Muslim representatives via an official body (Zwilling 2010: 189–191).

There are also several youth organisations, most notably the Young Muslims of France (*Jeunes Musulmans de France, JMF*), which were founded in 1993 with help of the UOIF, and the French Muslim Scouts (*Scouts Musulmans de France*) in 1991 (ibid.: 190). The Union of Young Muslims (*L'Union des Jeunes Musulmans, UJM*) has been active in Lyon since 1987, and the Muslim Students of France (*Étudiants Musulmans de France, ÉMF*) since 1989.

Around 2,150 mosques were counted in France in 2006, most of which are located in private houses or former factories, while only about 120 are actual mosque buildings. There are 20 large buildings with minarets and about as many again that can host over 1,000 worshippers (Zwilling 2010: 191–192). Important building projects are planned or under construction in several cities. No religious education is given at public schools. There are private religious schools, most of them Catholic, but a handful of private Muslim secondary schools have opened in the past decade. Often it is also possible for Muslim children to attend Christian schools and receive Islamic classes there. Most religious education is carried out by mosque associations, often with a connection to a particular country of origin (ibid.: 193–194). The majority of imam training courses are only offered by private institutions (e.g. *Institut Avicenne des Sciences Humaines*), and one programme is also offered at a Catholic faculty, teaching "Interculturalism, Secularism and Religions", which is made use of by imams from the Grande Mosquée de Paris, but has not yet been more widely accepted. Since 2009, the University of Strasbourg has been the first state institution to offer a masters degree, specialising in Islamic studies (ibid.: 194).

The most controversial issue caused by the secular state policy has been the *affaire du foulard*, or the headscarf affair of 1989, when three pupils were suspended from school for refusing to remove their headscarves in the classroom. A long and heated debate was fought among politicians, state institutions, headmasters, defenders of a stricter form of *laïcité*, religious authorities, human rights groups and parents (Fetzer/Soper 2005: 78–79; Gaspard/Khosrokhavar 1995). The Conseil d'État, the highest court of administrative law, ruled that a *hijab* could be worn if it did not disturb the functioning of the school in any way. Thus, it usually remained the decision of the principals, some of whom granted veiled girls access to their schools, while many others did not and banned all religious symbols. Some cases were taken to court and the students got reinstated, but in other cases the girls either studied by distance learning or dropped out of education altogether (Fetzer/Soper 2005: 79–81). Sharif Gemie points to the manifold meanings researchers have found to be attached to the veil by those who wear it, and especially to the usually strong commitment to being French (2010: 38–42). Nonetheless, a law was finally passed in 2004, banning all religious symbols from public schools (Sénat 2004). The debate was reignited in 2008 when discussion of the face veil, referred to as *burqa* or *niqab*, led to an investigative committee passing a law in 2010, to take effect in 2011, banning the face veil from all public places (Assemblée Nationale 2010; Le Monde 26/01/2010).

Public discourse has in the past few years been marked by discussions on the visibility of Islam, often still focusing on the headscarf, more recently on the face veil and minarets (Zwilling 2010: 200), but including Islamic swimsuits in public swimming pools. The polemics of the extreme right-wing party *Front National* have often stirred a debate on Islamophobia (Libération 04/01/2011). That France continues to struggle with defining the status of Islam and of immigrants more widely was demonstrated in the national identity debate in early 2010. Nicolas Sarkozy's government initiated the debate in which citizens were asked their opinion on what it meant to be French, on values, patriotism and minorities, and which was strongly criticised by observers of different political backgrounds as being specifically derogatory to Muslims (Time Magazine 12/02/2011).

Islam and Muslims in the United Kingdom

First contact between Muslims and Britain is traced back to the Bengali and Kashmiri sailors of the British East India Company, who arrived in the UK in the nineteenth century. They were joined by sailors from Yemen from 1869, and Indian soldiers also fought for the British in World War I (Ansari 2004; McLoughlin/Abbas 2010: 545–546). But as with Germany and France, major immigration did not take place until after World War II. The 1948 British Nationality Act granted British citizenship to any person from a Commonwealth country, so that many migrants from India and Pakistan in particular came to the UK, but laws passed between 1964 and 1971 restricted access again, and in 1981, the concept of the initial Nationality Act was revoked (Penn/Lambert 2009: 42). Subsequently, a restrictive migration policy was introduced alongside a commitment to a pluralist and multicultural society, protecting and even encouraging ethnic and cultural differences, including the formation of ethnic communities – in great contrast to both France and Germany (ibid.).

For the first few decades of Muslim presence in Britain after 1945, the size of the population could only be guessed at, and estimates ranged from 550,000 to 3 million, or usually around 1 to 1.5 million. The 2001 Census provided the first reliable numbers, estimating the total number of British Muslims to be 1.6 million, which then rose significantly in the following decade (Gilliat-Ray 2010: 117). According to Sophie Gilliat-Ray, the strong increase was due mainly to a high birth rate among Muslims, but also to recent immigration, some conversion to Islam and a stronger identification with the label "Muslim" in the post 9/11 environment and the "war on terror" (ibid.). In 2009, the Office of National Statistics published a figure of 2.4 million Muslims living in the UK, amounting to 4% of the population (The Times 30/01/2009). Countries of origin are predominantly Pakistan (43%, based on the 2001 Census), Bangladesh (17%) and India (9%), with some smaller minorities from West and East Africa, the latter coming originally from India (McLoughlin/Abbas 2010: 546; Gilliat-Ray 2010: 120). Like in France and Germany, the Muslim population shows a significantly young average age. In 2001, they already had the youngest age profile with around one third (34%) under the age of 16, compared with one fifth (20%) of the general population. Also, the 16- to 34-year-olds make up another third of the Muslim population, but only a quarter (25%) of the general population (Office for National Statistics 2004: 3). The growing birth rates will have increased this proportion even more.

The relationship between religion and the state is a matter of the UK's constituent countries England, Wales, Scotland and Northern Ireland, each of which has a different approach; for instance, the Church of England is the only established religion that has no counterparts in the other nations of the UK. There is no general law that determines how the state should treat religions, but some modes of practice have evolved over time (McLoughlin/Abbas 2010: 546–547). Moreover, there is no constitution that protects the freedom of religion as a fundamental right, as is the case in Germany and France. The state has, however, developed a "pragmatic approach to religious pluralism", and protected minority groups, but the legal status of Muslims is not fully determined (Fetzer/Soper 2005: 34). Since 1992, a few committees have been established by various governments to increase the interaction between faith groups and the state (e.g. the Faith Communities Consultative Council). The terrorist attacks of 7 July 2005 ("7/7") have put the spotlight on Islam and security issues, and the Preventing Violent Extremism programme has become one of the major points of contact between Muslims and the state (McLoughlin/Abbas 2010: 548).

The earliest Muslim organisation reaches back to 1970, when the Union of Muslim Organisations of the UK and Eire (UMO) was founded, but it was not able to exert much influence. After the Rushdie Affair in 1988–1989, the UK Action Committee on Islamic Affairs (UKACIA), which was particularly successful at fighting against religious discrimination, formed the Muslim Parliament of Great Britain. In 1997, the Muslim Council of Britain (MCB) evolved out of the UKACIA and has been one of the main organisations, although it has had an unsteady relationship with the government owing to some extremist statements made by individual members, and only a proportion of British Muslims feel represented by the Council. Other bodies include the Islamic Society of Britain, the Muslim Association of Britain (MAB) of mainly Arab background, the British Muslim Forum, consisting chiefly of Pakistani Muslims, the Sufi Muslim Council, and separate umbrella organisations in Scotland, Wales and Northern Ireland. The Quilliam Foundation was founded in 2008 by former *Hizb ut-Tahrir* members as an "anti-extremism think tank", researching British Islam and identifying radical currents (McLoughlin/Abbas 2010: 548–551).

The largest youth organisation is Young Muslims UK (YMUK) with regional bodies and local youth groups. Islamic societies at British universities have been represented by the Federation of Student Islamic Societies (FOSIS) since 1963. The Muslim Youth League UK (MYL UK) are a branch of the international movement *Minhaj ul-Quran*, founded by Muhammad Tahir ul-Qadri in Pakistan and promoting a moderate, anti-extremist interpretation of Islam. There is also a scout group, the Muslim Scouts Fellowship (UKMSF). Additionally, some authors add the radical group *Hizb ut-Tahrir* to the list of youth movements, because it has been particularly attractive to young Muslims (Gilliat 1997: 105–106).

The number of mosques in Britain today is not easily measured, as not all of them are registered with local authorities. Estimates therefore vary between 850 to 1,500 (Gilliat-Ray 2010: 181) or 2,000 (McLoughlin/Abbas 2010: 551). As in other European countries, their buildings and functions vary significantly, and only a minority of mosques have been purpose-built. Mosques also take over most of children's religious education, where the demand for new teaching methods is starting to be met. State schools teach general religious education, though with a Christian emphasis, but there are also Islamic schools, both publicly funded (11 primary or secondary schools) and many more privately funded ones (ibid.: 552–553). Imam training is not offered at public universities, some of which, however, train teachers and youth workers within their Islamic studies curriculum. Several private Islamic institutions train imams, often taking over models from Islamic countries, but other approaches are also taken by the Muslim College in London and the Cambridge Muslim College, which was founded in 2009. As for clothing norms, there are no restrictions on wearing headscarves at schools or in public offices, including the police and armed forces, as part of the uniform. The face veil and long coats are also increasingly common, although they may not always be permitted, for instance, by school headmasters (ibid.: 557).

The recent public discourse has first and foremost dealt with many forms of radicalisation: an organisation that has kept reappearing under different names (lately Islam4UK) was banned for its extremist incitements, and the national Prevent Violent Extremism programme continued to target radicalisation, especially of young people, with questionable success (The Independent 31/03/2010). At the same time, right-wing extremism and populism was discussed, particularly after the formation of the English Defence League in 2009, which allegedly fights Islamic extremism, but in reality opposes all forms of Islam and the presence of Muslims in England (Euro-Islam 13/09/2009). Islamophobia continues to be a point of discussion (The Guardian 20/01/2011), and in a more subtle form entered a debate stirred up by David Cameron, when he claimed in 2011 that multiculturalism had failed in Britain. After the French decision to ban the face veil, the issue was also discussed in the UK, but a ban was never likely to be introduced owing to the country's longstanding recognition of (visible) cultural differences (BBC 18/07/2010).

Research Setting

Apart from providing a short overview of Muslims in Germany, France and the UK, the background information presented also highlights the setting in which this research project took place. Despite different migration histories, all three countries have already had a significant Muslim population for decades, and they also have the largest Muslim minorities in Europe today. Islam is not only present, but also institutionalised to varying degrees and has become a part of public life. Ties with countries of origin are upheld, but in most cases the main focus has shifted to the European home country. The religion's manifold and diverse character is not only illustrated by great variations in religious practice, but also by the demand for a number of different organisations, which, despite their dissimilar orientations, do not even represent the entirety of Muslims in the respective countries. The population is in addition remarkably young, which bestows an increasingly important role upon Muslim youth.

Most importantly, however, the research took place in a turbulent post-9/11 and post-7/7 environment. Before 2001, Muslims had already been living in non-Muslim spaces, and some issues of living together had also given rise to discussions then. But since 9/11, and in the UK especially after 7/7 as well, Muslims have been in the spotlight where they may not even have been recognised as

Muslims before, but perhaps rather as people with a Turkish, Algerian or Pakistani background. Since then, they have not been able to afford *not* to take a position on Islamic extremism. They have had to deal with heightened security measures against their communities, at times with a general suspicion against members of their faith, and with the reality of Muslim radicalisation, abusing the religion as a lethal weapon. This has often led to a stronger identification with Islam (e.g. Gerlach 2006; Gilliat-Ray 2010), and despite some resignations, in many cases also to an increased desire to explain one's faith in order to reach a stage where Islam can be thought of independently of terrorism. This has been of particularly vital concern to young, believing members of the Islamic faith in non-Muslim environments, who will spend their entire lives as Muslims in these countries. It is in this setting that Islamic youth culture has developed.

About This Study

The idea for this research project developed in stages. Studies at the American University in Cairo (2004–2005) exposed me to very devout young Muslims, who were consuming a lot of American youth and pop culture and who were not shy about expressing both their piety and their fashionability. On my return to Europe, I researched the 2005 riots in French *banlieues*, and while I focused more on youth, segregation and urban conflict (Herding 2007), in the course of this research I came across examples of an Islamic youth culture that combined youth cultural expressions with a strong religious commitment. I began to wonder why I had not seen manifestations such as religious rap or fashion items with Islamic slogans in the Islamic world and what it was that made them so specifically European or Western. Not finding any satisfying answers in the academic literature, which had hardly even touched upon this phenomenon, I decided to look at Islamic youth culture in more depth, and I present the results of my research endeavour in this book.

Writing on Islam in Europe is always a minefield, because many people have many and divergent opinions on this complex field. I am certainly not free from writing from a particular angle myself, but my intention is not to give an evaluation of Islamic youth culture or to judge it. This study is an analysis of what Islamic youth culture is, why it has come into existence and what its wider implications are. Very often, the data speak for themselves.

The title of this book, "Inventing the Muslim Cool", is adopted from an informal conversation with a producer of Islamic youth culture, who put this forward as the major goal of his media company. It also alludes to a documentary film, "New Muslim Cool" (Taylor 2009), which depicts the early stages of a similar scene of young and cool Islam in the United States. Moreover, the title is a hint at the fact that the study focuses on the *process* of making Islamic youth culture.

To set the scene for the empirical findings and their analysis, Chapter II introduces the theoretical framework and the methodology applied in this study. Chapter III is a comprehensive presentation of Islamic youth culture, both descriptive and analytical, introducing artefacts and examples from the areas of music, comedy, fashion and the media. Chapter IV is a discussion of my findings from participant observations among the consumers to show what the phenomenon looks like in practice and how it can be grasped as a youth culture. From an analysis of interviews with the producers, I have developed a typology, which I will present in Chapter V. Going beyond the empirical findings, in Chapter VI, I will discuss their implications for the phenomenon and its context, as well as for the theoretical literature. Finally, the Conclusion recapitulates the most important insights gained from the entire research project.

II. Setting the Scene

A. THEORETICAL CONSIDERATIONS

As a cultural phenomenon, Islamic youth culture can be perceived through various lenses. Since this study is at the intersection of different cultural perspectives, and of novel complex experiences, it has to borrow from and to combine different kinds of cultural theories. Historically, there is no such concept as youth culture in Islam. It was and often still is common for young Muslims to make a gradual transition from childhood to adulthood, or from their parental family to founding a family of their own, which was especially true for girls. Even if there were a few spaces particular to youth, like the school or political movements of young Islamic revivalists, traditionally there was hardly any concept of leisure, fun and entertaining pastimes specifically for them. No activities or places catered only for young people, as forms of entertainment like weddings, religious or cultural festivals were always enjoyed by all generations. Young Muslims' consumption of youth cultures is a result of encounters between Muslims and European-American youth culture, which requires a thorough understanding of youth culture to be part of the theoretical discussion, to allow for generational issues, everyday culture and extravagant expressions to be made sense of. At the same time, this phenomenon calls for conceptualisations of cultural encounters. Great insights have been made by the notion of hybridity and by looking at how hybrid objects are created through the reaction to and appropriation of global cultural flows. Moreover, in this context I am not looking at the participation of Muslim youth in already existing youth cultures, but specifically at an Islamic youth culture in a non-Islamic context, which touches upon issues of Islam in Europe, including (post-)migration, multiculturalism, religiosity, secularisation and the relationship with the non-Muslim environment.

In this part of the chapter, I will set out the various theoretical approaches towards Islamic youth culture and review the few works that have looked at a similar population or at the phenomenon itself. Together with Part B on methodology, the chapter as a whole will set the scene for my own empirical exploration of this field.

1. Youth Culture

Understanding the phenomenon as a youth culture is not the only, but one of the most important ways of grasping it, since it bears two significant issues: a generational aspect of something being relevant to people at a certain period in their lives, and an emphasis on leisure activities, entertainment, fun and the meanings attached to these by young people. Abundant literature has dealt with questions of the constituent elements of youth culture(s): adherence and membership, production and consumption, and meanings of styles and symbols for specific social groups, which will help clarify the way in which the phenomenon in question can and should be grasped as a youth culture.

For an overview of the sociology of youth culture, I have found Andy Bennett's account one of the most useful, because it traces the historic development of academic interest in youth cultures with its different terms and perspectives, while it subtly highlights the most important theories relevant to his study on locality and popular music (Bennett 2000: 11–33). In the following, I will therefore partly adopt this structure, but will amend it to emphasise the concepts most worthwhile for the study of Islamic youth culture and to extend the UK-centric focus of Bennett's account.

Early Youth Cultures and Theories

In Europe and the United States, youth culture as a widely recognised mass phenomenon undoubtedly began after World War II, and mainstream sociological research also increasingly dealt with it as an area of investigation from that time. However, even if Talcott Parsons coined the term "youth culture" in 1942[1] or the

---

1   Parsons used the term "youth culture" in an article on sex roles and behaviour in relation to gender and age group to denote distinct behavioural patterns among the young American population in contrast to adult cultures. He also contrasts the romanticised American youth culture with the politicised German youth movements (Parsons 1942: esp. 606, 616). He certainly focuses on a limited, if important selection of themes within youth culture (gender, age group, inter-generational conflict, political involve-

word "teenager" was used by American advertisers from 1944 (Savage 2007: xiii), there is no reason for locating the very origins of youth culture itself around that period. As Jon Savage shows in his comprehensive account of early youth cultures between 1875 and 1945, both young people and policy makers attempted to define and negotiate the status of youth from the late nineteenth century onwards (Savage 2007). Recounting the transnational history of youth movements as diverse as the British Boy Scouts, German *Wandervögel*, American jazz in Europe, early mass consumerism, *Hitlerjugend* and Nazi resistance from the White Rose, the Swing Kids and the French *Zazous*, Savage sheds light on the period prior to what is commonly seen as the rise of youth culture. With this selection of trends, his concerns are the outstanding examples rather than the average youth (ibid.: xvii), but it is sensible to highlight the extraordinary in order to discover and draw attention to the origins of youth culture, which are almost necessarily the forerunners of later mass movements. Some early youth cultural practices have played an important role in opening spaces of flirtation and sexuality to young people, independent of family chaperonage. Among them were the dance hall culture of late nineteenth century Europe and the American dating culture from the interwar period onwards, but also the longstanding tradition of night bundling (*Kiltgang, Nachtfreien*), a partly sexual contact of unmarried couples, common in rural areas of Central and Northern Europe until around 1900 (Therborn 2004: 86, 139).

David Fowler starts his history of modern British youth culture in the 1920s, choosing a much later date than Savage, because he focuses on youth cultures generated by the 18 to 25 age group, rather than youth activities offered to them by adults, such as the Boy Scouts (Fowler 2008: 5). His account presents two strands of youth history, that of young urban lifestyles and broader youth activity fathoming new and alternative approaches to leading one's life (ibid.: 4), both being present in Britain before and after 1945.

In the German context, youth culture started with a different connotation in the educational movements of the 1920s. Youth culture then used to be a concept of the bourgeois youth to oppose the authoritarian education of Wilhelmian Germany (Hartwig 1980). Teachers and educational reformers put forward a special lifestyle that was supposed to form a distinct youth culture. In particular, the *Wandervogelbewegung* should celebrate juvenility as a way of life (ibid.; Savage 2007: 101–112). From the beginning, however, as Helmut Hartwig points out, class differences limited the universal value of the youth movement,

ment), but also points to the role of the very distinct national histories in the development of youth cultures.

which did not reach out to the working class and later did not attract many young people; this 1920s understanding of youth culture in Germany soon vanished, although there had also been a few other youth groups during the Weimar Republic such as the *Wilde Cliquen* of male working class rebellious youth (Peukert 1983).

Even before 1945, therefore, sociology began to develop an interest in youth, in some cases as early as the 1920s and 1930s. In an article from 1936, for instance, Edward Reuter discusses the existence of an independent world of adolescents (Reuter 1936), while the "Chicago School" established this research branch with the focus that went on to determine youth research for a long time, i.e. juvenile delinquency and how to explain it from a sociological rather than a criminological perspective. This meant grasping deviance as "normal" from the perspective of youth, as for example in William Whyte's study *Street Corner Society* (Whyte 1943), and taking it as a starting point for subculture by creating norms and values around it. Deviance and delinquency then remained the main points of focus within subculture and youth research (Bennett 2000: 14–17). After World War II, a second strand began to flourish. Parsons had already described a change in young people's values from emphasising productive work to hedonistic consumption and enjoying life (Parsons 1942), but with the economic growth in the United States, Britain and other European states in the 1950s and 1960s, youth and consumer culture discovered each other. Commodities such as fashion, accessories and music – portable in the form of the new 45 rpm records and transistor radios – became available to the majority of young people (Bennett 2000: 12). Consequently, consumerist and expressive subcultures increasingly became the subject of sociological studies, in Germany (Tenbruck 1965; Bell 1965; Lindner 1981) as well as in Britain (most notably Hall/Jefferson 1976; Hebdige 1979; Brake 1980).

By that time, and after initial controversies, research had acknowledged the status of "youth" as a category not just of age, but also of semi-independence and other features that can lead to the development of specific behaviour both in terms of deviance and of cultures, even though the term is far from having a fixed definition. Some also regard the category of youth as a "social achievement" rather than a given category, structured for instance by consumption and spending power, creativity, education and surveillance (Lipsitz 2005: xiv; Maira/Soep 2005: xviii). With a general agreement on youth as a meaningful category, denoting a life phase of early sexuality, between belonging to one family and founding one's own, between legal immaturity and economic independence, and with an increasing ability to make life choices (Scherr 2009: 19–21; Therborn 2011: 157–158), all but French sociology now seems comfortable with youth research (Bruno 2000). According to Bourdieu (1980), "[l]a 'jeunesse' n'est qu'un mot" – "youth" is just a word – because he regards this age group as much more differentiated by class than being held together by some sort of culture – although there is no reason to assume just one youth culture for all. He ruled out the possibility of youth culture as a concept as such, including youth cultures in the plural, and with it the term "youth" as a meaningful concept, which largely prevented French sociology from developing a sociology of youth and youth culture. Researchers did, however, develop ways to deal with the topic, mainly by applying a framework of delinquency (Mauger 2009) or of *banlieue* research (Milon 2000; Lepoutre 2001; Faure/Garcia 2005), or by focusing on more specific genres like rap music (Boucher 1999; Pecqueux 2007), and more recently a few works have opposed Bourdieu's paradigm (Lahire 2006: 497–556).

The situation in non-Western societies, however, is a completely different one and requires special attention. Although there is little research about the concept of youth and adolescence in non-Western countries, a few distinct observations provide important amendments to the Western notion. In their study on the "construction of adolescence", John Caldwell et al. (1998) suggest that the concept was brought to non-Western countries by global economic, institutional and social changes during colonialism and globalisation, for instance through longer education, delayed marriage or the idea of romantic relationships preceding marriage (ibid.: 149). They claim, however, that traditions still account for the majority of cultural practices around sexuality, marriage and reproduction, and downplay the influence of global youth cultures on social change. Whichever emphasis one chooses, the study indicates that the concept of adolescence is even more recent in non-Western than in Western societies, and that it may not even have such a large impact, with traditional practices still being very influential.

Cultural differences of the youth concept are widely acknowledged, emphasising a gradual initiation of children into adulthood instead of a disjuncture in more traditional societies, as for example Gill Cressey points out for rural Pakistan and Kashmir (Cressey 2006: 163, 172). In traditional Islamic contexts, boys after puberty are expected to spend less time with women and children and to visit the men's section at the mosque, while girls before marriage are regarded as needing protection and are therefore closely supervised by the family (ibid.: 163; Caldwell et al. 1998); a gender divide becomes established, with girls being married off particularly early, therefore not usually having a distinct and independent youth phase (Therborn 2004: 161). Yet a *concept* of youth in Islam is barely existent. Adolescence is not explicitly mentioned as a distinct phase in the Quran, although a succession of life stages is outlined that indicates the gradual

transition from childhood to adulthood, determined by changes in the relationship with the parents and a growing individual responsibility (Cressey 2006:
169–170). For instance, a time where parents are socially and religiously responsible for their children is followed by a phase of learning, preparing the children
for their roles in the religious community and their future families, which is
again succeeded by a period of increased accountability. Marriage usually sepa-
rates a young woman from her family, while the man, together with his new
wife, stays with his parents. In both cases there is no demarcation from the parents, and Islam does not suspect young people to be particularly prone to sin or
trouble (ibid.).

Cressey therefore concludes that youth is no autonomous category in Islam
and therefore the central themes of the Western youth concept – including rebel-
lion, sexuality and acquisition of nearly full independence – do not traditionally
correspond to young Muslims. I would add that this also holds true indeed for
the formation of a youth culture. Whenever youth movements and cultures in
non-Western contexts are studied, authors usually see their emergence as a result
of cultural globalisation and Western influence, certainly with much local adaptation, as will be discussed towards the end of this section on youth culture (see
also Kahane 1997: 207–216).

Subcultural Theory

Subcultural research cannot be thought of without Birmingham's Centre for
Contemporary Cultural Studies (CCCS), active from 1964 to 2002, and one of its
major publications, *Resistance through Rituals* (Hall/Jefferson 1993, first published 1976). Its studies established subculture as a substantial part of youth culture research, which they changed in two ways. First, they shifted the focus away
from gangs and towards "style-based" youth cultures, such as teddy boys, rock-
ers, mods or skinheads. Second, the CCCS took the deviance of subcultures as a
collective reaction and resistance of working class youth to the structural changes of the post-war period. Young people of the working class were considered
the origin of style-based youth cultures, as class in general formed one of the
main interests of the CCCS (Bennett 2000: 17–18). Another important assertion
in this respect is the understanding of subcultures as the particularly tangible
form that some youths express in response to their situation, while the majority
perhaps either never participates in a subculture or takes part in several, but on a
fleeting, non-fixed basis (Clarke/Hall et al. 1993 [1976]: 16). However, the responses that are uttered in the form of subcultures are symptomatic of the struggle of the working class, and to the youth they offer a means of resistance and
coping, albeit no solution; problems are solved in an "imaginary way" instead of

at the material level (ibid.: 44–48). The ethnographic studies in *Resistance through Rituals* investigate, among other topics, specific youth cultures like the Teds (Jefferson), the Mods (Hebdige) and the Skinheads (J. Clarke), and more generally young people's pastimes (Corrigan on "Doing Nothing"), style (J. Clarke) and the role of girls in youth culture (McRobbie/Garber; all 1993 [1976]).

Another classic work that has emerged from the CCCS is Dick Hebdige's *Subculture: The Meaning of Style* (Hebdige 1993, first published 1979), in which he gives the most detailed account of style and its significance to subculture. To him, the adoption of styles, along with images and ideologies, creates a space where an alternative identity can be constructed that deliberately plays with visible difference and "Otherness", which allows members of the group to question and counter-stipulate class and gender attributes – but only on a symbolic level (Hebdige 1993: 88–89). Style is defined as endowing subcultural participants with identity, especially by breaking with norms taken for granted by a vaguely defined mainstream society; style thus becomes "intentional communication", for example through clothes, the choosing of which must always be interpreted as meaningful (ibid.: 100–101). A major strategy in creating a style, also in order to irritate, is by stripping well-known objects of their usual context to give them a new meaning; this is what Hebdige calls "bricolage" (ibid.: 102, 106).

Even though the CCCS largely dealt with style-based subcultures, Hebdige's account points to other constituent elements of youth cultures. Expressions and manifestations catch any outsider's attention immediately, but motivations, origins and goals of subcultural participants must also be taken into account, such as their own value systems and behavioural norms (Brake 1980; Brake 1981: 18). Albert Scherr includes in the definition of style any typically used or newly created cultural form, in particular language, fashion, body language and music (Scherr 2009: 183), the latter playing the most central role in historical and contemporary youth cultures. As a general description of the composition of youth cultures, Scherr mentions substance and style, a certain group size, a readiness for action including provocation, and features specific to age and stratum (ibid.: 188). Rolf Lindner, furthermore, distinguishes between style as an end in itself and style as the expression of an attitude of protest; this distinction is also used by members of subcultures themselves to separate between "real" and "fake" members (Lindner 1981: 191) and underlines the importance of an idea or ideology to the members of a subculture.

Despite and because of its classic status in the field, the CCCS has received various criticisms. One might wonder whether the theory has possibly aged with its subject and whether it was particularly valid for the subcultures it studied without being able to offer a timely approach to later forms. One of the points of critique is the nearly exclusive dealing with class and the application of a neo-Marxist interpretation, which is seen to outshine empirical and thorough ethnographic research and to cause ignorance of the subjective interpretations of youth in favour of an inadequately sophisticated analysis with a certain political agenda (Bennett 2000: 22; Hodkinson 2007: 6). Also, the focus on the most visibly outstanding youths has been criticised, as their dealing with class, their practices and motivations were essentialised and at the same time, youths who were less involved were entirely ignored (G. Clarke 1990). Another major criticism is the vast absence of young women from the studies of the CCCS, which cannot be justified by a lower number of girls in the most prominent subcultures, but is rather due to the choice of subcultures studied. Only one article of *Resistance through Rituals* dealt with girls and indoor locations like the "teenage bedroom" (McRobbie/Garber 1993), while all others investigated outdoor, street-based male subcultures. Angela McRobbie herself extended the criticism in a volume on popular music that incorporated more studies into subculture, gender and sexuality (McRobbie 1990; Frith/Goodwin 1990). Similarly, ethnic minority subcultures were not adequately dealt with as they were mainly regarded as influencing white subcultures, for instance in music, or in the context of racism and "moral panic" (Nayak 2003; Hodkinson 2007: 7). Bennett furthermore indicates the failure of subcultural theory to consider local variations of music and style and especially of commercialised products (Bennett 2000: 23–24).

Scenes and Lifestyles

As a response to the important, but in parts unsatisfactory class-based analyses of style-based subcultures, various other notions have tried to replace the term "subculture". From the 1990s, youth cultures have been analysed more independently of young people's social background and therefore as less fixed and binding in terms of membership. Ronald Hitzler and Michaela Pfadenhauer promote the term "scenes", underlining the non-committal character of voluntary and temporary engagement of post-traditional collectivisations (Hitzler/Pfadenhauer 1998: 78; Hitzler/Honer/Pfadenhauer 2008). Scenes have alternatives and are freely selectable options, and they also include purely leisure-focused scenes like techno (Hitzler/Niederbacher 2010), which seems to grasp the change within youth cultures adequately. The 1997 German Youth Survey, for instance, diagnosed contemporary youth cultures as being fast moving and diffuse, with a central desire for fun replacing most political protest (Jugendwerk der Deutschen Shell 1997).

Alternatively, Bennett discusses the use of the term "lifestyles" for a very similar understanding of juvenile forms of leisure as more flexible and fluctuating (Bennett 2000: 25–27). He sees the greatest benefit in Richard Jenkins's first application of lifestyles – still in the context of working class youth – because it emphasises the interconnectedness of "subcultures" between each other and with wider society (Jenkins 1983; Bennett 2000: 25). This is taken much further in Bo Reimer's account of lifestyle orientations among Swedish youth, in which lifestyle is used to break down the relationship of class and taste in popular entertainment into many more influences. According to Reimer, lifestyle orientations result not only from a combination of class, gender, education, income and civil status, but also from young people's choice of entertainment that is not dependent on their socio-economic background (Reimer 1995: 135; Bennett 2000: 26). Although Iain Chambers does not use the term lifestyle himself, Bennett also interprets his understanding of popular culture in this way. Chambers, too, moves away from the concept of class and reflects on the role of the local in the generation of meaning around music or fashion: the meanings of such products are not completely made by the culture-producing industries, but are finished by the consumers (Chambers 1985; Bennett 2000: 26–27).

Paul Hodkinson and Wolfgang Deicke present several newer concepts, including scenes, lifestyles and also (neo-)tribes (Hodkinson/ Deicke 2007). David Hesmondhalgh, in the same volume, rebuffs all of these concepts, at least in their application to popular music studies, for adding no analytical value and being too contingent; in his opinion, the rejection of too narrowly defined concepts like class has led to another extreme (Hesmondhalgh 2007). Instead, he calls for use of the more confined terms of genre and articulation (ibid.: 45–48). This does not seem, however, to be a major step forward for a broader understanding of youth and subcultures, even if it may be useful in subsections of research like popular music. Precision is certainly needed, although perhaps more in the form of clear definitions than in the introduction of yet another term. As outlined above, however, French literature on youth cultures has taken this direction of zooming in on specific youth cultures as genres, possibly to circumvent discussions of how to define the broad concept of youth culture.

Ethnicity and Religion in Youth Culture Research

The general opening up towards different research interests and models of explanation within youth culture research has also made room for ethnicity. Studies focus on the strategies of young people to overcome parts of their migrant parents' culture and to deal with fitting into the Western environment. Some apply a postcolonial framework here, as do Raminder Kaur Kalhon and Virinder Kalra, who denote the hyphenated identity in the term "Br-Asian" (1996). Others focus on various forms of an ethnic identity among youth, taking shape in the fusion of the popular and some forms of the traditional (Bennett 2000: 29). This overlaps with research on hybrid cultures (Möller 2010), but a special focus on youth is still found in many studies, the majority of which specialise in music (e.g. Baker 1991; Maira 2002; Bax 2006; Murthy 2007; Gazzah 2008), while a smaller fraction deals with other forms or a more comprehensive view of youth cultures consisting of other elements rather than music (e.g. Aitsiselmi 2000; Soysal 2001; Projektgruppe JugendArt 2010a).

Still, even if some of these studies look at youth of Turkish or Pakistani background, they do not deal with an Islamic youth culture and focus on ethnicity instead. It is therefore necessary to explore the link between the sociology of youth and religion, which has most recently been done in a volume edited by Sylvia Collins-Mayo and Pink Dandelion (2010). It compiles the research conducted on the sociology of youth religion in a sub-project of the British AHRC/ESRC-funded Religion and Society Research Programme (2007–2012).[2] Significant changes are outlined in the transmission of religion, which is no longer simply passed on from parents to children, while the secularism of the post-war baby boomer and 1968 generation does not seem to replicate either in all youth contexts (Woodhead 2010: 239). Thus, themes of the book include generational analysis, globalisation and media, sacralisation, individual life choices, identity, religious diversity and transmission. An important contribution comes from Collins-Mayo and Tom Beaudoin, who analyse how the "Generation X" (born in the 1960s and 70s) grew up largely without religion and with the consumption a much popular culture, so that the Church responded to the drop in membership numbers by incorporating pop cultural elements and producing Christian popular culture like television programmes and comics, mainly in North America, but also in Britain. Beaudoin's concept of "virtual faith" furthermore denotes the use of religious symbols in music videos, in fashion and accessories and in cyberspace, where these symbols are mimicked and yet reflect a somewhat spiritual, if distorted relationship with religion (Beaudoin 1998; Collins-Mayo/Beaudoin 2010). Both questions – whether or not religious popular culture is a top–down or bottom–up case of action and what religious symbols in popular culture mean to the consumers – are interesting points of discussion in the context of Islamic youth culture, even if used to demarcate it from the "GenX" experience. Part III of the volume restates the widely acknowledged thesis that young people have moved from religiosity, in an institutional sense, to

---

2 http://www.religionandsociety.org.uk. AHRC=Arts and Humanities Research Council, ESRC=Economic and Social Research Council.

spirituality, and that spiritual expression can take an array of forms including witchcraft, shamanic practices and transformative experiences resulting from euphoric drug use and electronic dance music (Tacey 2003; Collins-Mayo/Dandelion 2010: 63, 65–111). In the light of this, and compared with such rather extreme forms, the emergence of Islamic youth cultural practices may not be so surprising; they still even appear much more institutionalised. Building on theories of individualisation and boundless life choices, Part IV deals with identity and that being religious requires from young people an active choice, not to mention hard work at times. Pia Karlsson Minganti explores these issues for Muslim women in Sweden, yet focuses on questions of gender, ethnicity, experiences of racism and generation and not on pop or youth culture (Karlsson Minganti 2010; Collins-Mayo/Dandelion 2010: 113–155). Finally, Part V discusses religious transmission, but while it is acknowledged that families and Churches no longer transmit religion in the traditional way or at all, the contributions concentrate precisely on these two factors, and religious socialisation through youth culture is ignored (Collins-Mayo/Dandelion 2010: 157–189). This will be an important aspect in the study of Islamic youth culture.

Youth Cultures and Globalisation

Finally, youth cultural research on globalisation and non-Western contexts draws attention to the relationship between the global and the local. There is no need to be a migrant to experience and experiment with different cultures, but they will flow to young people even if they are not even "leaving their own bedrooms" (Maira/Soep 2005b: xix). Widely acknowledged that globalisation does not simply equal homogenisation (e.g. Lukose 2005: 931), a global perspective on youth cultures allows for structural differences to be seen not as a given, but as exerting dissimilar influences on youth cultures depending on the national and social framework. Local meanings are also added to globally travelling cultures, especially to commercialised American ones, or, in turn, global trends and problems are interpreted nationally (Skelton/Valentine 1998; Androutsopoulos 2003; Wise 2008). For example, Mark Liechty demonstrates how youth in Kathmandu have to reconcile the images of a modern future, conveyed by the Western popular culture, with the realities of Nepal and village life; in fact, here as well as in many other countries, "youth" was not recognised as a distinctive phase until the late twentieth century (Liechty 1995: 191). Mike Brake has also drawn attention to the limitations of an Anglo-American focus in terms of resistance. He takes the example of Canada to show that youth resistance there only ever took an individualistic rather than a collective form owing to structural differences as simple as vast distances and severe winters, hindering collaborative gatherings

(Brake 1985: 145). Fiona Smith shows how the state can distort and challenge youth cultures, as in the case of East German youth resistance (Smith 1998). On the level of consumerist youth cultures, Ritty Lukose unmasks the local conditions for young people in Kerala, India, for exploring "new spaces of consumption", finding those conditions to be heavily marked by colonialist and nationalist categories (Lukose 2005: 916, 919).

Vered Amit-Talai and Helena Wulff also take an anthropological, ethnographic approach with youth at the centre (Amit-Talai/ Wulff 1995). Amit-Talai points out that the everyday cultures of youths are necessarily multicultural because their environments already consist of countless diverse influences. Thinking of youth cultures as non-multicultural would be far from the reality of today's societies (Amit-Talai 1995: 231–232). This is backed up by Mary Bucholtz, whose study focuses on youth cultural practice to actively integrate transnational elements, capitalism and local culture (Bucholtz 2002). Sunaina Maira's and Elisabeth Soep's collection *Youthscapes* applies a more political, perhaps less celebratory approach to global youth cultures by focusing on power relations in youth and popular culture (Maira/Soep 2005a). George Lipsitz, in the same volume, points out how globalisation also opened up the view of global injustices that very much affect youth, like hunger, poverty and death (Lipsitz 2005: ix); therefore, the study of their youth cultures should look at how they "continue to make something beautiful" with a meaning for themselves out of the global raw material they are given and under circumstances out of their control (ibid.: ix, xi). Maira and Soep thereby regard youths as key players in the dynamics of nation and globalisation (Maira/Soep 2005b).

Göran Therborn, on the other hand, sees contemporary youth cultures as strongly imbued with global cultural history (Therborn 2011: 160). Adding a historical dimension and a large-scale global perspective, he calls to mind that worldwide information flows do not only carry media, entertainment and arts, but also values, norms, models, standards and other ideas (ibid.: 117). They now often travel in the form of popular and youth cultural products; an international exchange is taking place in the new media, in the social networking of blogs, used by hundreds of millions. The official trade of cultural goods (e.g. sound media, film, visual arts) amounted to one per cent of all goods in the early 2000s (ibid.: 115; UNESCO 2005); as a matter of fact, the distribution of popular culture, due to illegal copies and copyright breach, is likely to be much higher. The "global youth world" that has developed from the 1970s and 1980s, is marked by global variation and connection, and has its hegemonic centre in Western Europe and North America (ibid.: 159–160). However, the emergence of regional centres of cultural production has started to challenge this hegemony, so that Therborn also acknowledges the decline of the North American-centric cultural flows (ibid.: 116). East Asian pop culture, Japanese and Mexican telenovelas, Arab and Latin American film production alongside that of India (Bollywood) and Nigeria (Nollywood) (ibid.), have all contributed to this challenge and added to global cultural flows in various directions.

Summary

Before going on, I will recapitulate what can be learned from youth cultural theory and how I am going to apply it in this study. Although "youth culture" is a generic term, I am not convinced by its rivals either – all of them seem to have some persuasive, but also questionable, elements. I will therefore remain with "youth culture" to denote the Islamic specimen under study, but not without borrowing from the concepts of subculture, lifestyle, scenes and their ethnic, religious and global occurrences.

Early youth cultural theories have first of all discussed "youth" as a meaningful category where young people, among other things, try out ideas that are important to them and are also eager to show them, if not boast about them, to the outside world. These theories have also paved the way for two main research interests, i.e. delinquency and expressive cultures, of which I am focusing only on the latter. At the same time, it is important to keep in mind the historical absence of a concept of youth, let alone youth culture, in Islam. Also in Islamic societies today, where adolescence has become more distinct as a life phase in the twentieth century, this is mainly a result from direct or indirect Western influence, despite local variations.

Subcultural theory, especially surrounding the CCCS, has emphasised style as being central to subcultures, and I take some of this on board. I do not regard it as the "base" of any youth culture, but as one of several basic, constituent elements. Hebdige's observations of style as a space for constructing identity, and his concept of "bricolage", the stripping of objects of their context and awarding them a new meaning, are very useful for looking at Islamic youth culture. Some authors have also stressed the importance of an idea or even ideology within a youth culture, on which I will place as much significance in the following as on style. The basic understanding of the CCCS of subcultures as a shared reaction to structural changes in society comes from the very different perspective of the 1960s, but is in a general application indeed relevant here, as the possibility of a collective response to a post-9/11 environment cannot be denied. I do, however, share most of the criticism expressed against subcultural theory, and will not consider (working) class as the origin of style-based youth cultures nor as a sufficient explanation. Neither will I fade out young women nor, obviously, ethnic minorities, and the failure of subcultural theory to incorporate religion is another deplorable aspect. With a strong emphasis on empirical research rather than on preconceived theories, this study also seeks to counter this very criticism with which much of CCCS research was confronted.

I follow the concepts of scenes and lifestyles in that they acknowledge their participants' individualism, choice and stronger independence of their social background, which appears more adequate for today's reality. Also, lifestyle theory takes into account a great variety of influences on someone's lifestyle orientation, with a focus on entertainment choices, which also plays a large role for Muslim youth. Very important is furthermore the recognition of an industry–consumer relationship and the fact that consumers finish the cultural product presented to them. In Islamic youth cultures, there is another level between the two, as the big brands of youth consumer culture are only taken as an inspiration that producers then turn into something relevant to their consumers, but these producers are small players and part of the scene rather than faceless industries. The idea that scenesters participate in more than one scene or with a temporary engagement only, is partly relevant. It is sensible not to essentialise the followers of Islamic youth culture and to notice that some of them may also enjoy listening to techno, but the idea of an entirely non-committal, fluctuating membership does not apply in this context where the idea is significant and participation is not just for the sake of leisure. Wherever these concepts drift towards a mere arbitrariness of denoting anything and nothing, they will not be applicable in this study.

Research into ethnic youth cultures has underlined the notion of fusion, for instance of the popular and the traditional, which will be dealt with more deeply when looking at hybridity in the following section. It also usefully emphasises the role of identity in ethnic youth cultures. The sociology of youth religion, then, contributes further to this framework by thinking of young people's religious belonging as an active choice, strong commitment and also as identity construction. The concepts of spirituality in less institutionalised settings and the top–down approach of hail-fellow-well-met Churches will play a role in Islamic youth culture, even if only in demarcation. The idea of virtual faith may also be employed in a contrasting way, as religious symbols are indeed pop-culturally processed, but not so much in a mimicking, rather in quite a straightforward way. Research into new methods of religious transmission is equally important, precisely because it has so far excluded youth culture as a possibility.

Finally, the worldwide perspective is useful for reflecting on the global significance of a youth culture on the one hand, and on the influences of globalisation on the other, both of which are relevant to Islamic youth culture. The appropriation of global flows of culture for local purposes as well as local conditions and constraints are important to notice when comparing the situation in different countries. Even if only a fraction of global cultural resources is picked up on, the fact that the flows are not unidirectional and that regional centres of cultural production have emerged, may explain an increased self-confidence in off-centre cultural production. The reminder that any globalised entertainment products, even if they are replenished with local meanings, also carry norms and values from their original location, is helpful for grasping the form not only as a neutral form; Islamic youth culture could otherwise too easily and wrongly be understood as having Western form filled with Islamic substance. Lastly, a global perspective is indispensable if dealing with a topic of global religion, paired with a political dimension of worldwide concern in the early twenty-first century.

These concepts have informed my understanding of Islamic youth culture as a "youth culture", and I also deliberately use the singular form to describe the whole of the movement and its inner connections between its constituent parts of performing arts, fashion and media; style, idea and action; consumers and producers. Also, this ranks the phenomenon as one among many other youth cultures – plural this time – although this is not to suggest an isolated view, ignoring the many overlaps. If there are other youth cultures based on Islam, for example, in Islamic countries, they are not included here, but they would then require of the plural form of Islamic youth culture*s*.

2. Hybridity

The mixing of cultures, or any of its synonyms like mélange, fusion, collage, blend, montage, cannot be thought of without another equivalent, the concept of hybridity. Historically though, the term carries colonial and indeed racist baggage, and was only converted into a positive term in postcolonial contexts – despite and because of its heritage. Originally a biological term, hybridity in that context denotes the mixture between two botanical or zoological species. Racist ideologies applied the term to the "impurity" believed to result from the mixing of a superior white "pure race" and non-white Others, a doctrine that summarised the essence of colonialism and determined much of its policies (Prabhu 2007: xii; Kuortti/Nyman 2007b: 4). Some authors have therefore cautioned against the continued use of the term hybridity, in order to avoid its associated racist ideology (Young 1995: 10, 27), but contemporary cultural theories have incorporated it primarily in two ways: to denote non-biological but cultural combinations of mixed and "hyphenated" identities (Brooker 1999) and to reverse the erstwhile supremacy of the white in a "counterdiscursive manner" (Kuortti/Nyman 2007b: 4–5). Today, the notion of hybridity rejects any essentialist understanding of culture as being fixed, absolute and heritable like genes, and repudiates with it the idea of an inherent assessments of superiority and supremacy.

Pinning Down a Fluid Concept

From a global perspective, hybridity generally refers to a mixing of cultures from all continents, with the process of hybridisation referring to the "making of global culture as a global mélange" (Nederveen Pieterse 1995: 60). However, not only cultures from places that are far apart are blended, in fact not just *cultures*, but also religious elements. Pnina Werbner's definition speaks of inversions, juxtapositions and fusions of "objects, languages and signifying practices from different and normally separated domains" (1997: 2), thereby including the possibility of mixing dissimilar elements from arenas that do not usually overlap.

Werbner also makes an important distinction between intentional and unconscious hybridity, the latter taking place throughout history with cultures evolving "through unreflective borrowings, mimetic appropriations, exchanges and inventions" (1997: 5), which differs from intentional hybridisation in its deliberation and the idea behind it, and this is the idea I am interested in exploring within Islamic youth culture. Because deliberate hybridity – Werbner also speaks of "artistic interventions" (ibid.: 5) – brings together what is widely regarded as incompatible, there is also a strong political dimension to it, of seeking to challenge and overthrow the public discourse of what is considered normal. Different academic traditions have chosen to place different emphases in this respect, which is why Jan Nederveen Pieterse has suggested a spectrum of hybridities, ranging from assimilationist hybridity, moving towards the cultural centre, to destabilising hybridity, which more actively blurs, reverses and subverts this centre and its normative canon (Nederveen Pieterse 1995: 56–57). The latter approach has brought the hybridity concept fame, especially in postcolonial studies, owing to the works of the "three great contemporary prophets of hybridity" (Werbner 1997: 13): Stuart Hall, Paul Gilroy and Homi Bhabha.

Postcolonial Perspectives

Hall argues from the perspective of cultural identity, which to him is always a matter of proclaimed "unities" in a "play of power and exclusion" (Hall 1996: 5). He therefore grants identity the potential of a vision to mobilise people in a struggle of hegemony and counter-hegemony (Werbner 1997: 13; Hall 1990). While Hall often applies a psychoanalytic understanding within his postcolonial thinking, this is not the approach I am taking; what is useful, however, is how he links hybridity and identity together, and his processual understanding of the latter. Because he conceives identities as a process of "becoming rather than being" (Hall 1996: 4), he also sees them in the context of using historic, linguistic and cultural resources (ibid.), pointing to hybridisation. Relevant in the context of Islam in Europe is Hall's understanding of a diaspora of identities as a constantly new production and reproduction, making use of transformation and difference; he rejects a definition of diaspora derived from purity and essence, and instead underlines that it is defined by heterogeneity, by identities based on difference, and thus by hybridity (Hall 1990: 235).

Bhabha, in the colonial context, primarily sees hybridity as a "contesting, antagonistic agency" (Bhabha 2004: 277). The overall goal and political achievement of a hybrid agency is therefore to counter the hegemony of a cultural authority, most palpable in a colonial power, by breaking the norm of a binary opposition of cultural groups that are otherwise treated as homogeneous in themselves (ibid.: 296). The aim is not to reverse the power distribution and to achieve supremacy, but to negotiate the cultural norm by offering various hybrid, at times ambiguous, alternatives (Bhabha 1996: 58). Avoiding a simplistic model of a third arising from two originals, Bhabha conceptualises hybridity as the "third space" that paves the way for other approaches to come about (Bhabha 1990). The third space restructures authority and establishes new political initiatives (ibid.: 211), thus hybridity is here closely connected to actively shaping the political context and to taking over agency. Despite some parallels, the situation of Muslims in Europe should not be directly equated to that of colonised peoples, and Bhabha's take on hybridity is not a sufficient interpretation to help explain the rise of Islamic youth culture in Europe – for example, I would not reduce the situation to a battle of antagonistic powers or cultures, and indeed not a binary one. Bhabha's insisting that hybridity brings about the unexpected and even the unwanted, however, is a useful reminder to question the context in which the phenomenon takes place and what is at stake for its key figures.

Gilroy's account of black cultures in the African diaspora and particularly in Britain well illustrates the processes of hybridisation. By way of examples, especially from the music scenes, Gilroy underlines how cultures are not fixed and watertight entities, but how the forms change and build on various other influences that are also historically scattered (Gilroy 1995: 217) – the original parts of a hybrid culture are therefore not to be seen as completely "un-hybrid" either. Gilroy's view also highlights the more complex processes behind a hybrid culture and where it leads to, by stating that the black cultures have disentangled cultural practices and their origins and were thus able to make use and sense of them in a new context. In this way the cultural practices contributed to a collective identity, not only within one black subculture, but also reaching beyond and thus creating new forms "with even more complex genealogies", including, for example, a culture shared between different ethnic groups, as happened with the British Asian interest in hip-hop and its various cultural resources in 1980s London (ibid.). With this view, Gilroy places much weight on the role of culture in the development of a black and British identity, which is a valuable prime example for the discussion of a European Islamic consciousness or collective identity, and to what extent it is shaped by a subculture, like that of Muslim youth.

In his discussion of the "black Atlantic" (Gilroy 1993), the transcultural generation of black diasporic cultures, Gilroy criticises both English and African-American theories and political cultures for having an essentialist, nationalistic outlook (ibid.: 4, 5–19). His concept of the "double consciousness", borrowed from W.E.B. Du Bois, expresses the difficulties of internalising an American – or European – identity while being black, yet it serves as a model for showing that such a dual perspective is possible and has shaped the hybrid cultures of the black Atlantic (ibid.: esp. 126, 188). With the global Islamic community of the *ummah* finding itself confronted with a similar issue – that of whether or not Western cultures and Islam are compatible – the idea of the double consciousness is a useful comparison, especially because compatibility has been denied from all sides. This is worth pursuing, even though the historic starting points of the respective diasporas differ strongly and the *ummah* has always been a transnational project; and yet, one that still has to deal with these questions of conflicting interests.

Global Cultural Flows

The hybridity concept has been used in a vast array of disciplines and research perspectives from the cultural critique of colonialism to the description of many other scenarios of transculturation (Hannerz 1992: 13), and it is rather these transcultural processes of how hybrid cultures are created that I explore in this research project. While hybridity has become a general term, other concepts denote very similar practices. Ulf Hannerz, for instance, prefers to speak of creolisation, and underlines that the emerging creole languages and cultural forms often live very much by the dynamics of mixture, whereby constant hybridisation becomes a continuous feature (Hannerz 1997: 14). Syncretism is another term that has mainly been used to describe the merging of religions, such as West African deities and Catholic saints, which hints at a similar direction, but is less useful in understanding combinations of more unlike domains like subculture(s) and Islam (Hannerz 1997: 15; Nederveen Pieterse 1995: 56).

Hybrid cultural production takes place on a micro level, showing in examples of local music fusions or localised interpretations of styles of dress. At the same time, however, it is inherently global, whether one grasps globalisation altogether as a process of hybridisation (Nederveen Pieterse 1995) or at least as strongly influenced by global cultural flows (Hannerz 1992, 1997; Wise 2008; Therborn 2011: 115–117) or, in turn, if hybridity is taken as the form in which these flows come together. In any case, the notion of flows adds a processual understanding to the analysis of cultures and how they come into being. The flow metaphor opposes a static view of culture, but it can also make processes of merging appear too smooth by ignoring uncertainties, losses and unexpected innovations (Hannerz 1997: 6). The study of Islamic youth culture benefits from the concept of global cultural flows in that it provides a global framework to a micro level phenomenon and thus acts as a reminder to distinguish the global flows that come together in this subculture, from ideas and designs from the Islamic world to African-American and Caribbean music, to European forms of youth activism. This is still the case if activists themselves claim to act only locally, picking up on the subcultures of their city, refusing to identify with a migration experience of their own and taking Islam as time- and place-independent. The concept of flows also helps to see the processual character of the subculture coming into being, although it should not mask the actors' intentionality; cultural flows do not just happen to passive recipients, but are set into motion because of people's consumption, adoption and remixing practices of cultural (re)sources.

Criticism

The greatest benefits of the hybridity concept – in general and for this particular project – lie in its counter-essentialist understanding of culture, which makes it an apt notion for studying cultural encounters of Islam, youth and subculture. However, the theory also poses a few problems. It can drift towards utter randomness, as either a hybrid culture is celebrated as an uncommon mixture of two "pure" cultures, or these original cultures are also thought of as hybrid, but then everything is hybrid, the newly created culture is nothing special and the theory merely states the obvious. This is also seen by some authors (e.g. Bhabha 1990: 211; Werbner 1997: 15), and Hannerz provides a sensible solution by stating that all cultures are indeed to some degree hybrid; if Creole is a hybrid language, partly made up of English, this does not mean that English is a language free of influences from Latin or French. The only importance is that the cultures have gone through separate historic developments, even if they have resulted from various influences (Hannerz 1997: 14–15). Also Therborn's concept of cultural belonging allows for an understanding of cultures as distinct from others, without having to assume an essentialist purity. Three main features of cultural belonging – having an identity different from the rest of the world, controlling a cognitive and symbolic code and having acquired particular norms and values (Therborn 1995: 128) – can be regarded as a starting point for global flows, while there is no reason to assume that these cultures have not gone through hybrid encounters themselves. This view acknowledges at least some social continuities instead of dispensing with them entirely.

Another often mentioned point of critique is the celebration of the concept and the "self-congratulation" of those using it (Werbner 1997: 15; Friedman 1997; Hutnyk 1997). It can certainly act as an important political force in discourses of colonialism and inequality. However, sometimes the concept seems to be primarily applied because it is politically favourable, which is problematic if it means that the outcome, i.e. the detection of unequal power relations, is already clear at the beginning of the research; empirical research always needs to be open-ended.

Summary

As for my own use of the hybridity concept, I would summarise it as a notion that allows cultural fusions to be looked at in terms of local practices of combining (parts of) cultures and in terms of global cultural flows. I focus chiefly on studying the process of how the hybrid forms come into being, what their sources are and which elements are adopted while others are rejected. Assuming an intentional act, I also study the reasons for creating hybrid cultural products, not by confining this to a postcolonial reading, but by remaining open to other motives and contextual influences. Finally, Islamic youth culture does not only fuse unalike and seemingly incompatible elements, but I would also argue that it is an *improbable* mix, as there are several conflicts between the properties and goals of various subcultures and those of religious beliefs and practices, and between some Western and Eastern traditions. Indeed, the fact that youth culture is not an Islamic concept in itself requires to study the phenomenon from a hybridity perspective.

3. Islam in Europe

In the past three decades, literature on Islam and Muslims in Europe has flourished greatly, especially in response to explosions of planes and trains in New York, London and Madrid. This has lead to a plethora of works, amounting to several thousand, as Frank Buijs and Jan Rath already estimated in their useful and comprehensive literature review in 2002 (Buijs/Rath 2002: 3, 28), and there is no reason to believe that academic production in this field has slowed down. A review of this body of literature would fill a second book without resulting in the provision of a useful analytical tool for grasping the emergence of Islamic youth culture. I therefore chose to indicate only very briefly the main directions of research in this field, and mainly to focus on the themes relevant to this topic – Muslim youth, European Islam, inter-generational conflict – before reviewing the few works bordering on Islamic youth culture itself.

General Approaches

Many collective works try to capture the situation of Muslims in Europe as a whole, either in the form of country reports from many European countries (Nielsen 1995; Haddad/Smith 2002; Maréchal 2002; Al-Hamarneh/Thielmann 2008; Nielsen et al. 2009, 2010), or as a transnational presentation of selected topics (Allievi/Nielsen 2003; Maréchal et al. 2003; Al-Azmeh/Focas 2007), or an overlap of both (Gerholm/Lithman 1988; Hunter 2002; Escudier et at. 2003). Distinction has been made between a longstanding Muslim presence, chiefly in the Balkans and the southeast of Europe, and Muslim immigration to mainly Western Europe (Buijs/Rath 2002: 4). Even though the vast majority of works deal with the latter, this – alongside local developments – has also sparked an increased interest in the Southern and Eastern European situation (e.g. Norris 1993; Popovic 1994; Nonneman/Niblock/Szajkowski 1997; Bougarel/Clayer 2001). The body of literature on immigration to Western Europe, then, deals with an array of topics: immigration, integration, Islamic practice, institutionalisation, the relationship between Muslims and the State, the relationship with non-Muslims, participation, education, citizenship, media and public opinion, security, terrorism, extremism and racism – to name but a few. The works themselves can hardly be summarised in thematic categories because of their constant overlap, convergence and at times also contradictory perspectives; rather, each topic corresponds to several of the most common research directions.

Thus, the literature on Muslim citizenship deals with immigration, multiculturalism, national law and participation (Shahid/Koningsveld 1996; Koopmans et al. 2005; Modood et al. 2006; Brown 2010). The many works on mosque construction look at the institutionalisation of Islam as well as conflicts with the host country in terms of religion in the public sphere, pluralism and xenophobia (Cesari 1994; Buijs 1998; Rath et al. 2001; Häusler 2008; Allievi 2009). The headscarf issue has produced literature on values and value-based conflicts, Islamic practice, and gender (Coppes 1994; El Hamel 2002; McGoldrick 2006; Amir-Moazami 2007; Winter 2008; Dreher/Ho 2009). Most publications on Islamophobia are more recent – although the issue was identified in the 1990s – and touch on the relationship between Muslims and non-Muslims, right-wing extremism, urban development and the media (Runnymede Trust 1997; Council of Europe 2004; Allen 2010; Morey 2010; Schneiders 2010; Yaqin 2010; Esposito/Kalin 2011; Morey/Yaqin 2010, 2011). The literature on converts deals with the relationship between Muslims and non-Muslims, Islamic practice, proselytisation, Muslim leadership and gender (Beckford/Gilliat 1998; Allievi 1999; Wohlrab-Sahr 1999; Nieuwkerk 2006; Reddie 2009). Cultural identity, again a topic across many studies, looks at Islamic practices in the cultural sphere, identity politics, often with an ethnographic approach (Baumann 1996; Basit 1997; Jacobson 1998; Tietze 2001; Werbner 2002; Sackmann/Peters/Faist 2003; Keaton 2006; Tiesler 2006; Kabir 2010). Some of these will be reviewed in more detail in the following section, since many also focus on youth. In addition to the purely academic studies, there are several accounts by Muslims themselves, dealing with their faith in the European environment (Ramadan 2003; Malik 2007), and very frequently also on how and why they either converted to Islam (Bushill-Matthews 2008) or renounced their faith or extremist orientation (Warraq 2003; Husain 2007; Ali 2008; Abdel-Samad 2010).

Muslim European Youth

With such a vast number of publications on various aspects of Muslims in Europe, it is surprising that the selection of works dealing with youth is rather limited. The few works that comment on their situation in Europe as a whole or in a particular country sketch the context and focus on religiosity and the identity issues in various forms. Apart from the necessary mentioning of the geopolitical context and major clashes between Islam and the West, the context mainly features inter-generational differences and the formation of a European Islam, both of which are closely related. Differences between generations inevitably occur in a post-migratory setting, and have been identified, for example, by Valérie Amiraux and Gerdien Jonker as one of three major differentiations young Muslims express in reaction to the stigma of "Muslim" imposed on them from the outside. These differentiations can show in the way some young Muslims distance themselves from non-Muslims, for instance through radicalisation, or in their distinction from other ethnic or Islamic groups by identifying (with) a "real Islam", or indeed in a disconnection from the parent generation that possessed authority over mosques – often ethnicity-based centres – and religious interpretation (Amiraux/Jonker 2006: 11–12). Olivier Roy describes the "process of de-ethnicisation" (Roy 2006: 149), in which many European-born Muslim youths follow either of two ways: either they take on a *banlieue* subculture of mainly

African-American origin or they become religious. If they do choose to practise Islam, this is done without reference to any ethnic background, in fact with a clear rejection of cultural traditions and an affirmation of Islam as universal and "true". This approach is applied by many and may result in "liberal", pop-cultural or also radical practices; in any case, it is first and foremost a matter of intergenerational conflict (ibid.: 146–154). Moreover, Roy has largely dealt with the "uncoupling" of religion and culture in many revivalist religions today and has aptly contextualised Islam in this global development (Roy 2007, 2010); hence, there is room to adopt new cultural traits. Roger Penn's and Paul Lambert's quantitative study proves that the children of migrants, mainly from Islamic countries, clearly adopt the popular culture of their European home country, in terms of preferences for food, television, media and leisure activities (Penn/Lambert 2009: 111–123).

The other feature that marks the context for young Muslims' engagement (or non-engagement, for that matter) is the development of a so-called "Euro-Islam". Several authors have argued that the Muslim presence in Europe has challenged the traditional Islamic worldview and that this has led to a change promoted by European Islamic scholars. Traditionally, Islamic jurists have divided the world into *dar al-islam*, the "house" or territory of Islam or peace, and *dar al-harb*, the "house of war" or non-Muslim territories. Other jurists have also identified a third sphere, the *dar al-ahd*, as a territory of contract or agreement. While in the fourteenth century it was initially conceptualised as temporary or as located in between the two other domains, European Muslim scholars in the 1990s have adopted this third option as a long-term solution, for it was considered more apt to capture the permanent residence of Muslims in Western countries (Cesari 1998a, 1999; Mandaville 2002: 227–228, 2003: 127; Ramadan 2002: 218, 2003). In this way, they gave their blessing to the younger generation's participation and engagement in European society as their own and only society. Peter Mandaville is largely optimistic about the development of a European Islam in the twenty-first century as an "emancipatory theology", actively shaped by young Muslims born and educated in the West, who have internalised some European education patterns and therefore place more emphasis on personal choice and on *ijtihad*, the judgement of the religious sources (Mandaville 2003: 137).

Young Muslims in the German, French and British Context

Several other publications study more specific issues with a national focus that outline the setting of young Muslims in these countries. In the German context, religiosity is a major theme occurring across various studies.[3] Investigating both the German and the French situations, Nikola Tietze distinguishes four types of religiosity among young Muslim men in precarious social, economic and political situations. The types of religiosity include "ethisation" (belief becomes an ethos, an instruction for action, religion is stripped of any ethnic or cultural dimensions, morality informs one's behaviour, and if turning extreme, *halal* and *haram* become harsh boundaries); "ideologisation" (belonging to a community carries more weight than the faith itself, the community is imagined as oppressed by society); "utopisation" (religiosity is a process of individual perfection; spirituality and traditional scholarship are emphasised up to the point that the social world may become meaningless); and "culturalisation" (religiosity is determined by belonging to a culture to which Islam is secondary; integration into a certain milieu can lead to isolation, but is also open to changing tradition and adapting it to the current time and place, allows for creative *bricolage*) (Tietze 2001: 157-159). Tietze thereby contributes to a very nuanced picture of the role of religion in young Muslims' lives. Islam gives plenty of options, first for collaging an identity and second for integrating with that identity into society – or not. While parts of her analysis correspond to people involved in Islamic youth culture, her types do not fully match with their religiosity. The fact that most features of "ethisation" would fit, and some of "culturalisation", but not others, is mainly due to the different populations in terms of gender, socio-economic background and the study's focus, which does not take youth culture into account. For Tietze, moving between these types is possible, the dynamics of which differ between French and the German society because of factors like citizenship rights and colonial or migratory history. A disadvantage of her typology is that despite her empirical investigations it stays in many parts highly theoretical and abstract, and thus blurs the influence of the different national settings.

Halit Öztürk studies the *Lebenswelten* – "life worlds", a topic of interest in current German sociology – of young Muslims in Berlin and in particular their religiosity and integration into wider society, showing that a strong affiliation with Islam does not contradict, but at times fosters a commitment to German society (Öztürk 2007). Although the young people in his sample experienced

---

3   Very generally, a chapter on youth and religiosity in the 2006 Shell Youth Survey diagnoses three general degrees of religiosity among German youth: "religion light" in Western Germany, no religion in Eastern Germany and a strong religious affiliation among young migrants of either Islamic or various Christian backgrounds. A higher degree of religiosity among young Muslims compared with their non-Muslim peers is suggested, but was not made explicit in the survey (Shell Deutschland Holding 2006: 203–239).

forms of discrimination, they identified themselves as being integrated, and for most cases, Öztürk deduces from this that the more religious they are, the more integrated they are. Consequently, the "pathways of integration" – promised in the title of the book – sometimes appear as mainly one path, that of Islam, even if his exhaustive case studies help to add some more details to this. A decade earlier, Fred-Ole Sandt published a less optimistic study in this respect, researching the religiosity and views on religion of teenagers with a Christian, Muslim, spiritual or atheist background (Sandt 1996). From interviewing the young Muslims in his sample, Sandt concludes two main groups that differ in their religious practice; one of them following Islam while criticising modern individualism and the other one dividing the religious sphere of the family from the Western sphere of the school, leisure and youth culture (ibid.: 259). In many ways, these findings may correspond to reality, but they are also fairly two-dimensional. Islamic youth culture, which overcomes both these models, became more visible a few years later, which may or may not be the reason for the absence of a more nuanced interpretation.

Hans-Jürgen von Wensierski and Claudia Lübcke present a very detailed overview of Muslim youth in Germany (Wensierski/Lübcke 2007). "Muslim" is here used to describe a young person's heritage or cultural background and not necessarily a religious affiliation; religiosity and thus an Islamic way of life, on the other hand, are seen as one option among many. The authors call for a more complex view of young Muslims' situations, leaving behind the dichotomy of tradition versus modernity or a religious lifestyle versus a secular Western one (ibid.: 8–9). Wensierski's article in the same volume describes how young Muslims pick and choose parts of their biography, which follows modernistic traits like a prolonged education and mobility and taking part in commercialised and medialised everyday cultures, but that does not have the same individualistic, pluralised and gender-equal emphasis like most biographies of their non-Muslim peers: an Islamic, selectively modernised youth phase (Wensierski 2007: 76–78).

In France, Muslims have to deal with the situation that religion is widely absent from the public sphere, and in turn, Islam blurs the boundaries between the private and the public (Cesari 1998b: 36). Jocelyne Cesari analyses the differences between generations of French Muslims and notices a more individualised religiosity among the young. They do not just accept what has been legitimated by tradition, but use their own reasoning to adopt Islamic ethics, as Mandaville has diagnosed for the European context in general. In France, this is part of the retreat of religion to the private sphere, as Islam can thus be used as a moral guideline, but does not need to show in everyday life (ibid.: 31). It is also part of a re-islamisation of many of the younger generation compared with the more ethnically-identifying migrant generation (Khosrokhavar 1998). Mohammed Berhil adds that the members of the younger generation reject, at least in retrospect, the harsh educational methods of some Quran schools and therefore choose their own individual approach to religion, which Mandaville had described as a change towards westernised educational preferences (Berhil 2003: 117). Cesari also describes the formation of youth organisations like *L'Union des Jeunes Musulmans (UJM)* as a means of religious transmission, founded by the "deuxième gé", the second generation, in 1987 (Cesari 1998a: 100–101).

Amiraux continues on the topic of the public sphere. She draws attention to the fact that publications only ever deal with the kind of Islam that is visible and traceable in public, usually taking shape in associations and institutionalised forms of engagement. To counter this, she presents case studies of Muslims who engage in society in many ways, an activity that is informed by their being Muslim and acting as such, but that cannot be grasped in terms of public or private religion (Amiraux 2006). She calls them "invisible Muslims" and a "silent majority" (ibid.: 48), showing that social commitment can be diverse and indeed combine one's Muslim identity with a presence in public.

Trica Keaton adds a new perspective with her study on Muslim girls and her particular consciousness of their African, often black, background (Keaton 2006). Although a high number of Muslim immigrants come from West Africa and the Comoros, Islam in France is often reduced to Maghrebine issues. Keaton paints a rather bleak picture of the incorporation of young Muslims into French nationality, who are confronted with even more barriers if they are girls. Her arguments return to a more ethnic debate, as she perceives social exclusion as still being the result of coming from an African background, but one that is enforced by the religious, and this is what laws like the headscarf ban from schools are directed at. The strong affirmation of her participants that they identify as being French is only part of the identity politics and still does not make them full and equal citizens.

The British situation again highlights intergenerational conflicts and identity formation. Jessica Jacobson addresses both in her study that tackles the reason why religion plays such a significant role in identity formation (Jacobson 1998). She claims that there are many sources of social identity available to second-generation British Pakistani, yet the majority seem to base their identity almost exclusively on Islam. One the one hand, her respondents explain this by the belief that religion is a matter of personal choice and reflection, while they regard ethnicity as fixed, natural and given, and on the other hand, Islam has precise guidelines and can establish social boundaries with non-Muslims. The combination of individual choice and collective Islamic prescriptions is not considered a contradiction, but appears to be characteristic of the generation under study.

Steven Vertovec regards young Muslims' debates with the parent generation as another dimension in a potentially conflictual relationship of sets of Islamic and Western values (Vertovec 1998). Their social, cultural and religious beliefs are not fixed, but result from interacting with both these spheres. Contradicting many other studies, Vertovec found that his respondents understand religion as culture, embracing the idea of belonging to a Muslim community while lacking religious knowledge. He furthermore describes the fear of the older generation, who see Islam threatened by the westernisation of their youth, while the respondents themselves were positively convinced of a feasible combination.

Expectations, aspirations and identity from a gender perspective are dealt with by Tehmina Basit in her study on British Muslim girls (Basit 1997). She describes how these girls negotiate their aspirations, only partly influenced by their parents and teachers, by playing with and trying out their various identities of being female, Muslim, family members, students and career-orientated British Asians; at the same time, their aspirations also shape the way they perceive themselves and perform in everyday life (ibid.: 172). Islam informs an ethos that sets up the widely supportive family framework, but does not play a major role in the girls' endeavours. The importance of black Muslims, to mirror the French context, and the role of black converts, are dealt with by Richard Reddie (2009).

Philip Lewis widens the view with his portrayal of British Muslim youth in general (Lewis 1994). As in many publications of the 1990s, he also identifies a crisis of transmission of Islam, as scholars did not reach out to the younger generation. The youth, however, took the initiative on a social level, for instance to overcome "victimhood" and complaint, and thus have become fully familiar with diversity, democracy and being British. Lewis's account tries to do justice to the complex diversity of this population and to British Muslim youth as a whole, and thus sets out a few general features like intergenerational tensions, a demand for an English-speaking Islam and a positive commitment to being British and Muslim. Nahid Afrose Kabir continues a similar format, but does not add much depth to the analysis of the situation of young Muslims in the United Kingdom (2010). It is instead a well-meaning plea for society cohesion, empowerment and the acceptance of "biculturalism", both by those who are directly affected, the bicultural youth themselves, and by wider society. What her account affirms, at least, is a very diverse picture of young British Muslims and their widely positive identification with Britain, which is expressed in an explicit loyalty to the country, sharing hobbies like sports and music with their non-Muslim peers and embracing a set of values corresponding to society at large.

Despite the structural differences in migration and citizenship in Germany, France and Britain, which provide different frameworks for young Muslims, a few constant features have become palpable. In the post-migratory situation Islam mostly becomes a choice, and if chosen, it is stripped from the ethnic ballast of preceding generations; intergenerational conflict has been an issue, especially in previous decades. Engagement with society is widespread and is sometimes facilitated where a religious identity is chosen over an ethnic one; even if religiosity does not determine every young person of Muslim background, it is a most welcome option for many.

Before finally approaching research on Islamic youth culture in Europe, an all-pervasive concept requires to be mentioned. Youth culture, hybridity and Islam in Europe do not only represent different cultural encounters, but also cannot avoid touching on *identity* again and again. However, identity is a tricky concept because it has been used to explain everything and therefore nothing, and, thus, as a cultural researcher, one cannot live with it nor without it, as Rogers Brubaker and Frederick Cooper have demonstrated so shrewdly (Brubaker/Cooper 2000). Instead of attaching the term "identity" to anything, they call for using more precise terms to indicate the specific sub-concepts that are subsumed under "identity". Of the three terms Brubaker and Cooper propose – identification, self-understanding and commonality/groupness – the first is most applicable in this study. Identification relates to categorisation and to the membership in a group with a categorical attribute like ethnicity, language, citizenship, gender and many more (ibid.: 15). The authors emphasise that studying the "work of identification" is more legitimate, and possibly more intriguing, than assuming identity as a necessary outcome; thus, the concept studies a process rather than a condition. I would add that this process of identification does not only involve placing oneself into a particular category or wondering which would be the most adequate – although this exploration is also meaningful – but that it also includes altering and renewing the categories if they do not correspond to one's self-perception. Another aspect is that the concept looks at the agents carrying out the identification and at the distinction between self-identification and the categorisation of oneself by others, such as the state, adding a power dimension to the analysis.[4] These uses of the term identification are the most useful for studying the coming of age of young Muslims in Europe, the categories that they and others use for them, and in what way Islamic youth culture is used in this process.

---

4   The term "identification" has another dimension, the psychoanalytic sense of identifying as someone, which some postmodern authors have picked up on, but this will not be applied in this study.

Islamic Youth Culture

To begin with, I will take a brief look at the few publications on consumerism and fun in Islamic countries. Patrick Haenni and Husam Tammam describe the emergence of consumption, or market Islam, for instance, in Egyptian shopping centres (Haenni/Tammam 2003), but also in Turkey and Indonesia, which Haenni calls a "conservative revolution" (Haenni 2005). It features a "light" form of Islam, practiced by an urban upper class, partly because of its chic accessories and partly owing to the morale of free market policies that has entered consumption Islam, leaving behind both official and political Islam (Haenni/Tammam 2003; Haenni 2005). One of the key figures is Egyptian televangelist Amr Khaled, who preaches Islam to young people in their language and in a modern style. At the same time, he employs a form of "Protestant ethic": spirituality is balanced with a call to become active, rich and successful, which will then serve as a role model for others on both the economic and the spiritual levels. This religious–entrepreneurial model, American style, has become very popular in Egypt (Haenni/Tammam 2003). A journalistic account by Allegra Stratton takes a look at the youth cultural scenes of the Middle East and uncovers a close connection between money-loaded pop cultural production and devoutness. Again, the fans embrace Islam and some conservative religious values in a light version that does not hold too many moral restrictions against sexy dress codes (Stratton 2006).

Asef Bayat sheds light on the relationship between Islamism and fun, and why the extreme regimes of Iran, Saudi-Arabia and Afghanistan under the Taliban rule out many forms of pleasure (Bayat 2007). Quoting many examples of policies suppressing leisure activities, non-religious pleasures, mixing of the sexes, music and other sources of joy, Bayat is able to show the inner logic of the desperate striving to maintain power based on fear; if fun challenges people's fears, it also threatens the regime itself. Islam is used as a moral framework to provide the rules of controlling fun and pleasure. However, Bayat also observes a significant change from this type of political Islamism to the "faith and fun" of what he still calls Islamism, but transformed into a "post-Islamist piety", away from political severity towards a religious conservatism that is now able to incorporate fun (Bayat 2002: 23). He supports Haenni's view of Amr Khaled as targeting upper class, affluent youth and women, but contradicts the assessment of "Islam light". Khaled's popular style and ethical values do not mask a very orthodox religious understanding: "While his style is highly imaginative, his theology remains deeply scriptural, with little perspective to historicize, to bring critical reason into interpretations" (ibid.). On the one hand, Bayat interprets the Amr Khaled phenomenon as the demand of a new youth culture as Stratton described it – with some inherent contradictions or swinging back and forth between different realms – and on the other hand as a new form of *dawah*, or proselytising.

In Europe, Islamic youth culture may or may not be seen as part of the same movement, depending on the author. While I will argue that this youth culture follows a different dynamic and features other characteristics, some authors mainly see economic reasons at work or regard Amr Khaled as the origin of the European phenomenon. A short introduction to Western "cool Islam" is given by Amel Boubekeur (2005). Presenting a few examples of Islamic street wear, music and Mecca Cola from the United States and Western Europe, she argues that a comfortable consumerism has replaced political Islamism, similar to Bayat's view, which allows Muslim pride to be shown in an inconspicuous way. However, I cannot quite follow her statement that this new culture is a form of secularisation. She argues that because it is based on elements from the secular sphere, it facilitates integration into Western societies (ibid.: 12). The latter part of the argument may be true, and there is a matter of overlapping spheres at work, but this does not justify the claim of a secularised culture; in fact, the reverse is true, that non-religious objects are being imbued with religious meaning. Also, she narrows the movement down to an individualistic consumer culture and thereby ignores the entangled networks among the youth as well as the producers and the manifold intentions behind it.

Julia Gerlach was one of the first authors to give a comprehensive description of the movement in Germany that she first termed "Pop Islam" (Gerlach 2006). Her journalistic account gives intriguing empirical insights into the phenomenon in Germany that she interprets as a continuation of the Amr Khaled movement, since according to her, Arabic-speaking German youth consume his preaching via satellite television and the internet. Khaled's ideas and style, she claims, resonate with young Muslims in Europe because of the geopolitical situation that fosters anti-Islamic sentiments coupled with their search for moral values in the Quran, as they embrace the young, fashionable outlook on Islam. Gerlach sees great potential for integration in the "remix of life-styles", in the embrace of Islam and globalised popular culture (ibid.: 11). She points out that the "Pop Muslims" show a strong social commitment to society, which prompts her to assume that an engagement in Islamic pop culture and communal work will keep them away from Islamist violence. But she also observes an explicit conservatism in an occasional display of anti-Western opinions that might again be open to extremist views. Altogether, drawing a parallel with the Arab world is useful, yet leaves the European situation unclear, and as I will show, has very little to do with the movement in Europe. In a later contribution, Gerlach revisits the concept and acknowledges that European Muslims have adapted the Arab influences to meet their own needs (Gerlach 2010). The book, however, fails to provide an analytical framework to explore the reasons for the emergence of Islamic youth culture, or perhaps it does not make the claim to do so.

There are several other journalistic and pedagogical treatments of the scene aimed at the general public, one of which is found in a special issue for schools and teachers (Müller/Nordbruch/Tataroglu 2008). The issue portrays the style, soundtrack, media and associations of Islamic youth culture, first to inform about what young religious Muslims are into, and second to distinguish between Islamic and Islamist tendencies. The purpose of the publication is for young people, social workers and teachers to be able to look at Muslim youth without prejudice and to understand their own culture, but also to be wary of extremist currents, preachers and organisations. The publication shows how Islamic youth culture has started to attract the attention of wider society. Two of the authors, Götz Nordbruch and Jochen Müller, also run the association and online information portal Ufuq, dealing with migrant youth cultures and political education.[5] The website and its regular newsletter (2007–2011) are aimed at Muslims and non-Muslims, at academics, journalists and educators, suggesting a balanced approach to prevent radical views on both sides (e.g. Ufuq 2011). Nordbruch has further emphasised the pluralistic aspect, the clear commitment of young Muslims to being German, as well as the question of how to address extremism in social youth work (2009, 2010). Another portrait of German Islamic youth culture is found in a collection by the Youth Culture Archive (Archiv der Jugendkulturen e.V.). It presents insights into the annual youth meeting by the organisation Muslimische Jugend in Deutschland (MJD) and interviews with participants and organisers (Projektgruppe JugendArt 2010b).

In Wensierski's and Lübcke's collection, most contributions deal with non-religious activities and biographies of young people of Muslim background – controversially still referred to as Muslims. Also, Lübcke's article, an overview of various German Muslim youth cultures, includes those that are ethnically rather than religiously influenced (Lübcke 2007). First, she looks at some common, non-Muslim youth cultures like punk, left-wing alternative and consumerist hedonistic subcultures to discover whether young Muslims are part of them, which they are only to a small extent. Then she explores a variety of subcultures that are dominated by people of Muslim background – hip-hop, the multiethnic clubbing scene, Turkish and multiethnic cliques, the Turkish or Muslim homosexual scene, the Turkish and Muslim art scene, young Muslims in associations,

---

5   Ufuq – Jugendkultur, Medien & politische Bildung in der Einwanderungsgesellschaft: http://www.ufuq.de.

and, finally, religious youth culture. The latter is the focus of my own research into Islamic youth culture, so defined because it is the only youth culture that is explicitly religious; Muslims certainly take part in any other youth culture as well, but without this clear reference. Lübcke confirms my observation that the participants in Islamic youth culture are usually well educated, and that women are as much present as men. She also credits the movement with a conservative stance, and considers Islam in this context to be far from modernised or western-ised. Indeed, she finds that Western pop culture is merely used as a vehicle to transport traditional values (ibid.: 312). The article offers a valuable insight into the presence of Muslims in various youth cultures, and yet it does not go into depth on the development of an explicitly Islamic youth culture, nor does it ex-plain why it occurs and what exactly the youth are trying to achieve with it.

For the British context, Mandaville has provided an important introduction to this topic in an article on popular culture and Muslim youth in the UK (Manda-ville 2009a). He relates the phenomenon to issues of identity formation and so-cio-political attitudes, and detects several themes that dominate young British Muslims' popular culture: one such theme is having an Islamic version of main-stream popular culture, leisure activities and also middle class lifestyles, partly as an alternative, but also in order to continue taking part in the mainstream. Another theme is the use of youthful expressions by organisations such as Young Muslims UK, but also by traditional religious scholars in order to reach out to young people (Mandaville 2009a: 165–167). Mandaville correctly notes the urge of this age group for adapting Islam to the time and place where they live, but looks at it from the perspective of consumers only, without taking into account that of the producers to find out why they offer Islamic popular culture.

Very few other publications deal with what I would consider sub-genres of Islamic youth culture – music and fashion – but they treat them as independent phenomena or in frameworks other than youth culture. Fashion is one such ex-ample: it can be considered part of youth culture, but also of an age-independent consumer culture, femininity or bodily display. The works of Emma Tarlo (2010a+b) and Annelies Moors (Tarlo/Moors 2007) rank among the most im-portant contributions in this field. These authors show how the alleged contradic-tion of Islamic sartorial prescriptions and trendiness is challenged by Muslim women worldwide. From Turkey to Indonesia, from Egypt to Iran, women mix local, ethnic and global styles with various forms of Islamic dress. Europe is no exception, but the non-Muslim environment adds another dimension in that Mus-lim fashion takes influences from the immediate surroundings and from a reli-gious background, which creates "a variety of hybrid styles that blend concerns with religion, modesty, politics, and identity with a creative engagement with both Western and Eastern fashions" (Moors/Tarlo 2007: 138). Tarlo gives a vivid and extensive overview of the abundant options of female Islamic dress, either designed specifically for Muslim women or made to fit in an Islamic way by the women themselves (Tarlo 2010a). She looks at the practices and intentions of both consumers and producers, the rich creativity on both sides, and how biographies are crafted through fashion. Her ethnographic journey ends with the conclusion that all of this feeds into a "global Islamic fashion scape" that offers an increased choice of carefully crafted and re-combined styles (ibid.: 224–225). Tarlo's concern is not with fashion as part of a wider youth culture, nor does she limit it to young people, but her findings are widely applicable to the specific case of young urban Islamic fashion and in parts also to the other genres of Islamic youth culture.

Miriam Gazzah researches into Dutch-Moroccan youth culture and the significance of music for the identification process in a post-migration context (Gazzah 2008, 2009). By looking at their music, she explains how young Dutch-Moroccans place themselves in society and in what way the political context as well as their social, religious and cultural background has an effect on their music (Gazzah 2009: 424). However, she also places the music into a wider context of an Islam-inspired youth culture, in which "Islam is used to give music, fashion, food, style or cultural imagery in general an Islamic touch" (ibid.: 413), even though she states that Islam and ethnicity remain equally important for the population she studies. As a youth culture, it provides the option of being a "cool Muslim" as an equal alternative to being a goth or a hip-hopper (ibid.: 425). Relating the phenomenon back to the wider context, Gazzah points out that young European Muslims do not only speak Dutch, French or English fluently, but that they also master the language of youth culture (ibid.: 404) – from that perspective, the widespread demands for a European-language Islam are very similar to the translation of Islam into youth culture.

Summary

The overwhelming amount of literature on Islam in Europe requires a narrow focus to be chosen. However, even the publications on young European Muslims treat issues ranging from the post-migration context and the geo-political situation to inter-generational conflicts, the formation of a European Islam, social engagement and religion as an active choice. The national contexts stress different aspects, such as religiosity and the definition of Muslimness in Germany, the French issue of religion in the public sphere, or the role of religion in identity formation and Islamic diversity in the United Kingdom. The contrast with Islamic consumerism raises questions about how much of Islamic youth culture is a

Western phenomenon and whether it is mainly an economic one. The few publications that have already studied this phenomenon indicate that the relationship between the global and the local is not easy to trace, that Western societies are at times unsure how to deal with Islamic youth culture, and they underline the importance of not studying it as an isolated culture or a single option for young Muslims to express themselves. The recurring concept of identity in this context requires a precise use of the term as identification, focussing on the process of working on one's identity whatever the outcome, and on the agency of self-identification as opposed to being categorised by others, including the alteration and renewal of these categories. Used in this way, it helps to elucidate the relationship between young Muslims and their environment and what young Muslims are trying to achieve with Islamic youth culture.

Conclusion: Lacunae in the Literature

This chapter started from noticing that there is no distinct concept of youth nor of youth culture in Islam and that the literature does not provide any satisfying bridge for this gap. Several lacunae remain that show the inability of the theoretic literature to sufficiently understand and explain Islamic youth culture, that is to say to explicate its nature, reasons and implications and those of similar cultural phenomena.

The literature on youth and subcultures has provided some useful concepts for the understanding of Islamic youth culture, including the acknowledgement of youth as an analytical category, an emphasis on style and an underlying idea of subcultures, and the importance of individual choice, commitment and identity formation. But many questions remain unanswered: How can youth cultural theory be transferred to Islam? How can the origins of subcultures be conceptualised other than on the basis of class? Where is there space for religion in theories on both mainstream and ethnic youth cultures? And from the perspective of youth and religion research – why the affiliation with pop culture (if not used by Churches to woo young people or used by them to mimic religion)?

The global perspective on youth cultures along with hybridity theory have proven useful in drawing attention to global flows and their local adaptations, and both concepts facilitate understanding the phenomenon as a hybrid fusion and how the combination comes about. But notions of global encounters and hybridity are often applied to the merging of two cultures, rather than a culture and a religion, or a globally flowing culture and its local adaptation. Here, however, two global "ideas" (a global religion and Euro-American youth culture) come together and meet with some local conditions (whereby the local is not the most central trait, but rather the German, French, British context). Moreover, the theories do not explain the reasons why the combination is carried out. Why should youth culture and Islam go well together? What is gained when Islamic youth culture is classified as hybrid?

The literature on Islam in Europe has been a useful hint to the main themes that determine the context in which the phenomenon is taking place. Despite a few intriguing case studies, there were only few investigations into the situation of youth and in particular youth culture among young Muslims. This results in lacking to explain the reasons of the emergence of Islamic youth culture, as resulting from the relationship with the environment, and a clarification of the consequences for this context. If "identity" is one aim or outcome, the application of this concept needs to be very clear and to shed light on this relationship. The empirical inquiry will therefore be undertaken to reveal what Islamic youth culture tells us about the situation of young Muslims in Europe.

Altogether, theories on youth culture have thus far not been conceptualised in the context of Islam, and certainly not in a combined application to a non-Islamic, Western environment. The empirical study of Islamic youth culture intends to amend each of these theories as outlined above, and to demonstrate that they need to be combined in order to understand cultural phenomena composed of national and (post-)migration contexts, global youth culture and a world religion.

B. Methodology

1. Asking Questions

Tying in with the issues raised and the lacunae pointed out in the discussion of the literature, empirical research questions are required to complement the design of this study. The phenomenon of Islamic youth culture in Western Europe raises a wealth of questions, but I have decided to focus on two broad areas: the character and the development of this subculture. The former corresponds to several questions regarding what the phenomenon actually represents: What is Islamic youth culture and what are its inherent and basic qualities? How does it manifest itself? What cultural references does it put into practice? This does not only explore its constituent parts, but also what the subculture is *not* made of or what it is a demarcation of. Furthermore, this set of questions investigates who the key figures and the followers of the phenomenon are, where it takes its form

and how transnational it is. Finally, it poses the question: Is it a religious practice, is it youth culture or is it something else?

The second set of questions concerns the development of the subculture:
Why is Islamic youth culture created? What prompts someone to create or contribute to Islamic youth culture? What are the biographical, (sub)cultural, religious or societal reasons for this engagement? What meaning does Islamic youth
culture have for the producer and how does the person explain and account for
his or her motivation? Apart from the questions that zoom in on the individual
perspective, this set of questions also takes into account the context and investigates the role of the contextual setting.

2. Designing the Research

Overall Design: Ethnography and Reconstructive Research

An explorative study into a relatively recent scene, unfamiliar in large parts of
the literature, lends itself to ethnography. Adopting an ethnographic research
design as the framework for the study as a whole allows an in-depth study of a
small-scale setting or group to be conducted in the everyday context of the field,
involving the researcher's participation over time and the collection of various
kinds of data (Hammersley/Atkinson 2007: 3). Such a research design also permits several qualitative methods to be triangulated under the ethnographic umbrella, in the process of both data collection and analysis.

The choice of a qualitative approach here is mainly informed by the research
object. It requires to be studied with qualitative methods: first, to discover the
traits of a new phenomenon, before it were possible to test hypotheses on it. Especially at this stage, but also for substantive reasons, a subculture should not be
reduced to separate variables, but should rather be studied in its complexity and
everyday context with methods that are open enough to represent this (Flick
2002: 5). Second, and apart from the reasons suggesting an ethnography, the
qualitative approach to this topic is a commitment to interpretive sociology and
reconstructive research.[6]

---

6   Interpretive sociology and reconstructive research in German-speaking sociology are
    most clearly addressed in Hitzler 2002; Kruse 2009; Bohnsack 2010;
    Przyborski/Wohlrab-Sahr 2010, among others. Anglo-American sociology usually
    provides a historic overview of qualitative research traditions, starting with positivism
    and its challenges through naturalism (e.g. Esterberg 2002; Hammersley/Atkinson
    2007) and further concepts, among which are social constructionist and interpretive
    approaches (Esterberg 2002: 15–16).

A very general definition of interpretive sociology would be the reconstruction of meaning (Hitzler 2002: [3]) that informs everyday practices (Bohnsack 2010: 10). The epistemological assumptions behind this approach originate from Max Weber's *verstehende Soziologie*, interpretive sociology, that tries to understand and reconstruct an agent's subjective meaning, rather than explaining his or her actions in seemingly rational and objective terms (Weber 1990 [1922]). Interpretive sociology is further based on ethnomethodology, symbolic interactionism and social constructivism (Kruse 2009: 9–10). Each in its own way, these theories understand "reality" as being socially constructed. In the case of ethnomethodology, this is thought to happen through people's everyday rules and practices (Garfinkel 1967), in symbolic interactionism through their interactions in the form of symbolic codes (Mead 1934; Blumer 1967; Koob 2007) or in social constructivism by their reproduction and modification of the constructed reality they find (Watzlawick 1984; Glasersfeld 1995). The different "versions of reality" are not arbitrary, however, but draw on a stable core, and any variations beyond this are based on meaningful rules that can be reconstructed (Wernet 2009: 13–14). These assumptions guide reconstructive research along the principles of interpretation and openness in the sense that one's own theoretic knowledge is suspended and that meaning is reconstructed from the data, rather than imposed on the data (Kruse 2009: 11–12).

For the research on this topic, these assumptions imply that the emphasis lies in investigating how the social space of Islamic youth culture is constructed and what the phenomenon means to the population under study. This subjective meaning is to be reconstructed in the course of the research, and specifically by means of in-depth interviews. The interview analysis follows a hermeneutic analysis that seeks to decipher an objective meaning from the interview text (Oevermann 1993).

Thus, while some quantitative research questions would generally have been plausible (What percentage of young people follow Islamic youth culture? What is their distribution of gender, age, ethnicity, education? What variables are the factors that cause someone to engage in Islamic youth culture?), there are plenty of reasons not to include them in this research, but to leave them to a potential follow-up study to this qualitative exploration. The target of this research project is not to test concepts or hypotheses, nor to use standardised tests to study causal relationships and distributions, but to reconstruct the concepts of the studied population in a continued process of interpretation.[7]

---

7   Several researchers now argue that the distinction between "qualitative" and "quantitative" methodologies is ill-advised, and that the notions of "reconstructive" and "hy-

I thus planned a data collection that had three elements to it: gathering examples and artefacts of Islamic youth culture on the internet, at events and at festivals; participant observation among young Muslims as the "consumers" of this youth culture; and formal interviews with "producers" of Islamic music, comedy, fashion and media. The three differed in place, degree of formality and nature of the data, but overlapped in time and were intertwined, each contributing distinct knowledge to the exploration of the subculture.

Similarly, the analysis took three different paths, and indeed required such, since the first part of data collection resulted in images and objects, the second manifested itself in field notes, while the third yielded audio files and text. While most ethnographers move back and forth among data, analysis and theory generation, and therefore apply a less formalised analysis at all stages (Hammersley/Atkinson 2007: 158), I carried out a thorough analysis, mainly after the fieldwork. In dealing with the artefacts, I used chiefly "thick description" (Geertz 1973). I analysed the field notes from participant observation by identifying and generating more general concepts. For the interviews, I applied a balanced combination of interpretive (hermeneutic) and content analysis in order to develop a typology.

Such a combination of various data collection and analysis techniques fits into the general framework of an ethnography. Data-source triangulation as well as methods triangulation can help both to complete the picture of a certain phenomenon, which is intended here, and to check whether patterns identified at one stage of the research are plausible at other stages. One should, of course, keep Hammersley's and Atkinson's warning in mind that this is not unproblematic, as different kinds of data can also contradict each other (Hammersley/Atkinson 2007: 184), but as they also state, comparisons between different empirical observations and more abstract concepts, including potential discrepancies, are the "stock-in-trade of ethnographic work" (ibid.: 161). The various sources and methods employed in this project have been chosen carefully in a complementary and knowledge-enhancing way, and a re-integration of the conclusions drawn from each stage will be carried out in Chapter VI.

Interview Design in Detail

I have chosen a particular emphasis within my approach to the topic that affects the methodology and the research design as a whole. The artefacts – songs, lyr-

---

potheses testing" methods are much more meaningful (Hitzler 2002: [1,14]; Bohnsack 2010: 10; Przyborski/Wohlrab-Sahr 2010: 27).

ics, fashion items, magazines, websites – give an account of what Islamic youth culture consists of. Participant observations among the young consumers of these items reveal how those are perceived, who participates in the youth culture, where it takes place, and to a certain extent give an idea of why it emerges, considering the role of the context in shaping a demand for it. These two stages will therefore mainly address the first set of research questions. However, the second set of questions, particularly the issue of why Islamic youth culture is created, can only be fully explored by approaching the key figures and asking them about their aims. For this reason, I decided to interview producers of Islamic youth culture and to place a particular emphasis on these qualitative interviews within the methodological framework, and although I integrate all the data into one ensemble at the end, I consider the interviews not only to be the main data source, but I also used them for a more complex analysis.

Another reason for selecting producers rather than consumers as interviewees was that the key figures of a movement may be more consistent or stable members of a potentially fluid youth culture; they would probably have reflected upon their motivation when committing to their activity, whereas the younger consumers may not necessarily have given as much thought to the development of Islamic youth culture. A focus on action and actors is an important ethnographic technique (Hammersley/Atkinson 2007: 168). It also allows for a theoretic perspective of cultural production. Finally, research practicality was in favour of interviewing producers: they were easy to identify as members of the scene and could be contacted individually and without difficulty, since most of them either had websites or performed at public events. This focus once more called for a qualitative approach to the research topic as a whole: the population of producers is rather low in number and would not have satisfied the demands of a representative quantitative study. Researching this sample with qualitative methods, on the other hand, permitted me to interview the population nearly in its entirety.

Interview Format

My chosen interview format overlaps with several types, but is largely based on one that is most relevant for my purposes and that I follow in a slightly adapted form. One of the only partly related forms is the narrative interview, which is particularly used in biographical research (Flick 2002: 96–104). My approach relates to biographical interviews in the sense that the activity of the producers is in many ways linked to their biography, not just because they are or have become Muslim, but also because their own youth – seen as phases of living subculture and development of their expertise in hip-hop, urban design or the like – has influenced the activity they pursue today. The activity also reflects very personal beliefs and values, and so the interview had to address how they developed over time; and first and foremost, it was directed at how the interviewees developed their idea of the activity, which again often connects to biographical events. However, I decided against narrative interviews for this study, because I wanted to focus specifically on the topic of Islamic youth culture and its creation, and for that I needed to be able to ask a few thematic guiding questions rather than purely open-ended ones. My aim of developing a typology of motivations also required repeating the main questions with every interviewee in order to be able to group similar responses to a topic later on.

Hence, the interview needed to be of the semi-structured type, which itself has several sub-types, such as the focused, problem-centred, expert or ethnographic interview (Flick 2002: 74–95). The expert interview would have been partly relevant because the interviewee was questioned as an expert in "a certain field of activity", i.e. Islamic youth culture, and represented a group, or in this case, a part of a movement (ibid.: 89). On the other hand, the expert interview would not have fully served the purpose here, because it regards the individual as being less important, and this conflicts with the fact that most interviewees are artists on some level; therefore, the individual does play a role, in addition to the biographical reasons.

The type of semi-structured interview that was the most fitting for this research project was therefore the problem-centred interview, as suggested by Andreas Witzel (1985, 2000; Flick 2002: 85–89). Within this interview format, questions and narrative stimuli are used to gather "biographical data with regard to a certain problem" (Flick 2002: 86), although I would interpret the specific issue in question not necessarily as a "problem" in the sense of a difficulty or nuisance – which would be an ill-advised start to researching Islam – but rather as a research problem or puzzle. In this case, this was to be the emergence of the phenomenon of Islamic youth culture and its underlying aims, intentions, motivations and conditions that fostered its development. This approach allowed the interviewees' opinions, positions and subsequent actions to be taken as a focal point, because they were interviewed as experts and had been chosen for that reason (Witzel 2000: [12]), which corresponded to my sampling strategy. The interviewer is required to keep a balance between openness to the interviewee's narrative without superimposing any theory and guidance, and a focus on the research problem, while stimulating narration of what is relevant to the interviewee (ibid.: [3]). This is achieved through a mixture of questioning, conversation and listening techniques on the side of the interviewer, which I applied both during the interview and when designing the interview questionnaire.

Interview Questionnaire

The interview questionnaire observed a balance of structure and openness (Helfferich 2004; Kruse 2004: 146–148; Kruse 2009: 70–72). It neither reduced the conversation to a highly structured question-and-answer game in which the interviewer alone sets the agenda, nor did it allow for a completely unguided monologue by the interviewee. The semi-structured questionnaire, or guide, was a compromise between the two and left enough room for situational questions. It was composed of six guiding questions, each of which covered one main substantive field with a few further questions added as follow-ups and to keep the conversation going (to illustrate the structure, the first question is displayed below; see the full interview questionnaire in Appendix A; format adapted from Kruse 2009: 66–67). Before starting the interview, I introduced my study and my particular interest in the interviewees' activity by restating my interest in Islamic youth culture and in the people who contribute to it, and that I was therefore interested in their personal experience and why they did what they did (adapted from Kruse 2009: 93–94). This was to provide a direction to the interview and a focus on the main issue (Witzel 1985: 246). I also emphasised that I would ask open questions, inviting the interviewee to tell me anything that they felt was important, without any interruptions (Kruse 2009: 94), in order to underline my openness and to let them take the lead; the balance of open and structured interview design was therefore laid out from the beginning.

Table 1: Interview questionnaire (question 1)

Question #1		
You produce young, Islamic music (fashion, media etc.). How did you develop this idea? Tell me a little bit about it.		
Substantive aspects	*Questions to keep going*	*Follow-up questions*
Initial idea	Substantive questions	Could you describe to me a very typical piece of your work (or music/fashion etc.)? Why is it typical?
Ties with biography	And then?	
Motivation	Is there anything else that gave you the idea?	
Wider aims	Anything else?	What do you want to achieve through your music (fashion)?

The first question, as laid out above, opened the conversation by addressing the interviewee's initial idea for his or her activity, aiming to unfold its entire development so far with the use of further questions to keep the narration going. One follow-up question already addressed the overall aim, asking what the person wanted to achieve through their activity, to study whether this claim was maintained throughout the interview. The character of this first question was casual ("Tell me a little bit about it"), but also prompted the respondent to position him- or herself as I started with an ascribing statement, "You produce young, Islamic music" (or comedy/fashion/media). While some interviewees accepted this label, others immediately picked up on it to counter or clarify it, thereby providing a definition of their activity. This question is a typical opener for a problem-centred interview (adapted from Witzel 1985: 246).

The second question (see Appendix A) enquired about any influences on the interviewee's activity, ranging from subcultural and spiritual inspirations to structural impacts, including a reflection on the role of being a Muslim in the respective country. The third question seemingly moved away from the personal by asking how the respondent defined youth culture, thereby addressing his or her subjective definition of youth culture in general and Islamic youth culture in particular, which was aimed at revealing their personal stance and how this was reflected in the person's own activity. In most interviews, especially in those relating to the German scene, I also asked for an opinion on the term "Pop Islam" (Gerlach 2006), partly to uncover more information about the nature of Islamic youth culture, but mainly because this led to insightful reflections about the role of Islam in Western cultures, their compatibility and non-Muslims' attempts at labelling Islamic phenomena.

With the fourth question I tried to find out about the producers' relationship with young Muslims by enquiring about their target group. Although an artist's desired target group often differs from their actual target group, and indeed many claimed they addressed "everybody", the sub-questions forced them to take an outsider's view of their own activity, also explaining why there was a need for it and thus what they saw as the gap they were filling. By the fifth question, it was time to raise more controversial issues and ask about criticism from Muslims and non-Muslims, and how the interviewee dealt with it. This was supposed to stimulate narration about perceived or actual obstacles, strategies for coping and for self-presentation, and about how the initial idea strengthened. I also wanted to observe how the respondents reacted to unpleasant criticism and asked them to give me detailed examples of such situations.

The sixth and final question took a wider perspective of Islamic youth culture and its transnational character. Asking about the movement's key figures in the country and abroad, I tried to find out whether the interviewees were able and willing to locate themselves within the framework of a larger movement, how aware they were of any transnational elements and if they felt interconnected with others among the sample. At the end, I gave the interviewee the opportunity to raise any other points that we had not discussed, and particularly after I stopped the recording, there was another chance for comments "off the record".

Apart from the interview questionnaire and the audio recording, I also employed two more gathering techniques that Witzel suggests as the four elements of a problem-centred interview, i.e. a short survey and a postscript (Witzel 1985: 235–241; Flick 2002: 86). The latter – which was applied in a few cases only to keep the data to a manageable amount – captured the interview setting, atmosphere, relationship between interviewer and interviewee, conversation dynamics, conspicuous themes and any exchange before and after the interview (see also Kruse 2009: 101). This postscript could later be drawn upon during the analysis to check a certain interpretation and it also formed part of my ethnographic field notes. The anonymous short survey gathered data on age, city of residence, gender, job, education, migration background, nationality and religious affiliation (Sunni/Shia; converted or not). It helped to collect a few pieces of structural data for background information, without having to incorporate this into the interview, which was supposed to concentrate on the interviewee's narration on the main topic.

Sampling

Since I selected a sample based on insights from the data rather than on a preconceived theory, my overall sampling strategy was a "theoretical" one, as proposed by Barney Glaser and Anselm Strauss (1967: 45–78). It involved revising my sample based on what I found out, particularly during the first stage of collecting artefacts, as this contributed to defining the phenomenon, and also extending it later on in the process. For instance, the decision to interview producers rather than consumers was already an outcome of the first observations of the phenomenon before starting fieldwork. To arrive at a heterogeneous sample that would reflect the variety in the field, I looked for a maximum of differences (Glaser/Strauss 1967: 56; Kelle/Kluge 1999: 45). The collection of artefacts suggested three main fields – music, fashion and media – from which I aimed to recruit interviewees (again, at a later stage of the fieldwork, comedy evolved as another genre and was combined with music into performing arts).

My choice of countries should also be discussed in relation to sampling. Since France, Germany and Britain are the countries with the largest Muslim minorities in Europe, Islamic youth culture has developed there faster than in other countries, and its study reveals important insights into state policies and societal reactions to Islam in these places. From a practical research point of view, these three countries were manageable in terms of language, as otherwise Belgium, the Netherlands, or some Northern and Southern European countries would have been interesting to study, too. However, this, as well as the inclusion of North America, would have gone beyond the scope of this research project.

I therefore aimed to gather interviewees from the performing arts, fashion and media and from the three countries. While my goal was a total sample of 30 interviewees, I did not plan an exact number for every genre, country or gender, which turned out to be a wise choice. This way, the sample reflected the dynamics of the production of Islamic youth culture; even more so, as it was a nearly complete sample of the total population – a narrowly defined and therefore very small population, of course – since I interviewed almost every representative of the producers within this small movement. I finally interviewed 14 representatives of the performing arts (music and comedy, although mainly the former), 9 people involved in fashion and 9 dealing with media; 10 of these interviews took place in Germany, 7 in France and 15 in the UK, which already gives an indication of the subculture's centres of gravity. With a final number of 32 interviews, the size of the sample corresponded to, or slightly exceeded the amount common in reconstructive research, providing enough cases for a typology, but staying within a reasonable number in order to carry out a meticulous textual analysis (see the list of interviewees in Appendix B).

Owing to the "handpicked" selection, I recruited most interviewees by directly contacting them. As semi-public figures, they usually advertised their products or themselves on a website and could easily be contacted even before I arrived at the respective fieldwork site (see the letter in Appendix C). Others only caught my attention during the fieldwork, when I attended events at which they performed where I could immediately ask them for an interview. The remaining, although comprising the lowest number, were recommended to me by other interviewees (snowball system).

Giving all respondents as much time as possible to tell me their story, each interview had a duration of 60 minutes on average, with some lasting significantly longer. Each interview was transcribed at full length in the original language – French, German or English – and as close to the spoken word as possible to have a complete and wholly accurate basis for the interpretive analysis.

3. Searching for Answers: Fieldwork

The Field

When I finally embarked on fieldwork, I found the "field" to be a seemingly obvious term. Before venturing "out there", sometimes during the field research and also afterwards when writing up the findings, the field does not always appear to be a clearly defined space. By a narrow and more space-based definition, my field would be the cities I chose: Frankfurt, Marseille and Birmingham, or perhaps only those districts that are "relevant" to young Muslims. A wider and topic-based definition of the field would include all places, events and situations that can be linked to Islamic youth culture, including the interviews with producers in other cities and online research for audio and visual artefacts. Broadly speaking, one could claim to be "in the field" wherever and whenever data are gathered.[8] I adopted the second approach for this study, and I took the opportunity to participate in events as they appeared, also outside the places I had initially planned to focus on. In the end, the cities turned out to be "base camps" for explorations and for trips to my interviewees – Islamic youth culture being a small scene, there was scarcely more than one producer in one place; they were scattered all over the country, particularly in Germany and France. In the UK, the scene was much more centralised, and because most of my interviews took place in London, the focus shifted slightly from Birmingham to London.

I had initially chosen these cities for their social structure, particularly regarding immigration from Islamic countries, but it would be a false claim to present complete ethnographic accounts of the three cities at large or even of their scenes of Islamic youth culture. My aim was to follow the scene wherever it manifested itself, in order to observe whether it was connected to the cities without presupposing that it was. Also, because of their extremely diverse nature in terms of history, economy or immigration (to name but a few), the set-up was not a comparison to explain differences, but rather to look for what the scenes had in common *despite* the different settings, and thus to reach a more refined idea and definition of the youth culture.[9]

In 2008/2009, I spent three months each in Frankfurt and Marseille, and another three to four months split among Birmingham, London and Cambridge. Events I attended included religious festivals, Islamic rap concerts, youth camps,

---

8   This was suggested by Darin Weinberg in our discussion on field research and its definition(s) in May 2009. For a thorough discussion of the term "field", see Gupta/Ferguson (1997).

9   I thank Gary Alan Fine for his advice on this during an ethnographic workshop series in Cambridge during the Easter Term 2009.

Friday prayers and more, at places as diverse as mosques, fast food restaurants, exhibition centres, universities, markets and youth hostels, among others. I gained access in a variety of ways. In Frankfurt, I was lucky enough to experience the "Day of Open Mosque" at the very beginning of my fieldwork stay, on the national holiday of 3 October, where I met several people who later served as "gate keepers" and invited me to other events; one often paved the way for the next. I also established contact with the largest Muslim German youth organisation, *Muslimische Jugend in Deutschland (MJD)*, and participated in their annual youth meetings. In Marseille, structural circumstances resulted in more observation than participation, while in the UK, information about events was widely available on the internet and was also passed on to me by my interviewees (see Chapter IV).

The Role of the Researcher

Any form of qualitative and ethnographic research, and particularly the question of access, bears the issue of the role of the researcher. In reconstructive research, by assuming a reality constructed by human interaction, it is uncontested that the researcher *has* an effect on the people and the issue under study; many authors comprehensively discuss reflexivity in the research process (Hammersley/Atkinson 2007; Davies 2008; Kruse 2009; Przyborski/Wohlrab-Sahr 2010; among many others). What differs from one project to another, however, is *how* the research is affected. As Charlotte Davies points out, it is especially vital to be aware of this when societies and cultures are studied in which the researcher is personally involved (Davies 2008: 5). Rather than researching youth in Islamic countries, I shared being European with those I studied – also being German, living in Britain – and therefore sharing, for instance, some of the same subcultural references. Too close a proximity can be detrimental to the research process, as it leads to overlooking practices, habits or statements because of their familiarity, and an attitude of conscious defamiliarisation is therefore an indispensable measure (e.g. Amann/Hirschauer 1997). On the other hand, I was not part of my study population, especially by not being Muslim myself, and did not have any previous contacts in that field. Again, this carries problems, as it can be a barrier to trust and access, and one has to take into account one's own potential prejudices and, in fact, to deal with these on both sides. Not knowing a culture from the inside may result in overamplifying minor details or misunderstanding more important issues, but consciously negotiating this and overcoming it is at the heart of ethnographic research. It can also be beneficial: a contrasting background can be useful for uncovering details that are normal and inconspicuous for members of a community. Also, there is the danger of self-absorption, where there are no more boundaries between the researcher and the researched, which can render an investigation impossible (Davies 2008: 5). However, many informants were interested in my personal motivation for this research. While I was not seeking to convert to Islam, which some of them hoped, I met their approval in that I had spent a year in Egypt and knew Arabic, which was a fortunate trust-building asset whenever the question of my motivation came up.

Furthermore, being a woman granted me access to intimate all-female gatherings, which would not have been possible otherwise. Of course I was excluded from male environments, such as the men's prayer rooms, and my interaction with male respondents was almost certainly different to that of a male researcher's – for example, on rare occasions a male informant seemed uncomfortable shaking hands with a woman, and at times it was impossible for me to pay the bill at a café. All of this had to be taken into account for field reports and for the context of interviews, but the positive side of such interactions is that it sharpens the view of gender-based issues. Finally, my role as a researcher was generally welcomed, especially when informants compared this to their experience with journalists. I always proactively stated my background as a sociologist and my research interest. Very rarely, and more out of curiosity with regard to this technique, I carried out some covert research, for instance at a Friday prayer – which understandably sparked hopes of my eagerness to convert. For my purposes though, I found this neither fruitful nor ethical, and thus continued to carry out overt research at all times.

Participant Observation

Observing the field and participating in events took up the largest part of my time during the fieldwork. Most ethnographers rightly disentangle the two terms and speak of participating and observing (e.g. Gold 1958; Esterberg 2002: 60–61; Hammersley/Atkinson 2007; Davies 2008: 77–104). Many discuss which of the two terms is the more important one and whether one only serves the other, initially proposing that they mutually enforce each other in a "dialectic spiral" (Rabinow 1977: 80) or that the researcher takes one of four roles in the spectrum between complete observer and complete participant (Gold 1958). Davies identifies a preference for participation in current research, but rejects the assumption that this is an indicator of research quality (Davies 2008: 84). In my own research, I primarily realised that multi-sited ethnography can lead to great differences in the observation/participation balance, and that this could reveal a great deal about the research object. In Germany, for example, I participated more than I observed, which was partly due to the high degree of organisation among youth groups, facilitating participation, even for an outsider. In Marseille, where this was not the case, I often employed an "observation flottante" (Pétonnet 1982) – letting one's attention "float" around, absorbing any information without a filter based on one's previous theoretic knowledge, making oneself available for unexpected observations (ibid.: 39) – and thus observed more. This did not only lead to different descriptions of the scene, but was also telling of the structural differences between the two places. To conclude, beyond designing, planning and reflecting upon the methodology while applying it, I also relied to a great extent on what might be most useful in fieldwork: fortunate coincidences, and the presence of mind to grasp them.

4. Finding Answers: Methods of Analysis

Analysis of Artefacts and Field Notes

Although the process of analysis is never completely detached from data collection in qualitative research, analysing the data requires a range of additional techniques that also have further methodological and epistemological implications. For each of the three methodological stages I have employed different forms of analysis that varied in technique, rigor and outcome.

I applied first and foremost a "thick description" (Geertz 1973: 3–30) to analyse the artefacts. This was an essential part of the study as an ethnography of a fairly new subculture that has not been described in detail by the literature. In line with Geertz's concept I did not confine it to pure description, but included analytic and interpretive observations (ibid.: 15–16, 20; see Chapter III).

To analyse my field notes of the participants' observations I used the approach of generating concepts, as commonly used in ethnography, uncovering a structure in largely "unstructured" data (Hammersley/Atkinson 2007: 161–162). The same authors distinguish "spontaneous" analytic concepts that are used by participants, and "observer-identified" concepts, as proposed by Lofland (1971; Hammersley/Atkinson 2007: 163). While notions of people in the field may sometimes be the most apt to circumscribe a concept, and I also understand "observer-identified" concepts to be directly derived from participants' accounts and actions, I made use of this latter form in the second part of my analysis. Here, I looked at the consumers' perspective and compared my observations with the concepts of youth and subculture as discussed in the literature. In Chapter IV, I propose a conceptual way to grasp the phenomenon as a youth culture by identifying its three constituent elements.

Balancing Hermeneutic and Content Analysis

Most scrutiny was dedicated to the analysis of the interviews. The process involved transcribing each interview, working in an analysis group with a colleague, carrying out a sequential analysis to identify the main motifs and relevant categories, coding all interview transcripts with these categories using qualitative data analysis software, writing summaries and analytic memos of the single cases, before carrying out a comparative analysis of all cases and finally creating a typology. The methodological background was composed of hermeneutical analysis and content analysis, both aimed at the discovery of patterns and motifs in the interview text using different techniques.

There are many persuasive elements to the hermeneutic methodology. The method of objective hermeneutics ("Objektive Hermeneutik") was first introduced by Ulrich Oevermann (1981, 1993). He proposed that an objective meaning can be interpreted from a text, such as an interview transcript, based on a variety of linguistic, stylistic and semantic indicators, and by focusing on how something is expressed, instead of overly empathising with the interviewee and claiming to know what he or she really meant (also Wohlrab-Sahr 1999: 100). Cornelia Helfferich, Jan Kruse and Heike Klindworth (2005) developed and refined the method of "integrative, text-hermeneutic analysis", focussing on linguistic and communicative phenomena. Berg gives an overview of similar "interpretative", if less systematic, approaches (2009). All of these are reconstructive approaches, aimed at the reconstruction of meaning as apparent from the text. Any analysis, whether in the form of description, categories or interpretation, is here derived inductively from the text rather than projected onto it. It is latent more than manifest content that is searched for, or the meaning underlying the physical data (e.g. Berg 2009: 343–345). I adopted the methodological assumptions and some techniques of the hermeneutic methodology, searching for "central motifs", collecting various interpretations before deciding on one only at the end of a case analysis.

I carried out the first analysis of the interview transcripts on paper in an analysis group, as highly recommended in objective hermeneutic analysis in order to avoid subjective interpretations, but rather to share them intersubjectively and to maximise the variety of possible interpretations (Kruse 2009: 159–163).[10] Each of our group members selected a key passage of around four pages for each discussion – often the beginning of an interview or another dense sec-

---

10 Our group consisted of two members. My colleague Martin Langebach of the University of Düsseldorf worked on youth and political party membership, and we exchanged transcripts and discussed them over the phone on a weekly basis over a period of about 18 months.

tion that revealed some of the main patterns. My group partner and I first read and analysed the passage individually and then again together. We applied a sequential or line-by-line analysis, paying attention to linguistic details, and followed the content as it unfolded without linking it to later statements in order to understand the structure and the way in which the speaker had chosen to present his or her account (Deppermann 2008: 53–78). It was also an open-ended reading with no applied categories; rather, we collected the addressed themes and the modes in which they were expressed. We particularly searched for the "central motif" of the passage, referring to any recurring images, themes, structures, positions or symbolic figures (Kruse 2009: 156). The outcomes were usually one or two of such motifs, several interpretations or perspectives, and important themes that could later turn into categories.

I did not apply the hermeneutic method to the full, however, as I focused more on the semantic level, or the meaning and diction, than on the level of micro-linguistics, interaction and syntax (e.g. Kruse 2009: 147–148). From a practical point of view, the hermeneutic method is also extremely time-consuming, and because in this case the interview analysis was embedded in an ethnography involving many other data, it was advisable at some point to find a realistic and efficient method of completion. This point followed the sequential analysis that identified motifs and categories, after which I primarily applied a more content analytic approach.

Content analysis works stronger with categories and emphasises the content over linguistic and communicative elements. A content analytic approach also fits the research purpose, because the problem-centred interview already focuses on a thematic area.[11] Of the several approaches to content analysis,[12] Mayring has proposed a very systematic method (Mayring 2000, 2004, 2010). In defining the method, he stresses that it does not only deal with the actual content, but also with language and symbols of the entire communication process, and that it might more adequately be called a category-driven text analysis (Mayring 2010: 13). It focuses on condensing and categorising the data, which at this stage also prepared the way for the final aim of developing a typology, as this required categories. However, content analysis of this kind is often very theory-driven from the start, which I suspended in favour of an open interpretation at the beginning. That way I avoided merely combing through the text with preconceived categories and arriving at premature conclusions.

---

11 Despite Kruse's palpable aversion to content analysis (2009: 164–165, 194–196), he also recommends a "content analytic to hermeneutic analysis" for problem-centred interviews (Kruse 2009: 62).

12 For an overview of content analysis in its various forms see Berg 2009: 338–377.

I continued the analysis using computer assisted qualitative data analysis software (CAQDAS). I used the programme Atlas.ti to code every transcript in its entirety, by assigning quotes from the text – a paragraph, a few sentences or words – to a category. These categories were derived from the research questions, interview questionnaire and the previous step:

- Activity (sub-codes: Description, History/Development, Influences, Success, Target group)
- Youth (sub-codes: Definition of youth culture, Islamic youth culture, Young Muslims)
- Islam (sub-codes: Personal experience, Subjective Islam definition)
- Motivation (sub-codes: Aims, Incentives)
- Central motif (sub-codes: the individual central motifs)[13]
- Free motifs (sub-codes: the individual free motifs)[14]
- Medium
- Gender
- Perception of society
- Criticism
- Transnationalism
- Key figures

In the process of coding, the categories served as "containers" for collecting the relevant text passages. I also confirmed the central motif from the previous step or identified a new one and distinguished further free motifs, to both of which I usually ascribed in-vivo codes, choosing an interview quotation as the name. The difference between central and free motifs was that the former was the most important of all motifs in relation to the research questions and corresponded to the interviewee's account of why he or she was engaged in Islamic youth culture. Because I had prompted the respondents with this thematic outlook in my intro-

---

13 Examples included: "Aufmerksamkeit wieder auf Werte zu lenken, die wirklich Bestand haben"; "Divorced from the streets and married to Islam"; "Evangelists of Muslims as regular consumers"; "Help in the development of the new identity"; "Leur ouvrir le cœur"; "Nouveaux créneaux"; "Ne Grenze setzen"; "Partager la lumière"; "Religious self-positioning".

14 Examples included: "Changer l'image qu'on a de la femme voilée"; "Communication"; "Dawah"; "Demarcation discourse"; "Hijab"; "Humour"; "Kulturpessimismus"; "Mein Herz war tot, danach wurde es lebendig"; "Urban streetstyle"; "Véhicule des valeurs".

duction to each interview, it was present at least in the back of their heads. Free motifs were any other important themes and figures with no special focus.

The use of Atlas.ti very much facilitated the work compared with coding on paper. Not only did it abolish the pre-digital practice of cutting quotes from the paper transcripts and putting them into boxes labelled with the respective codes; this was done much more quickly with the help of a CAQDAS programme and also allowed multiple codes to be attached to one quote. Moreover, it also made it possible afterwards to display all the passages that corresponded to one code, within one or across all transcripts, commonly known as the "code and retrieve" function. This was essential for the next step of writing memos and preparing the way for the horizontal analysis and typology. A common criticism of programmes like Atlas.ti is that they can tempt the researcher to rather obsessive coding without ever closely reading the text. I solved this significant problem by carrying out the first steps on paper and by working without any categories at that stage.

After coding each interview, I wrote a case summary, with the help of "memos". I searched within Atlas.ti for all quotes from one interview corresponding to one particular category and summarised what the interviewee had said. I also added analytic comments to it and turned the summary into notes or memos that were then saved as an attachment to the interview file. Each interview eventually had around twelve memos of the most important categories attached, which were usually the following (also see Appendix E):

- Subjective description of the activity and its development
- Central motif
- Free motifs
- Personal Islamic experience
- Subjective Islam definition
- Perception of society
- Youth culture
- Islamic youth culture
- Aims
- Criticism
- Incentives

With the help of Atlas.ti I compiled all the memos of one interview into a case summary; the output of this stage taking the form of one single text document for each interview, or 32 in total. Both the coding and the memo-writing process had a descriptive and an analytic dimension. The coding was more descriptive where it meant allocating codes to text passages, but more analytical where I had to decide which were the central and free motifs and which in-vivo codes would describe them best. The memos primarily served as a summary, but I also included comments, observations and analytical notes.

Many qualitative research projects use grounded theory either throughout the whole research process or as a method of analysis, referring to the procedure developed by Glaser and Strauss (1967) and substantially revised by Strauss and Corbin (1990). Analysis in grounded theory comprises an elaborate system of coding in three phases and establishing a hierarchy of categories by increasingly abstracting from the text. Applying a grounded theory analysis would have meant using categories from the start and in a very time-intensive way, while neglecting the advantageous techniques of the other two methods. What I have adopted from the grounded theory for this project is a general attitude of grounding one's conclusions in the data, keeping a close relationship between gathering data and conceptualising them at a more abstract level, going back and forth between stages in the data collection process, and being open about the outcome. Yet, for the various reasons outlined above, a combination of hermeneutic and content analysis seemed most sensible to me for this project: in short, coding the interview text with categories (content analysis) derived from previous interpretation (hermeneutic analysis).

The Typology

Following the single-case, vertical analysis, I moved on to a horizontal analysis across cases. Using Atlas.ti once again, I compiled all the memos of one category across interviews, to receive one document per category, or just over twelve in total. This was the starting point for developing a typology. I studied the results (quotes, summaries, observations) for each category in detail to discover a pattern and to see which would be the most relevant for the types, on their own and in combination with the others. It turned out that these were the central motif, the target group, the view on Islamic youth culture and the perception of society.[15] Interestingly, the personal Islamic experience – whether the person was brought up religiously, had converted or reverted to Islam – did not have any effect on the other categories.

I then used cross-classified tables for the categories and their characteristics to arrive at more refined patterns. I merged some characteristics to reduce the category's variety, which Kluge refers to as the quintessence of developing a typology (Kluge 1999: 101). In the process, it was important to reduce the op-

---

15 For a description of these categories as an analytical space, their characteristics and patterns, see the beginning of Chapter V.

tions to those most significant, in order to continue the combination with further categories (Kelle/Kluge 1999: 92; Kluge 1999: 279). This finally brought about four types of motivation, providing an explanation for the second set of research questions on the development of Islamic youth culture. While the respondents of one type have most of their characteristics in common, they differ strongly with those of the other types, to allow for a minimal internal and a maximal external difference (Kelle/Kluge 1999: 83). The remaining categories that did not contribute to the typology were later used in the characterisation of the types to provide a more rounded picture.

In the presentation of the final types, I have introduced a short case study for each to give an empirical example and to highlight some of the main characteristics, and I have opted for prototypes rather than ideal or extreme types. The latter would only be appropriate if the cases were located on a scale between two extremes, which is not the case here. An ideal type would have the advantage of abstracting from the single case and pointing out the most important and commonly shared features, but this also means that no empirical case corresponds directly to the ideal type and thus some variety, differences and contradictions would be lost (Kluge 1999: 280). Prototypes may have the disadvantage that all cases are different and one would have to be chosen over another, but this can be solved by carefully selecting the most classical representative, highlighting the typical and the individual traits, and by restating that it does not constitute the type, but rather corresponds to it (Kelle/Kluge 1999: 95). Because they have the benefit of being actual empirical cases – representing what initially served as the basis for developing the types – I chose to present prototypes as an introduction to each type (see Chapter V).

There are good reasons for working with typologies. To name but a few studies using typologies, Ellen Hertz (1998) included one in her ethnography of the Shanghai stock market, describing three types of stock market players that became apparent during her fieldwork. She did not develop the types herself, but picked up what had been reported by the local press and other observers of the market, thereby building on a classification generated by the field. Ric Curtis and Travis Wendel (2000) presented a typology in their ethnography of the illegal drug trade, focusing on forms of the social and technical organisation of distribution based on their own observations and interviews. Monika Wohlrab-Sahr (1999) studied what makes people decide to convert to Islam in Germany and the United States and proposed three types that take into account the person's biographical situation when ascertaining what they find attractive about Islam. Applying the methodology of objective hermeneutics, she developed a typology from her own reconstructive analysis of the interviews she conducted. Another enquiry that was helpful in finalising my own typology, especially in reducing and combining categories, was one by Dietz et al. (1997) on the career plans and delinquency of working class youth (presented for methodological purposes in Kelle/Kluge 1999: 87–90, 93–94).

What all of these very different studies have in common is that they use typologies in order to reduce the complexity of qualitative data. This allows for more general statements to be concluded – not about a large population, but at least about the entire sample, instead of just reconstructing single cases. I could have used my interview data in different ways. For instance, I could have integrated them in a more traditionally ethnographic way as equal sources of information among others, and used interview quotations for either a thick description or the generation of concepts, as I did with my other field notes. But I wanted to carry out a more systematic and closer textual analysis to find out what was behind the interviewee's accounts. Not just taking them at face value, I tried to uncover what prompted them to create Islamic youth culture; on the surface, Islamic youth culture may appear to be a unified movement with a common goal, but I aimed at discovering the various influences of a biographical, subcultural, religious or societal nature that would stimulate an individual to contribute to it. In order to make these findings intelligible, then, I developed a typology that condensed all this intricate information and encapsulated it in four distinct types.

Alternative typologies that would have been possible include, for instance, a cross-table of background features like the participants' nationality, gender and genre. But such an approach would have been prone to a fair criticism that is often raised against typologies: that they are too descriptive and therefore lack analytical value, and moreover, that they oversimplify complex issues by reducing them to black-and-white options in an unimaginative table. I have tried to circumvent this by gaining the categories for the typology not from hard facts but from a close textual analysis and by thus capturing the dynamics of what the participants were doing and how they articulated it.

Foreign-Language Data

To add a word on working with data in different languages, it should be noted that this certainly had an effect on the project, including challenges and benefits.[16] When carrying out fieldwork in another country, one might encounter

---

16 A native speaker of German, I am fluent in French and English, but there is always a difference to one's native tongue that needs to be reflected when working with language. I have shared some of the following thoughts with Jan Kruse in an email ex-

more difficulties and obstacles, or perhaps miss a spontaneous opportunity because of the slightest language barrier. If I had fewer interviewees or fieldwork experiences in France, I at least needed to consider that this was not only for structural reasons, but perhaps also because of my own interaction in the field, since I received many more responses in the UK; however, some structural reasons do seem to remain. Conducting the interviews in different languages was not a problem, only one concept raised difficulties: the notion of "youth culture" is widely understood in English and German, whether in everyday language or in sociology, but in French, it is not the case. With youth culture research keeping a low profile in France for reasons outlined above (Bourdieu 1980), there was little to build upon, but I also had to find out which of the possible translations would work best in everyday speech – *culture de (la) jeunesse, culture des jeunes* or *culture jeune*. It is the latter, but the matter led to an interesting misunderstanding during the first French interview. I asked my interviewee how he personally defined *culture des jeunes*, which he mistook as *culture du jeûne*, culture of fasting, and which seemed to make sense to him as a practising Muslim. As none of us noticed the misunderstanding, a peculiar conversation unfolded about how his comedy contributed to the "culture of fasting" – not at all an answer to my question, but intriguing in terms of language, subjective concepts and spaces of meaning on both sides. During my fieldwork, I came to cherish misunderstandings for the rich and unexpected insights they offered, at least in hindsight.

Foreign-language interview analysis can hold even more pitfalls for the researcher, especially because of the methodological difficulties of understanding the other person's account,[17] which becomes a literal issue here. I wanted to use all the interviews in their original language and asked native speakers to transcribe the recordings for me, as I could have missed some expressions of slang or other unfamiliar phrases; in turn however, I needed to proofread their transcriptions and fill in where background knowledge was needed to understand a certain phrase. During the analysis, the issue continued to exist, since a non-native speaker might always overlook an allusion, irony or a tone, which is even more important when the analysis requires looking at *how* something is presented as well as *what* is being said (Przyborski/Wohlrab-Sahr 2010: 308). In addition to repeated readings of the transcript and listening to the recording, I therefore also asked French or British colleagues for advice.

---

change in 2011 as a response to his survey on this topic for his book project (Kruse et al. 2012).

17 On the problem of the understanding of others ("Fremdverstehen"), see for example Kruse 2009: 20–24; Przyborski/Wohlrab-Sahr 2010: 28–31.

Again, at times I also perceived it as an asset not to be a native speaker, as it caused metaphors to catch my eye even more than in my own language where I was more used to them. A great example was the phrase of an interviewee who assessed the potential US government funding of his media project as being a "kiss of death". Since neither of us was actively familiar with the term, my analysis group partner and I spent a substantial amount of time discussing the metaphor and found – beyond the simple translation of "counterproductive" – many semantic fields around kiss, embrace, death, fellowship, treachery, Judas kiss and Christianity. Thereby the interviewee's choice to describe the relationship of the US government and Islamic activists in this way became much more colourful.

As for the presentation of foreign-language data in this book, I have chosen to quote all interviewees in their native language to reproduce the original tone and phrasing. I did, however, provide translations in the footnotes; all translations are my own and I hope to have replicated the characteristic style of each quotation.

5. Limits and Ethical Considerations

At the end of an ethnography or any qualitative research there often remains the generation of theories, especially when a grounded theory approach is applied, or at least an account of descriptive and explanatory analyses (Hammersley/Atkinson 2007: 158). In this research project, which studies a local yet transnational form of subculture, my aim was to provide a comprehensive ethnographic description, explanations of its manifestations and especially a well-founded typology of the motivations underlying this phenomenon. The application to other cases may be limited, as the result is not going to be one overarching theory, and I do not claim to explain the emergence of any religious youth culture, possibly not even any where Islam is involved. The typology is a step from the single case towards generalisation. Generalising results in qualitative research is not aimed at representativity, but at embedding cases in a larger framework that possesses the same rules or patterns as the cases, and at allowing the conclusion that related cases would behave similarly (Przyborski/Wohlrab-Sahr 2010: 314). Also, the explanations of all stages should be intersubjectively comprehensible (e.g. Kruse: 2009: 36, 142). Although the researcher's role has a large influence during data collection, the analysis should be traceable if the same data, methods and theories are applied again, which requires the researcher to disclose them at every stage. Still, a fraction of subjectivity always remains, as no researcher is completely free of preconceived concepts and ideas. I do hope, however, that my account of Islamic youth culture will be plausible and sound in the light of my chosen framework.

Finally, a word on data protection. Observing research ethics at all times was my highest priority. I obtained ethical approval for this project from the relevant university committee before carrying out any fieldwork, and I have obtained the written consent of all interviewees to record the interviews, transcribe them and use the data for my dissertation and its publication (for the consent form, see Appendix D). Still, one issue remained ambiguous in this particular context. It is common practice to anonymise the names and details of interviewees, as required by ethics committees with good cause. However, when dealing with public figures, such as musicians or actors, this leads to a dilemma, as they also need to be described and discussed in this role, but at the same time, their identity as participants has to be protected. I have addressed this issue by taking the following decision. Wherever I have given a description of the key figures in the Islamic youth cultural scene, I have referred to the actual person as they appeared in social reality, but I have only based it on information that was publicly available, i.e. online resources such as their own websites, artefacts like CDs or fashion items, and observations at public events (Chapters III and IV). However, in Chapter V, which deals with the interview data, their description and close analysis, the interviewee's identity was neither disclosed nor linked to their public description of the previous chapters. Personal details have been changed. On the one hand, this is unfortunate, as mixing the data might have provided a more rounded picture of even thicker description, but the alternatives – of either anonymising and forging the "real" key figures or disclosing the interviewee's identity – are not acceptable options. On the other hand, the interviews provide a completely different kind of data, and deserve to be treated in a distinct way. Including the participants of the study in two different capacities, therefore, appeared to be the most sensible solution.

As for the presentation of this entire ethnography, I regard the artefacts, the participant observation and the interviews with their respective analyses as three strands that, braided together, respond to the research questions in complementing ways. Therefore, I chose to structure the book around these strands, which is reflected in the chapter outline. Alternative ways of telling the story of Islamic youth culture could have followed the lines of places or countries, subcultural genres or any other themes. However, because the intention of this ethnography was to find out about the nature, appeal and purpose of Islamic youth culture, a presentation of what the artefacts, consumers and producers revealed about this seemed most pertinent.

III. "Portez vos valeurs":
Manifestations of Islamic Youth Culture

A. INTRODUCTION

This chapter introduces the phenomenon of Islamic youth culture on the basis of its artefacts and manifestations, structured by the three dominant genres: performing arts (music and comedy), fashion and media. For each of them, I will portray one representative from Germany, France and the United Kingdom, which may sometimes be the most typical or one that stands for the extent of variety among the key figures and artefacts. In a more condensed form, I will then also describe other examples of the genres, before concluding with a more analytic view of each genre as a whole and its role in Islamic youth culture.

The artists or the founders of companies presented here are for the most part also the people I interviewed, but for reasons of data protection I will not link them to any particular interview; interviews will instead be dealt with in Chapter V. The information given here is based on my collection of material gathered in the field and online, consisting of, but not limited to, music albums, articles of clothing, advertisements, video clips, websites and newspaper articles.

This presentation of artefacts can never be exhaustive. Many of the cultural products and companies, and in particular their online presence, are short-lived, which is perhaps interesting in itself, but which makes it impossible to ever give a comprehensive picture. Rather, this presentation is a snapshot at one particular point of time – in this case 2011 as the time of writing, although most examples have been collected continuously from 2007 onwards. Finally, this chapter will try to work towards a definition of the phenomenon of Islamic youth culture.

B. MANIFESTATIONS AND ARTEFACTS

1. Performing Arts: Music and Comedy

Ammar114

The best-known Islamic rapper in Germany is Ammar114. Born in Ethiopia, he spent his childhood in Frankfurt. During his teenage years, he started a commercial rap career, which he abandoned upon converting to Islam at the age of 19 in the late 1990s. He debated for a while whether or not to continue making music, and eventually resumed his career, but with a compromise: he carried on writing and performing hip-hop, but the content of his lyrics now entirely revolved around Islam.

Since taking this decision, Ammar114's career in "Islamic hip-hop" has developed successfully. In 2000, he launched a website where he offered his songs for free download and started performing at Islamic and other religious festivals. In 2004 he published his first CD, *"Mehr als Musik"* (More than music), gave many more performances and later released a second CD, *"Aus dem Schatten ans Licht"* (From shadow to light) in 2008. For the past few years he has been present at all major Islamic events all over Germany and has contributed to establishing the new genre of Islamic hip-hop in Germany. The name Ammar114 combines the name he adopted when converting and the number of *suras* (chapters) in the Quran, which he claims play a central role in his life (Qantara 04/12/2008).

In his lyrics and product design, Ammar114 often uses the shadow-and-light metaphor, which is a common, if not overused image in the contexts of religion, truth-seeking and a sudden change in lifestyle. In his songs, he mainly uses it for a before-and-after comparison that alludes to his conversion. It shows a photograph of Ammar himself against a dark background, with only his bent head and folded hands visible in a ray of light from above. His head is covered by a white crocheted cap, his hands hold a microphone and prayer beads, just above the title *"Aus dem Schatten ans Licht"* (fig. 1). The website[1] offers older songs for download, and there is a short introduction to Ammar himself, about his conversion and further stages of his career. His web presence therefore chiefly centres on the artist himself and the significant event of his conversion, all in the name of Allah. Many of the lyrics show a similar focus, albeit ranging from personal to religiously educational to political. Ammar114's first songs deal with this very

---

1 Ammar114: http://www.ammar114.de. For access dates of all websites, please refer to bibliography.

experience and describe how he repented of his former life as a street culture rapper and asked Allah's forgiveness, but concrete socio-political events also often constitute the subject matter. Many symbols recur that have a meaning for Muslims but less so for non-Muslims, and therefore act as – more or less – secret codes, like the numbers 114 (the *suras*) or 5:32 (a particular verse), phrases like *Allahu akbar* (Allah is great) or *takbir* (praise), or allusions to *shaitan* (devil).

The story in Ammar's very first song as an Islamic rapper, "*Allah vergib mir*" (Allah forgive me), begins with a clichéd teenage story – his girlfriend leaves him, he throws himself into a life of drug abuse, "hating everyone" and ends up lonely. Then, at a turning point and thanks to Allah, he realises that this is not what life is about, but that Allah is the only one deserving of his love. In hindsight, the rapper is grateful for what was, at the time, a painful experience, because it eventually brought him "back to Allah". The song's fatalistic, humble and devout character is typical of many of his songs (fig. 1).

Figure 1: Lyrics of Allah vergib mir *by Ammar114 and album cover*[2]

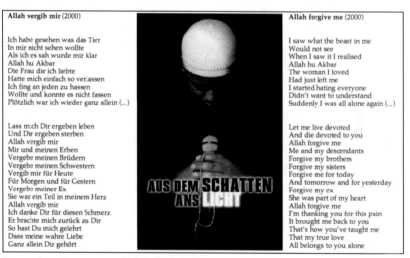

Allah vergib mir (2000)	Allah forgive me (2000)
Ich habe gesehen was das Tier In mir nicht sehen wollte Als ich es sah wurde mir klar Allah hu Akbar Die Frau die ich liebte Hatte mich einfach so verlassen Ich fing an jeden zu hassen Wollte und konnte es nicht fassen Plötzlich war ich wieder ganz allein (...)	I saw what the beast in me Would not see When I saw it I realised Allah hu Akbar The woman I loved Had just left me I started hating everyone Didn't want to understand Suddenly I was all alone again (...)
Lass mich Dir ergeben leben Und Dir ergeben sterben Allah vergib mir Mir und meinen Erben Vergebe meinen Brüdern Vergebe meinen Schwestern Vergib mir für Heute Für Morgen und für Gestern Vergebe meiner Ex Sie war ein Teil in meinem Herz Allah vergib mir Ich danke Dir für diesen Schmerz Er brachte mich zurück zu Dir So hast Du mich gelehrt Dass meine wahre Liebe Ganz allein Dir gehört	Let me live devoted And die devoted to you Allah forgive me Me and my descendants Forgive my brothers Forgive my sisters Forgive me for today And tomorrow and for yesterday Forgive my ex She was part of my heart Allah forgive me I'm thanking you for this pain It brought me back to you That's how you've taught me That my true love All belongs to you alone

Source: http://www.ammar114.de, lyrics added

Other songs are solely religious, such as the first track of the 2004 album, *Al-Fatiha*, the opening *sura* of the Quran, which Ammar recites in both Arabic and German. Not only a declaration of faith, this may also be aimed at teaching young Muslims. The song "*Im Namen der Demokratie*" (In the name of democracy) is more political and has stirred up much controversy, naming criminal

---

2 All translations of the lyrics are my own.

actions that have been executed by Western democracies, such as the CIA's secret interrogations in Europe, the Iraq war or the death of an American student who acted as a "human shield" against the demolition of Palestinian houses in the Gaza strip. A song much sought-after at festivals is *"Liebe Schwester"* (Dear sister), addressing all "sisters in faith" who wear the *hijab* or headscarf, but also relating to the 2003 headscarf verdict[3], encouraging a veiled teacher to fight for her professional rights. While some lyrics offer a rather simplistic black-and-white explanation of the world, Ammar does not defend crimes committed in the name of Islam. A song of that very name, *"Im Namen des Islam"* (In the name of Islam), denounces Islamic terror. The 2008 song *"[Fünf:32]"* ([Five:32]) tackles the issues of juvenile delinquency, honour killing and terrorist suicide bombing, clearly condemning any such violence on the grounds of parts of the much cited *sura* 5:32 of the Quran, which equates the killing of one person to the killing all humankind and saving one person to saving humanity. The message goes out to both Muslims and non-Muslims, shedding light on topics that many Muslim communities ignore for fear of discrimination and at the same time making the statement that Islam does not allow such crimes.[4]

Here, rap is clearly used as a vehicle for conveying a message. According to one of Ammar's own statements, he does not want to motivate young people to start rapping, in fact he would rather not, but instead make them think and move closer to Islam (Islamische Zeitung 21/05/2008). This is explicitly stated in one of his early songs *"Ich lebe für Allah"*: *"Du kannst mir Millionen bieten doch eine Sache ist klar / Das beste Angebot kommt immer noch von Allah"* (You can offer millions to me but one thing is clear / Allah still makes the best offer). On the other hand, rap is what Ammar grew up with and what he did professionally for a while, thus it is not surprising he uses the language of hip-hop for his ideas. Being a convert, he was less aware at first of the debate on whether music was allowed or not, but later solved the conflict by the subjective claim that the intention to provoke good deeds has higher value than the constraints against music (ibid.).

---

3   The "headscarf verdict" of the Federal Constitutional Court of Germany revoked the ban of a veiled Muslim teacher from her profession and called for a new legal foundation in an increasingly religiously pluralistic society on 24/09/2003. Currently, however, veiled women are not allowed to teach at German state schools.

4   Website of the song *"[Fünf:32]"*: http://www.fuenf32.de.

Le Silence des Mosquées

In France, the oldest group of the new genre is Le Silence des Mosquées, who have been performing since 1992.[5] Despite growing up in an Islamic environment as the children of North African immigrants in the suburbs of Dijon, the group combined different experiences of religious socialisation. While some were encouraged by their family to learn about and practise Islam, others were introduced to it from a cultural and traditional point of view and they only later taught themselves about religion until they "rediscovered themselves" religiously, as they put it. It seems symptomatic that this fact is mentioned even in a short introduction to the band on their MySpace page.[6] Many Islamic musicians have a conversion or reversion experience, and displaying it supposedly conveys an impression of an increased level of reflection about religion.

The group claim that for the first five years, before releasing any albums, they only performed for a Muslim audience, before later addressing a wider audience with a more general message. However, the change is a minor one. The first album features songs such like *"Allahou la ilaha illa llah"* (Allah, There is no god but God) and *"Wa soubhanallah"* (Glorious is Allah), all aimed at reminding the audience of basic Islamic principles and the beauty of their practice. The song *"Ya Allah"* (Oh Allah) sums up a reversion experience that wants to pass the experience on to another not-yet-believer: *"Je me sens mieux, grâce à Allah je suis plus heureux"* (I feel better, thanks to Allah I am much happier). The 2006 album also includes topics of social injustice, but does not cease reminding its audience of religion.

The song *"Cris de Bosnie"* (Cries of Bosnia) is the only political one on the 1996 album. It draws attention to the Bosnian conflict and the massacres of the Muslim population, but it also draws on Islamic solidarity and it calls for invocations to support Bosnian Muslims. The song was re-released on the 2006 album to recall the conflict, which also shows that both religious education and political engagement have been a stimulus for the group from the beginning. The 1998 song *"Pour ma sœur"* (For my sister) is of socio-political interest and resembles Ammar114's *"Liebe Schwester"* (fig. 2). Both songs are dedicated to veiled Muslim women and praise their courageous choice to wear the headscarf, despite the constraints of society or even their families.

---

5 Discography: *"Le Silence des Mosquées"* (1996), *"L'amour d'Allah et du Messager"* (The love of Allah and the Prophet, 1998), *"Message d'un chœur"* (Message of a choir, 2000), *"D'un Chemin à l'Autre"* (From one path to another, 2006).

6 Le Silence des Mosquées: http://www.myspace.com/silencedesmosquees, http://www. silencedesmosquees.com.

Reminders of the after-life are frequent and recur throughout many songs by other artists as well. In general, over their long performing career, Le Silence des Mosquées have touched on most aspects of Islamic practice and spirituality, on some Muslim-related politics and everyday anecdotes that act as reminders of the benefits of a religious life.

The music itself could be referred to as contemporary *nashid* (religious chant), but many songs might as well be classified as soft pop. Also, the language and context are "contemporary", as all songs are in French, except for a few Arabic-Islamic expressions, and are written from the perspective of practising Islam in France.

Figure 2: Lyrics of Pour ma sœur *and website of Le Silence des Mosquées*

Pour ma sœur (1998)	For my sister (1998)
O ma sœur, tu as les clefs	Oh my sister, you've got the keys
De la pureté, de la piété	Of purity, of piety
O ma sœur, tu t'es confiée	Oh my sister, you've confided
À Allah et son messager	In Allah and his messenger

Source: http://www.silencedesmosquees.com, lyrics added

Poetic Pilgrimage

In the British Islamic music scene, women play a significant role. Female duo Poetic Pilgrimage started performing together under that name in 2002, although they did not convert to Islam until 2005. Before their conversion, they had already been on a quest for religion and the meaning of life – hence pilgrimage – but like many, they put their musical career on hold when they adopted Islam. "They decided to stop doing music for a while and engaged in prayer and purified their intentions until they felt the time was right", says their MySpace profile.[7] The emphasis on "intentions" is not coincidental, as this is the main argument against the Islamic prohibition of music. Resuming their career, they continued their messages of peace and social criticism, but from a Muslim perspective. The 2006 album *"Pilgrims Love the Prophet"* mainly centres on the rap-

---

7 Poetic Pilgrimage: http://www.myspace.com/poeticpilgrimage.

pers' pilgrimage towards Islam and their love for the Prophet. Later, another theme became important to the duo, that of female performance in Islam, as the ban of music is often extended to women performing on stage. However, having confidently found statements and religious opinions in support of their cause, Poetic Pilgrimage proactively address this conservative viewpoint. The mini-album "*Something You Never Expected*" is dedicated to this matter, as is the song "*Unlikely MCs*" on the 2008 album "*Freedom Times*". It starts "*This is something you weren't expecting / Muslim chick, mic in hand, rappin'*", and continues discussing the unconventional change the audience would have to get used to.

Poetic Pilgrimage produce rap, which is also referred to as spoken word, i.e. poetry presented with no or little background music in order to focus on the substance. The latter means a lot to them, as their lyrics reveal: they are rather intellectual, less predictable than those of some of their colleagues, and social and political topics are well researched. What is also uncommon is that there is not only the usual criticism of conflicts where Muslims are victims, but also of those where they are among the perpetrators, such as in Darfur and Iran (fig. 3).[8]

Figure 3: Lyrics of Ode to Those Who Give a Damn *and album cover*

Ode to Those Who Give a Damn

I carry
The decrepit Legacy, of those wretched casualties,
Who've lost the faculty to fathom
What it means to be Free (...)

I'm an Iranian woman marching for equality
I'd rather die standing up than live on my knees
And it seems they didn't get the memo
That my soul was born free.

And rape is still being used as weapons of war
Invading what's pure
Those parading in Darfur (...)

But you'll see me
Hijaab tied tight
Black glove fist raised high
Chanting the war cry 'No Justice, No peace'
Till the day I lose life

Source: http://www.euterpemedia.de/Poetic-Pilgrimage-Freedom-Times, lyrics added

---

8   See "*Ode To Those Who Give A Damn*", cited in Mandaville 2009b.

Samia and Oriental Comic

A French-educated actress and comedian, Samia plays sketches on topics concerning Muslims living in France. She is a member of the theatre group Oriental Comic and has started her own show, playing with the oriental theme, as "Samia et les 40 comiques".[9] She performs in the centre of Paris in front of Muslim and non-Muslim audiences, both at public theatres and private events.

In her sketches, she mocks North and West Africans and their accents along with the French themselves. In a piece about the *hijab* she mimics all conflicting perspectives, including her own, adding a self-ironic touch while wearing a headscarf on stage (fig. 4). She makes fun of non-Muslims who are surprised to find her capable of using a debit card as well as of Muslim men who obsessively control the women in their lives. But apart from relating to the everyday experiences of French Muslims, she also intentionally leaves other topics out that a regular comedy show would have: there are no references to sex in the show that promises to be "200% halal". The concept is to provide entertainment for a wide audience, including all family members and people of different Islamic beliefs, and therefore to cut out any vulgar or offensive content. In fact, it is not just the audience that demands *halal* standards, but Samia and the other actors themselves do not feel comfortable performing in any other way and thus promote the benefits of this type of comedy.

Figure 4: French Comedian Samia

Source: Le courrier de l'atlas no. 24

Other Musicians and Comedians

The success of Ammar114 was fostered through his Frankfurt-based media company 114media, and the "brand" 114 is at the forefront of the German Islamic rap movement. Serkan114 produces songs on love – platonic love, family

9   Oriental Comic: http://www.orientalcomic.fr; Samia et les 40 comiques: http://www.samiaetles40comiques.com.

love, and Allah's love for the people – while Sayfoudin114 offers social criticism on the situation of Muslims in Germany.[10] Ammar has also had significant influence on another band, Amantu (Arabic for "I believe"), made up of two German-Moroccan rappers from Wuppertal. Both of them had a "reversion" experience bringing them back to their Muslim heritage, which influences many of their very spiritual songs. They often address the topic of how to get away from "questionable" moral conduct (drugs, materialism, extramarital relationships) and how to lead a good life.

Two women also form part of the German scene, Lady Scar and Sahira, both of them from Berlin. Lady Scar is of African-American and Puerto-Rican background and a classic rapper. Having spent much time on the streets with other youths of migratory background gives her the authority or "street credibility" to address related issues in her songs. Her strong language also distinguishes her from other artists on the scene who deliberately avoid any swear words, which are otherwise very common in hip-hop. Islamic references are employed in her lyrics on everyday life, for example in a song about life on social benefits, in which she thanks God (*"Al7amdulillah"*) for providing her with a brighter future if she keeps praying and wearing the *hijab*. Rapper Sahira describes 9/11 as a turning point in her life. At a time when Islam and Muslims were being maligned and generally suspected of terrorism, Sahira felt the need to form her own opinion and started studying the Quran, becoming more religious herself in the process (N-TV 07/04/2007). Many of her songs are autobiographical, but particularly the later songs speak of God and spirituality more directly. Through her music, Sahira aims to help teenagers with a migration background by enhancing their self-esteem and acting as a role model especially for young Muslim women (Berliner Zeitung 30/04/2007).

To name a different representative of the performing arts, Uma Lamo is Germany's first Islamic comedy group. The name of the three-man group, whose members have a Moroccan background, is imaginative, but alludes to both Arabic *ummah* and the Tamazight/Berber word for brother. Lamo abbreviates the Arabic statement of faith and also stands for the group's ideals of love, grace, empathy and readiness to make sacrifices.[11] In their sketches, they combine various influences of current popular culture, while the context is always Islamic, like in the skit on Conrad the Convert at a Cologne mosque. By their own account, the group seek to give religious advice (*nasiha*) through their plays, to-

---

10 Sayfoudin114: http://www.sayfoudin114.de.

11 "La ilaha illa Allah wa Mohammed rasulullah"; Liebe, Anmut, Mitgefühl, Opferbereitschaft. See http://www.sadaka-benefiz.de/index.php?pid=programm.

gether with humour and wisdom. They often perform at Islamic festivals and at events of the youth organisation *Muslimische Jugend in Deutschland (MJD)*.

In France, a few Muslim rappers have gained great popularity among a wider, non-Muslim audience, which is mainly due to the fact that they address more general spiritual or political issues. Although references to religion are clearly present, they are not as predominant as with other bands. One could argue that their works might not necessarily be classified as Islamic, but rather as music by Muslim artists. However, because Islam is clearly referred to in parts of the lyrics and the artists incorporate much of their religion into their performances and songs, they also form part of this genre, as well as of other genres perhaps. The most prevalent representatives of this current scene are Kery James, Abd al Malik and Médine (L'express 07/06/2004; Time Magazine 06/11/2005; Le monde diplomatique 09/2008).

The rappers of Réalité Anonyme from Montpellier are more explicitly religious. Of the two young men starting the group in 1999, Volont.R and Barseulo-né, only the latter has continued until today.[12] Without exception, all songs centre around religion, for example around the role of Islam in the quest for truth. Some lyrics express gratitude for being born Muslim, while others talk about the rappers' ideal of a future marriage, which should not be distorted by cultural customs, but guided only by the Prophet's rules.

The precursors of British Islamic hip-hop are the group Mecca2Medina, who currently consist of two male rappers. When they started in 1996, they were the only band producing Islamic hip-hop in the UK, and after releasing a number of albums, they have moved on to promoting the new genre and younger bands. They are also part of the campaign *"Proud to be a British Muslim"*, an initiative to promote the peaceful character of Islam and tolerance in British society with the "vision of a diverse, all inclusive and strong Britain".[13] The band Pearls of Islam are two sisters, brought up by Caribbean parents who converted to Sufism. All their songs are inspired by Sufi beliefs, many dealing with love and the need for spirituality and also playing with visual hippie references.[14] In musical terms, the Pearls of Islam are very diverse and skilled, employing rap, spoken word, vocals, piano, guitar and drums. Mohammed Yahya, who works closely with Mecca2Medina and Poetic Pilgrimage, has been active in various Islamic hip-hop, interfaith and festival activities ever since. He also performs in the duo

---

12 Réalité Anonyme: http://www.myspace.com/realiteanonyme, http://realite-anonyme-13.skyrock.com; see SaphirNews 16/07/2003.

13 Proud to Be a British Muslim Campaign: http://www.islamispeace.org.uk/itmc.php?id_top=24.

14 Pearls of Islam: http://www.myspace.com/pearlsofislam.

Lines of Faith with Jewish rapper Daniel Silverstein, and he has been the co-organiser of a monthly Islamic hip-hop event in London called Rebel Muzik that gathers together many and also less well known representatives of the British Islamic music scene.

Although many of these artists have found their own way into the genre, an important trend has been set by British-Azerbaijani singer Sami Yusuf, who has been at the forefront of modern Islamic music since 2004. Sami Yusuf became famous with the song *"Al Muallim"* (The teacher), in which he reminds his audience of Mohammed's teachings that have been forgotten by many – perhaps by those living in non-Muslim contexts, which might be one reason why he composes in English. His music videos resemble those of romantic pop songs, while the protagonists of his lyrics are, for instance, the Prophet or the singer's mother. Sami Yusuf has had the biggest economic success of modern Islamic artists and is widely popular throughout the West and Islamic countries. Perhaps because of his success and because he mainly lives abroad, he is less connected with the British Islamic music scene and appears only for large-scale events. Whether or not he has influenced other British Islamic rappers, he has certainly played an important role in the promotion of modern Islamic music on a global scale.

The Popularity of a Contested Genre

The unfortunate relationship between Islamic scholarship and music is among the most contested issues when trying to place music on a scale ranging from *halal* to *haram*. Very few verses in the Quran mention musical instruments, singing or amusement, while a few parts in the *Hadith* (anecdotes on the life of the Prophet) speak of the Prophet Mohammed's attitudes towards music. Both those in favour of and those opposed to music will find evidence to support their position. While some scholars reject music in all forms, others only disapprove of drums or wind instruments, which are believed to resemble Satan's voice, or entertainment, because they regard them as distracting from religion and allowing for the sexes to mix freely. Some deprecating attitudes of the Prophet towards musical practice are also interpreted in light of their particular historical situation, in which non-Muslims used music to overpower Quranic recitations. However, even those with more liberal viewpoints that allow music in general keep some restrictions in place: the topic of a song should not contradict Islamic teachings (e.g. not advocate alcohol), the manner of performance should not allude to sexuality, and excessive entertainment should not lead to the neglect of religious duties. Criticism is voiced by some imams, by Salafists, and by some other believers who also write to Islamic musicians, providing Quranic "evidence" for their alleged wrongdoing.

Despite treading on a minefield, many young, believing Muslims deliberately choose music – not just as their hobby, but precisely as a means of expressing their faith. They do not ignore the controversy; for instance, the website Muslimhiphop.com features a dominant disclaimer: "Before you judge: read our position on music in Islam", a position supported by scholarly articles arguing in favour of music.[15] However, the musicians suggest the emergence of a new genre that does not incorporate music, despite religious restrictions, but is in line with religion. In order to achieve this, the musicians provide a two-fold solution of intentions and rules.

Justifying making music with the "right intentions" is a very common approach, and the emphasis placed on the lyrics is therefore strong. If the music is concerned with the remembrance of Allah and the Prophet, the argument that music distracts from religion becomes invalid. Rap music in particular lends itself to this purpose, because it emphasised the words more than the music. Moreover, many musicians, especially the converted or reverted, display a strong proselytising attitude and make no secret of their intention of making *dawah*. Yusuf Islam – formerly known as Cat Stevens – holds that there are more important issues for Muslims to address than fighting about the prohibition of music, and that music should be used to educate about Islam and thus proselytise (Islam n.d.). All mainly spiritual songs can be interpreted in this way, although these certainly also address an audience who are already religious and the songs then have a reinforcing and community-enhancing effect.

Other problems that are negotiated through music are providing disadvantaged Muslim youths with self-esteem and showing them what they can achieve with the support of Allah. This is the reason why the artists so often give an account of their own youth, illustrating the underprivileged background they came from or the bad influence of a drug scene, and again how their faith helped them to become the personality and artist they are today. This is particularly often used by converts and reverts and can, besides the social function, also be considered a form of proselytism. On a different note, the music is also used to counter the negative image of Islam as often portrayed by the media and to draw attention to political and social conflict. Again, rap may appear particularly suitable for this purpose, as it is an art form associated with marginalised social groups and their fighting for rights.

The other justification for lifting the music ban is demonstrated when looking at what topics are *not* covered in the songs: sexual reference, love stories (unless clearly relating to marriage), vulgarity, strong language, references to

---

15 Muslim Hip-Hop: http://www.muslimhiphop.com/index.php?p=What_is_MHH/ Music_in_Islam.

alcohol, drugs or crime, partying or having fun as an end in itself. Some or all of these would be expected in hip-hop and any other youth cultural music scene, and their absence is a clear trait of contemporary Islamic music. Adhering to these rules – using hip-hop in a *halal* manner and disconnecting it from sex, drugs and violence – makes the prohibition less convincing. The musicians convey conservative values throughout to stay within the realm of Islamic teachings. Finally, in all cases either they were musicians first and then incorporated their Islamic faith later or they developed an interest in both at the same time; however, it was never the case that they became interested in music while already practicing Islam. Thus, as if music in general were not enough, young Muslim Europeans even choose Western types of music, such as hip-hop, as their preferred means of expression, and they do so in devotion.

Remarkably, radical German Salafists, who strongly condemn any kind of music for being *haram*, have recently become aware of the possibilities music offers to access and influence youth. Radical preacher Pierre Vogel recruited former "gangsta rapper" Deso Dogg to renounce his former involvement in rap and to start producing rap full of Salafist ideology. Under his new name Abou Maleeq, he now calls for young Muslims to fight Western troops in Afghanistan. This opportunist use of music only includes a capella songs without instruments, and all other (Islamic) music is still considered forbidden. As Islamic studies scholar Jochen Müller points out, this type of music appeals to less religious, marginalised youths who are open to politically radical views. He warns of the dangers and the antidemocratic ideology of Salafist rap, while he evaluates all other forms of young Islamic music as peace-oriented and affirmative of society (Deutschlandradio 16/06/2011).

While the similarities between the French, German and British scenes facilitate the outline of the new genre, a closer look at the differences will help to better understand its role in a particular context and how rap is used as "a tool for reworking local identity" (Mitchell 2001: 1–2). Indeed, the major themes of the songs resemble each other across borders as they are linked by the commonalities of Islam and have the global *ummah* in mind. However, ignoring the conspicuous differences between the three countries in context, the artists' background, the commercial structure or in fact some locally specific contents of songs would mean ignoring the genre's potential for identity negotiation and would disregard the fact that, without doubt, the artists fully engage with their national framework.

A conspicuous feature, accounting for both similarity and difference between the countries, is the language in which a song is written. On the one hand, the musicians from the three countries share the fact that they rap in their respective national languages – and not in that of any Islamic country. Like the switch from English to French or German, which according to Andy Bennett allows for increased accuracy between localised experience and its linguistic representation (Bennett 2003: 31), the switch from Arabic or Turkish to a Western language is representative of a life in the West. On the other hand, the different languages themselves hint at contrasting national contexts, both in terms of the local hip-hop development and of the musicians' relationship with society. Bennett claims that language itself, regardless of its lyrical content, is key to the interpretation of the meaning of popular music (ibid.: 36).

As for local musical traditions, the case of France clearly shows that the advent of contemporary Islamic music is not only connected with the global rise of Islam, but also with local musical traditions. In his short sketch of how French rap music developed in the 1980s and 1990s, André Prévos points out that after a decade of imitating US gangsta rap, French artists started to develop their own style (Prévos 2001: 45–46). While before the late 1980s French rap uncritically adopted what US rappers had on offer (ibid.: 45), simply changing the language, but nothing else that might localise it, the early 1990s were marked by typically French styles, repertoires and themes, which first and foremost meant: highly political music. Listeners of French rap will notice its deeply political nature, not least because it often evolved in the disadvantaged and politicised areas of the *banlieues* with groups from IAM to Zebda. Prévos also sees as the "central mission" of French hip-hop culture the urge to "vent the anger and the frustration of many disadvantaged and sometimes mistreated individuals, and to defend the cause of the poorest and least socially integrated segments of French society" (ibid.: 46). Taking this trajectory further, in the 2000s Islamic hip-hop shifted the focus from the purely political, which had up till then satisfied the need for social relevancy. This aspect also accounts for the slower development of Islamic music in France compared with Germany and Britain. Thus, on the one hand, the Islamic development followed in the footsteps of socio-politically relevant rap, and on the other hand, this tradition slowed the new development down until it proved to be meaningful to producers and consumers in a novel way.

In contrast, the development of the German rap scene has taken different routes. Its local production started later than in France, was barely political, and it was initially only middle-class Germans with no migratory background that produced rap at all. The scene diversified in the 2000s, but still largely mirrors these initial prototypes today. In his detailed account of the "birth of a genre", Mark Pennay (2001) states that in the 1980s African-American rap was consumed in Germany, but found little local imitation because the life circumstances alluded to were too different, and the political dimension was therefore largely ignored; language barriers also played a part. Pennay diagnoses a "general ignorance of and lack of serious engagement with rap as a medium of political expression" (ibid.: 117) throughout the 1980s. The only exceptions were a few immigrants who copied the American examples and rapped in English, and some influence of general American hip-hop culture on East German youth.

1993 saw the emergence of German-language rap with local references, started by the two groups Advanced Chemistry and Die Fantastischen Vier. While the former did indeed feature some critical songs, such as *"Fremd im eigenen Land"* (Foreign in my own country), which tackles the implicit racism of the middle classes, the latter instead focussed on everyday life scenes and witty to nonsensical lyrics, and successfully so. In the 2000s, German rappers have either developed this further or have moved towards "gangsta rap".

All of this leaves little room for Islamic rap in the mainstream and thus explains why it has developed purely in non-commercial subcultural circles, while Islamic artists in France are now well integrated into the commercial music business. It also gives a reason for the desire for a specifically Muslim genre, as even migrant cultures were underrepresented in rap – again, unlike in France. However, the fact that German rap, regardless of its substance, had established itself successfully in the German language was of great importance (Bennett 2003: 31–32) and a basis to build on for the Islamic rappers who fully relied on this language for their own songs. The 1990s also saw the emergence of a Turkish-German music scene, achieving success, however, only years later. Daniel Bax ascribes this to the point in time where the musicians started using the German language; the Turkish also has an influence on German hip-hop, with successful musicians like Muhabbet, but more in terms of oriental musical styles rather than substance, let alone religious lyrics (Bax 2006).

For the British context, David Hesmondhalgh and Caspar Melville have shown how the adaptation of the US influence can go far beyond the localisation of styles, a concept they reject as invalid. Instead of modifications of themes and accents, they perceive British hip-hop as having transformed its origins on a much larger scale (Hesmondhalgh/Melville 2001: 86). For instance, they focus on the British Asian band Fun-Da-Mental, who took up notions of African-American Islamic radicalism and black separatist politics combined with British Asian issues, to point to different frames of reference and significance. The range indicates a variety of cultural fusions and audiences, which may often involve a political stance, but not always in such an explicit way as in France.

The different developments of hip-hop in the three countries account for some of the contrasting elements observed in contemporary Islamic music. The diverse creativity of the British scene, especially with London as the hub for new genres, explains some of the differences in Islamic music between Britain, France and Germany. In Britain, the Islamic music scene is larger than in the other two countries in terms of number of musicians, albums and events, and has been around since the mid-1990s. There is a high degree of networking among the musicians, fostered by the pioneers Mecca2Medina and the regular event Rebel Muzik. Nearly all British artists are located in London and part of a strong network, while they are decentralised in the other two countries. In Germany, the label 114media is an active networker, in France perhaps the collective La Boussole, or other local event organisers, but in both cases the musicians are not all concentrated in the capital.

Many of the artists presented are converts to Islam or have had a reversion experience: about one third of the bands presented here either speak of a continuous religious upbringing or do not comment on this, while twice as many have converted or reverted, with most of them indeed having converted. This is evenly distributed across the three countries, with some more reverts in Germany. Approximately half of the bands come from a black ethnic background, and in fact, all converts are black British, French or German, most of them in the UK. So the ethnic background does not simply mirror Islamic immigration, but immigration as a whole, with a significant emphasis on conversion among black immigrants; Nation of Islam ideas are therefore another major factor in terms of African-American influence apart from hip-hop, and they have been more fruitful in the British context than in the other two countries. Conversion represents a trend, as Reddie has shown for young black men (2009), but also women. Thus, especially in the British context there are several music producing women, with almost none in France, and a few in Germany. Across the three countries there are three to four times as many male Islamic musicians, and a striking difference from other musical genres may be the absence of mixed bands, as these are all single-sex, even though at festivals and on tours some of them do perform together.

Comedy is a much more recent phenomenon among Muslims on stage. While this genre does not exclusively form part of youth culture, but rather belongs to popular culture in general, it adds to the understanding of youth culture in the Islamic context. Comedy as such is often part of youth-focussed shows and television programmes, but Islamic comedy shows, just like many of the concerts, are embedded into a family and festival environment, where they are to be enjoyed by, and must be compatible with, the whole family. As for music, although it may appeal more to young people, the moral soundness of the lyrics, just like the sketches, makes it possible to consume the performance in a family environment.

Even though the ideas to perform comedy have sprung up locally, they have a prominent American forerunner in the group Allah made me funny. These popular comedians tour around the world, and do not shy away from making people laugh about anything Islamic, which has encouraged groups in Europe to try Islamic comedy out. It is a genre that most profits from the tensions between Muslims and non-Muslims, because people on all sides are grateful if they may, for once, leave their kid gloves aside, and address their anxieties and anger with cathartic laughter. The comedians enjoy playing with the unexpected. Just as the music is stretching the boundaries of *halal*, Islamic comedy is testing how far the liberty of satire can be stretched and what the benefits are for Muslims and non-Muslims alike.

2. Fashion

Styleislam

The most successful German Islamic fashion company is Styleislam, founded in 2008 by a young, Turkish German couple, Melih and Yeliz Kesmen, in an industrial town of the Ruhrgebiet.[16] They sell sporty T-shirts, hooded sweatshirts and accessories with stylishly designed religious slogans. A classic Styleislam shirt reads *"I love my Prophet"*, with the name Mohammed in Arabic, and was the very first that founder Melih Kesmen designed (fig. 5).

Figure 5: Styleislam: I love my Prophet

Source: http://www.styleislam.com

---

16 Styleislam: http://styleislam.com.

All slogans are in English, not German, supposedly to match with American urban street wear and therefore to increase the "coolness factor", but also to serve a global customer base. They are often mixed with an Islamic-Arabic expression in either Latin or Arabic script, such as *"Al Akhira – The final destination"*, meaning the afterlife, a reminder of humility and the short stay in this world. *"Jannah – Under mothers' feet"* alludes to paradise *(jannah)* that is, according to a saying of the Prophet Mohammed, to be reached by obeying one's mother, while *"Ummah – Be part of it"* reminds people of the fact that Islam is not only religious worship, but also sharing religious principles in the community of Muslims. The slogans are accompanied by small illustrations. Sometimes they imitate well-known symbols, as in the case of *"Juma"* (Friday, day of prayer) that resembles the sports label Puma, replacing the jumping puma with a praying person – possibly intended as an alternative symbol of strength. The *"Go halal"* slogan is illustrated with a pig, gambling dice and a German style beer glass, all crossed out, as a concise but humorous reminder of how to adhere to Islamic principles (fig. 6).

Figure 6: Styleislam: Juma, Go halal

Source: http://www.styleislam.com

The examples highlight that nearly all slogans bear a religious message alluding to the Quran, *Hadith*, religious practice and the Islamic community. As with the lyrics in Islamic music, there is also a striking absence of themes such as sex, drugs, partying or anything similar that may otherwise be of youth cultural interest. Also the clothing cuts are in line with Islamic rules, with longer shirts and tunics available for women.

Figure 7: Styleislam advertisement banner

Source: http://muslime.wordpress.com/2007/12/26/zeig-mir-deinen-style-styleislamcom

The fashion is also very much anchored in Western popular culture, as illustrated by the company's advertisement banner (fig. 7). It features three men, each wearing a Styleislam T-shirt, *"I love my Prophet"*, *"Al Medina"* and *"Iqra"*. The latter is possibly inviting the viewer to read the Quran, as *Iqra* (Read) is believed to be its first revealed word; the middle one, a muscular basketball player, implies American street culture, while the first one is particularly interesting from a pop cultural point of view: the picture shows the upper body of a man, dressed in a suit and tie, who tears his shirt open to show what he wears underneath – a T-shirt with the slogan *"I love my Prophet"* and the name Mohammed in Arabic. This reminds the viewer of the famous gesture of Superman: whenever his everyday alias Clark Kent, in suit and tie, turns into Superman, he tears his shirt open, under which the big S and soon all of Superman's outfit appears. With the advertisement alluding to this scene, the beholder is invited to associate Mohammed with Superman (fig. 8).[17]

Styleislam, originally not planned as a money-making business, has advanced to a highly successful company within only a few years. It attracts great media attention for providing Islam with a novel look and for its strong identification with Germany.[18] The business recruits young people for apprenticeship training positions in design and merchandising, often giving preference to young women wearing the *hijab*, who may have difficulties finding a job elsewhere. The highly professional website offers separate online shops in various languages for ten European countries, Turkey, Canada and the United States, targeting a solvent consumer base that is ready to spend 20 to 35€ on a shirt. The products are sold mainly online and shipped worldwide, but the company's suc-

---

17 I owe thanks to the art historian Henry Keazor for drawing my attention to this.

18 E.g.: Berliner Zeitung 08/03/2008; Süddeutsche Zeitung Magazin 04/2010; Die Zeit 14/05/2010; Welt am Sonntag 29/08/2010; The German Times 10/2010; Frankfurter Rundschau 04/01/2011.

cess enabled Styleislam to expand and open shops in other countries, interestingly not in the West, but in Istanbul and Medina, where the outfits and accessories are sold to the affluent population. Incidentally, the Medina branch, where the customers are pilgrims from all over the world, is advertised as being conveniently located opposite the KFC fast food restaurant.[19]

Figure 8: Clark Kent turns into Superman

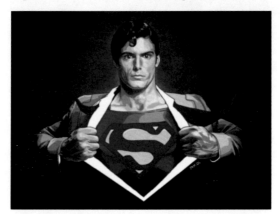

Source: http://www.fanpop.com/clubs/superman/images/
546265/title/superman-clark-kent-fanart

Ünicité

In France, one of the urban fashion companies is the brand Ünicité, alluding to "divine unity", the concept of monotheism.[20] It was founded in early 2007 as an online shop and first presented at France's largest Islamic fair in Bourget in April that year. The Paris-based company was planned as a community project, with some of the profit going to an Islamic charity, and with the intention of developing "Muslim wear" in France (Al Kanz 18/09/2007).

The name, logo and motto of this brand are heavy with symbolic meaning. Regarding the name, one could at first assume that the spelling of the French work unicité with the letter Ü was derived from Turkish, or much less likely, from German, but in fact it is supposed to resemble the letter "ta" in Arabic [ت], which is the first letter of the word *tawhid* (oneness, unity) in Arabic. Casually, it also provides the logo with a unique note. The logo is a stylised hand gesture of

---

19 Styleislam blog: http://blog.styleislam.com/styleislam-in-medina.

20 Ünicité: http://www.unicitewear.com. The company was active at the time of interview, but is currently offline and may have closed down like most of its counterparts.

a pointed index finger and the thumb enclosing the three other fingers, the gesture that accompanies the *shahada*[21] during prayer; the index finger symbolising divine unity (fig. 9).

Figure 9: Ünicité logo

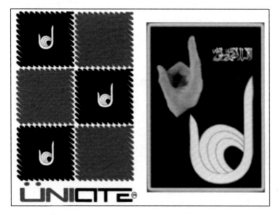

Source: Ünicitéwear Catalogue 2008

In this fashion context, the logo is employed as a recognition feature in two ways. Muslims will distinguish it as a central religious gesture, a sign of commonality in the non-Muslim context of France. As a fashion logo, it fosters brand recognition like any other label. The brand motto, *"Portez vos valeurs"* (Wear your values), suggests that there is more to the clothes than fashion and that the consumer would not just buy something that has a value itself, but actually a garment that would underline his or her values. The absence of particular slogans as in the case of Styleislam focuses the "values" on the notion of *unicité* and whatever is associated with it; it implies nothing more specific than the adherence to the Islamic faith, i.e. following no particular sect or cultural tradition, so that any Muslim could identify with it. There is, however, a noticeable absence of female-specific clothes and models; hence in terms of unity, the customer base might not feel fully represented. One of the main motives plays with bringing the brand's different features together. It combines the logo, name and slogan in a circle – in many religious contexts a symbol for unity, oneness and the divine. Beneath the logo are what looks like arbitrary brush strokes; rotated

---

21 The *shahada* is the Islamic statement of faith: "I testify there is no god but God and Mohammed is his Prophet."

clockwise by 90°, however, they turn out to be a calligraphy of the Arabic word *tawhid* (fig. 10).

Figure 10: Ünicité design: tawhid

Source: Ünicitéwear Catalogue 2008

In terms of style, Ünicité claims to be "prêt-à-porter street wear" and "Muslim wear", used to denote a clothing style combining urban fashion trends and spiritual Islamic references. This generally describes the trend as a whole; in the case of Ünicité, the style works with codes borrowed from urban style and religion, while being unobtrusive, but not inconspicuous.

Elenany

Elenany is a high quality and sophisticated fashion label, launched by the young designer Sarah Elenany with the help of her London university in 2009.[22] She combines urban styles with traditional Arabic types of forms found in mosques – such as repetitive and angular shapes – for the display of Islamic symbols. The simplified, thick stroke graphics resemble graffiti styles, while the religious symbols are probably what the designer regards as most central to Islam: like with Ünicité, the most important is the *shahada* gesture of the pointed finger, but interpreted not primarily as *tawhid* (unity) but as "testify"[23] and acting as the brand logo. Other symbols include minarets, possibly designed in response to the Swiss minaret ban, brotherhood, symbolised by stylised prayer gestures, or *dua*, two hands performing supplication (fig. 11).

---

22 Elenany: http://elenany.co.uk, The Guardian 21/05/2009.

23 From the *shahada*: "I <u>testify</u> there is no god but God and Mohammed is his Prophet".

Figure 11: Elenany's designs: minaret winter coat, dua and logo

Source: Courtesy of the artist

Styles are available for both sexes. While the clothes are long and loose and not revealing, they do not convey a particularly Islamic look. In most cases, the graphics are hidden on the inside of hoods and coats or used as an inconspicuous pattern; no slogans are added. Hence the styles and symbols appeal to Muslims without stigmatising them as traditionally clad, but rather using hidden, subcultural codes to be deciphered by those who are familiar both with the vocabulary of urban graffiti and Islamic symbols.

Figure 12: Elenany's Throw Yo' Hands

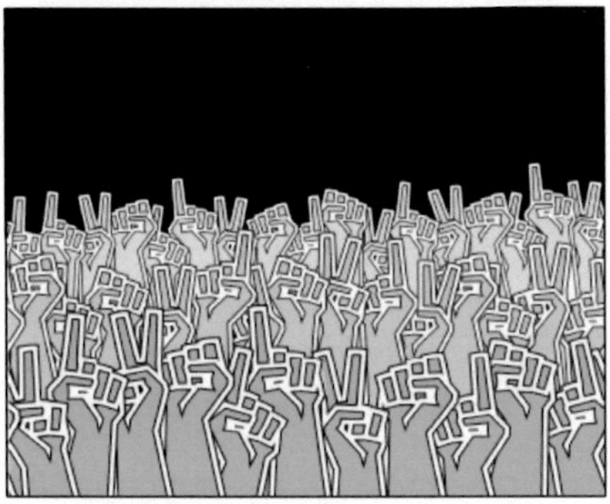

Source: Courtesy of the artist

The "Throw Yo' Hands" graphic, for instance, appears as an urban landscape made of a sea of protesters with fists raised – but not just fists, also the V sign and, again, the pointed finger of the *shahada* (fig. 12). At the same time, both presentation and design are sufficiently open to reach out to non-Muslims.

More Fashionistas

Styleislam dominates the German market, but two smaller companies temporarily joined the niche. Comuni-T and Muslim Shirt offer similar, though less well designed slogans than their successful competitor, since in both cases the owners only run it as a side business.[24] Comuni-T features a few more political statements on the situation in the Middle East, while the makers of Muslim Shirt go as far as claiming religious absoluteness with a shirt simply stating *"Islam ist die Wahrheit"* (Islam is the truth).

In France, there have been a few attempts at establishing urban style Islamic clothing, some of which only lasted for a short while. The first attempt to introduce urban Islamic clothing in France was made by French NBA basketball player Tariq Abdul-Wahad, a convert to Islam. He tried to launch the American Muslim clothing company Dawah Wear[25] in France, but it was not profitable, and a few more have come and gone in the past years, one of them being Ünicité (SaphirNews 20/05/2008). In addition to these, rapper Médine has launched a T-shirt collection that mainly merchandises his record label Din Records, carrying the titles from his songs.[26] The slogan *"I'm Muslim, don't panik"* has become the most popular.

Zaynab is a fashion brand catering for an entirely different consumer group. The designer specialises in swimwear and running outfits for women who wear the veil, and therefore covers the sportswoman up from tip to toe.[27] Her "coverkinis" are a full-body swimwear composed of leggings, a long-sleeved top and a

---

24 Comuni-T: http://www.comuni-t.com/shop/index.php. Muslim Shirt went offline, but was still active at the time of the interview with the producer at http://www.muslim-shirt.de. Some of their designs have been collected in a short article (Ufuq 28/10/2008).

25 Dawah Wear: http://www.dawahwear.com.

26 Le Savoir est une Arme: http://www.le-savoir-est-une-arme.com. *Din* in Din Records is Arabic for religion.

27 Zaynab: http://www.zaynab-styliste.com. The business is based on the Mediterranean coast.

hood covering the hair and neck.[28] Unlike Styleislam or Ünicité, where slogans "advertise" one's convictions in a sportive style, Zaynab's fashion encourages women to pursue sportive activity despite *and* in line with Islam. If interpreted as an emancipation of women, the fashion must also be seen as a start-up of religion, because it invades a field – sports – that is mostly rather indifferent to religion. Although Zaynab does not specifically target young people, her fashion is particularly appealing to them because of the significance of the beach and sports in young people's leisure activities.

A British medical student writes a very popular fashion blog, not to sell, but to collect and comment on Islamic fashion.[29] Even though she is not a designer, she creates styles by combining non-Islamic fashion items with the *hijab* and in layers to achieve a full cover and style. Urban Ummah is a British clothing company that again resembles the previous T-shirt producers.[30] It has an edge of its own by displaying an Islamic ethics that incorporates a care for animals' rights, traditionally strong in Britain, and up-to-date environmental and ethical concerns: *"Clothing to believe in"*. Tawheed Is Unity is another online shop that besides clothing also offers music and other urban art and thus claims to be *"The home of urban Muslim culture"*.[31] The logo is, once more, the pointed index finger of the *shadada* gesture. The slogans *"Tawheed is unity"* and *"Clothing for the tawheed generation"* coincide with the lyrics of one of Poetic Pilgrimage's songs,[32] and indeed, the business is run by them and a network of other British Islamic musicians like Mecca2Medina, Masikah and Mohammed Yahya.

Finally, not a fashion designer, but sharing the passion for hip-hop culture and "urban spiritual art", Mohammed Ali also expresses Islamic phrases in a subcultural way.[33] The Birmingham-based tagger sprays large graffiti with a short message in Latin and Arab script, such as *dhikr* (Remembrance of God) or *iqra* (Read). His graffiti are legal and sought after by cities around the globe.

---

28 This type of swimwear was first registered as a trademark by a Lebanese Australian, Aheda Zanetti, under the name "burqini", combining burqa and bikini (http://www.ahi ida.com). Because of the trademarketed term, Zaynab had to choose a different name.

29 Hijab Style Blog: http://www.hijabstyle.co.uk.

30 Urban Ummah: http://www.urbanummah.com.

31 Tawheed Is Unity: http://www.tawheedisunity.com; http://www.myspace.com/ tawheedisunity.

32 Lyrics of *"Hitchhiking to Heaven"*: So that's it / Pilgrims are just trynna see the face of our Lord / Trynna hitchhike to heaven / Ya this is for the tawheed generation / Tawheed is unity / Come follow me, listen / (Refrain 3x:) Put your tawheeds up / Ones in the air / And praise Allah.

33 Aerosol Arabic: http://www.aerosolarabic.com/v2/index.php.

Prêt-À-Porter Values

The term "Islamic fashion" evokes images of *hijabs, chadors* and particularly of female garments. Elaborate headscarf styles and other female attire is indeed found in Europe's young Islamic fashion, but this area is far from being limited to the ladies – on the contrary: it seems that male youths almost envied their female peers for being able to show their religion by their appearance, and were looking for a sartorial equivalent. Islamic street wear is the male response.

Women's garments in Islam are regarded, debated, written and fought over much more than men's. This attention stands in contrast to the Islamic sources of Quran, *Hadith* and *Sunnah* that prescribe more rules for male dress than the few allusions to what can be interpreted as a recommendation for women to cover their hair (Tarlo 2010: 7–8). And yet, female dress attracts more attention and is usually the focus of religious and political activism or commentary. As Emma Tarlo points out in her book *Visibly Muslim*, this goes as far as taking only "visible Muslims" as representatives of Islam, which can result in a simplified or essentialised view of Muslims, but also in a marginalisation of Muslim women who do not wear the veil (2010: 4–5, 12). Islamic street wear can be combined with a headscarf, but it also provides the opportunity for any non-veiling Muslim, male or female, to make their religion visible.

The fashion genre is the most visible of the three categories, compared to the performing arts and media, and on many levels this visibility is its most important feature. It sets an end to the hiding away of Western Muslims in the past, when many immigrants sought to live a more inconspicuous life, but as Tarlo rightly points out, it is also a way of responding to an already heightened visibility due to media coverage since 9/11 and 7/7. Media reports often depict traditionally-clad Muslims, rarely with any relevance to the story, but as a powerful statement suggesting alienness. Tarlo argues that the question for Muslims is no longer whether to be visible or not, but how to *manage* the heightened visibility (2010: 10–11). The choice of displaying obviously Islamic symbols and slogans can therefore be understood as a way to get back in control and to appropriate the discourse around the Muslim look. It plays with the alienness, at first by deliberately showing one's Muslimness, but then also by reversing it when subcultural and Western elements are referenced in the same object. Exhibiting an unexpected image of Muslims contributes to redefining what it means to look Muslim and to controlling ascriptions from the outside.

The designer, the person wearing the shirt and any observer who sees and reads it play a role in this process. Each designer proposes an image that he or she wants to sell to the customer, already with the wider public audience in mind; the producers therefore want to have an influence on both. The person who buys the shirt is a customer, but chooses from various offers whatever fits with his or her interpretation and preferences. There are many reasons to wear Islamic fashion: piety, politics and pride, among others. The "coolness factor" is another crucial one that underlines the feasibility of a cool Islam, both by fitting into juvenile cultures of the social environment and by openly identifying with Islam despite its widely negative image: the coolness of being the "underdog". In the process, the consumer of Islamic fashion also becomes an actor on the stage of the street, the bus, the school or the workplace. There is even potential for creating dialogue with people who look at the shirts and slogans in public, a dialogue very much intended by the designers. T-shirts as an advertising space for personal convictions or humorous messages is nothing new, but it is innovative to break down the potentially conflicted topic of religion and Islam in Europe into a short message or pictogram in order to evoke curiosity, to explain or educate. It can encourage both non-Muslims and non-practicing Muslims to review their image of Islam in a playful way. In front of other Muslims, symbols like the *shahada* or a stylised prayer gesture act as a sign of community, bearing an element of secrecy if the meaning is obvious to the knowing insider but requires explanation for a non-Muslim.

But visibility is not the whole story of Islamic fashion products; there is some important invisibility to it as well. All companies claim to sell more than fashion, a product that has values, expressed in mottos like *"Clothing to believe in"* or *"Portez vos valeurs"*. This may be highlighted for various reasons, such as targeting a certain customer base or making one's own profession appear less superficial and commercialised. It also stands for the claim that Islamic youth culture as a whole makes, which is a commitment to a balance between entertainment, fun, leisure, subculture, lifestyle and coolness on the one hand, and religion as something substantial and meaningful on the other hand. On a different level, the business around Islamic fashion remains rather invisible because it is almost exclusively dealt with online. The interaction between producers and consumers is not visible in the cities, but happens on the internet or sometimes at selected Islamic festivals, which somewhat lessens the visibility of the fashion.

There is money in this genre, perhaps more than in the others, if done at a professional level. Most products are not cheap and attract the more affluent customers. There is no indication, however, that economic success is the only motivation to run such a business. More money could probably be earned elsewhere. A side business, cheaply producing a few shirts, might be the product of a money-making idea, but those brands cannot be sustained over a longer period of time. The more professional designers dominate the niche, but they also display serious religious knowledge and commitment.

Islamic fashion shows a huge variety, and street wear in its various forms is only one recent contribution to it. It is certainly not at all the only option of dress for young European Muslims, but one that has become readily available, that is still unconventional and that resonates with the aspirations of many young people because of its visibility, stylishness and implicit values. Having become more widespread later than contemporary Islamic music, it has added to the options of expressing a young, Western Islam.

3. Media

Waymo

While there are few media products in Germany that cater particularly for young Muslims, there is one important internet platform for this purpose: Waymo.de has features of YouTube and Facebook, allowing registered users to upload videos, pictures and audio files that have a relevance to them in a wider Islamic sense.[34] Users can comment on the uploads and contact each other. The language is German; some contents may be in English, more rarely in Turkish or Arabic, in which case a translation is usually provided. The fact that this community is German and Islamic at the same time is illustrated by the virtual "poke" function, similar to that on other social networks. This way of greeting someone is called "salamen", an artificial word made up of the Islamic greeting *salam* and the grammatical suffix of German verbs (fig. 13). Waymo is closely connected to other representatives of German Islam, for instance the *Zentralrat der Muslime* (Central Council of Muslims) and their website islam.de, the youth organisation *Muslimische Jugend in Deutschland* (MJD), but also Styleislam, with whom Waymo organised a Muslim comedy contest in 2008.

This youth cultural "artefact" is different to those of fashion and the performing arts in that the makers provide a platform, but the content is added by the consumers. It is a web 2.0 feature that is developed further by being used. Embedded videos and other contents are not necessarily created by the users themselves, but found on other webpages such as YouTube. This also means that any subject and attitude can be posted onto Waymo, which raises the issue of controlling the content. The makers reserve the right to delete uploads and add a disclaimer on every page that Waymo is not responsible for the content of the upload nor the comments, and that they do not reflect the opinion of Waymo.

In some cases, this is necessary: at a random visit in 2010, the website featured an uploaded video of a radical religious leader in Britain, who claimed to

---

34 Waymo: http://waymo.de.

"disprove" the belief that Jesus was God and thus tried to invalidate one of the central beliefs to Christianity. Another video was a Salafist lecture, disseminating extreme gender segregation attitudes among a group of young male followers of a radical group called "Dawa Ffm". The radical preacher Pierre Vogel is also often present, which might suggest a growing popularity of Salafist thought among some of the younger Muslims. Such contents usually get deleted later, if they do not comply with Waymo's rules of ethics, which particularly rule out extremist and political contents or those of a kind that could lead to misunderstanding and insult.[35] For the organisers it is certainly difficult to draw the line when contents get many positive comments, such as a video presentation on "beauty tips for sisters", which recommended women to lower their gaze or to put on an attitude of shame instead of heavy make-up – clearly reinforcing strict and conservative gender roles, even if these contents are usually posted and welcomed by female users. Most other contents are typically *nashids*, pictures of mosques, videos of the hugely popular Ammar114, social awareness appeals, e.g. on Sudanese poverty by Islamic Relief, comic series (e.g. a Simpsons episode) if they contain Islamic references, and enthusiastic conversion accounts. This type of medium therefore faces issues of control and moderation, but is particularly interesting for the study of young Muslims, because the final, yet constantly changing product is interactively made up of a provided framework and of user generated contents.

Figure 13: "Waymo salamt dich!"

Source: Own photography

---

35 Waymo: http://waymo.de/rules.

A part ça tout va bien

Qualifying for the category of comedy as well as for media, "A part ça tout va bien" is an online project promoting Islamic comedy.[36] The name, indicating that "apart from that everything is fine", hints at a source of irritation that hinders people from feeling fully at ease. Indeed the project statement names continuing conflicts between Muslims and non-Muslims such as the headscarf ban at schools or radical practices like divorce due to non-virginity as the reason for a strong tension that divides the French. The project therefore tries to tackle mutual misunderstanding and distrust in a humorous way by encouraging people to laugh together, at each other and especially at themselves: *"Qui a dit que les musulmans n'avaient pas d'humour?"* (Who said Muslims don't have any humour?), is the motto of the allegedly first website of Islamic comedy.

A part ça tout va bien is not a performing comedy group, but uses the format of webisodes.[37] The videos are exclusively available online (fig. 14), receiving several hundred thousand views or up to two million per clip. The blog section allows for comments on the sketches, where users generally give enthusiastic feedback, with the occasional criticism that an episode was unislamic or misunderstands the basics of the French Republic. The founders are two young men from Bordeaux, one non-Muslim, one Muslim, the latter of whom also participates in the Paris-based comedy group Oriental Comic together with the actress Samia.

Among those mocked in the sketches are Islamic radicals, French racists, the French state for its unease with Islam, secular parents' speechlessness given their children's return to religion, Muslims in France and in the Maghreb. One series, "Islam School Welkoum"[38], features three young French Muslims who attend a religious school in Morocco in the search for the true Islam, escaping the distraction, temptation and corrupted Islam they have come to know in France. The punchlines characterise the religious education as so traditional and hypocritical that in the course of the episodes the three discover themselves as very French. Nobody escapes caricature, which helps relax the tension about topics often only aggravated by discussion. The sketches do not necessarily offer a solution as such, but rather a mindset for taking the tensions with a pinch of salt and in fact,

---

36 A part ça tout va bien: http://www.apartcatoutvabien.com, http://comediemuslim.apart catoutvabien.com.

37 A webisode, a portmanteau word of web and episode, denotes a short video released on the internet instead of television and is usually part of a series.

38 Islam School Welkoum: http://www.islamschoolwelkoum.com. This series has been produced for SaphirNews, a news website for Muslims living in France that often reports about popular and youth culture: http://www.saphirnews.com.

with self-irony. This way, any problems between Muslims and non-Muslims are removed from a politicised arena and boiled down to a question of perspective or attitude, which indeed may often be the problem's starting point. What cannot be detected is whether or not the intended target group – who would benefit from this kind of "education" – actually watches the sketches or whether the comedy is preaching to the converted.

Figure 14: A part ça tout va bien

Source: http://www.apartcatoutvabien.com

Gazelle Media

The relationship of Muslims with fun has also occupied the participants of the Muslim Café, an online television programme run by Gazelle Media.[39] It broadcasted debates from a Moroccan-style London café, where the participants discussed whether or not hip-hop or Harry Potter were *halal*, what they thought about dating and Islam, if Muslim women could have it all, and the question "Can Muslims have fun?" (fig. 15). All topics revolved around religion and entertainment and arose from living Islam in the West. The discussants were Muslims from all walks of life, mainly young people, occasionally joined by a non-Muslim. The programme successfully ran for a few years in the late 2000s, before going offline for site maintenance, or possibly due to funding problems, in 2009.

Gazelle Media, however, has carried on successfully. Working for clients as diverse as the BBC, the British Council, the Young Muslims Advisory Group and community initiatives, the company offers digitally produced media for television, radio, internet and print. Substantially, they provide "in-depth knowledge

---

39 Muslim Café: http://www.muslimcafe.tv, http://www.gazellemedia.co.uk/projects/ view/muslimcafe-tv.

of multicultural Britain and global communities" with the aim to help promote diversity. The focus on Islam is set by the team's interests and backgrounds. Most of the team members are Muslims and interested in the topic of Islam in the West. Highly professionally trained, they have worked for major companies, including the BBC and Channel 4, and have worked on these issues before, as for instance the executive director Navid Akhtar, who was a specialist advisor to BBC Radio 5 after 9/11, among many other projects.

The team's expertise in arts, music, culture, religion and history may go beyond the limits of youth culture, which is usually less concerned with highly intellectual debates. Also, the company works between reporting, creating and selling – and, age aside, the producers themselves are not necessarily part of an Islamic youth scene.

On the other hand, Gazelle Media places an emphasis on Muslim youth and the subcultural in several ways: products for television and online broadcasting have included pieces on musicians Sami Yusuf and Mohammed Yahya as well as a film on British Muslims, celebrating the younger generations for comfortably identifying with both the UK and Islam.

The company also offers training on Islam and creative expression, media literacy, production skills and on dealing with Islamophobia, understanding the latter as mainly resulting from the media coverage, particularly frustrating young Muslims and thus contributing to radicalisation. The courses are tailored for young people, schools, teachers, community organisations, journalists and others, whereby members of minority groups are particularly encouraged to participate.

Finally, director Navid Akhtar revealed a close link between Gazelle Media and Islamic youth culture in our informal conversation at the Islam Expo 2008. "We are inventing the Muslim cool", he shared with me, referring to both the Muslim Café and his vision for future projects.[40] Paraphrasing it in this way, he presented a commitment to developing Islamic youth culture as being one of Gazelle Media's major aims.

---

40 Incidentally, he also provided a book title.

Figure 15: Muslim Café by Gazelle Media Limited

Source: http://www.muslimcafe.tv

More Media Products

Not a great amount of media products for young Muslims have been able to establish themselves, and nearly all of them are based in the UK. The Platform Magazine professionally covered "Islamic urban music and culture", as the editor described the genre, and also contained "no blasphemy no nudity no profanity".[41] Financial difficulties caused the magazine cease production after three years in 2009. The magazine The Revival: Voice of the Muslim Youth caters especially for young British Muslims. Articles address spiritual topics in a way that relates to young people, and demand, for example, that British imams make themselves more acquainted with the situation of today's youth. Cover stories have included teenage pregnancy and drug abuse to provide advice, including from a religious perspective.[42] The magazine also hosts a very popular column of two cartoon characters, Ali and Jamal: Jamal is the "good guy" who prays five times a day, knows the Quran by heart, never goes clubbing and who finally leaves to pursue religious studies in Egypt. Ali is the "bad guy" with many girl-

---

41 This information was obtained in 2008 from the magazine's MySpace website, which is no longer available, and from issues of the publication itself.

42 Such advice can be of a very conservative stance. For example, while the female author of the article "Single, Muslim and Pregnant" calls for better sexual education in Muslim families and mosques to avoid teenage pregnancy, illegal abortion or "virginity fixing", she also comes to the conclusion that a Muslim girl in such circumstances is "guilty of one of the biggest sins in Islam" (The Revival 08/04/2008).

friends, little knowledge about religion, who likes drinking alcohol and eventually ends up in prison for drug dealing. The educational touch lacks quite a bit of subtlety, and as with many examples of Islamic youth culture, the "cool" format does not contradict a generally conservative character.

Unity FM is a Birmingham-based radio station run by young Muslims for the city's Muslim population. It caters for different age groups, and the programme includes spiritual broadcasts, entertainment, community information and debates. The diversity of the audience poses some difficulties as to what music can be played; most of it is *nashid*, but there is also some British Islamic hip-hop and even the occasional mainstream song. The supposedly "coolest online space for Muslim youth" is provided by the website MuslimYouthNet. Like Waymo, it features the option to create a personal profile to participate in forum debates, upload videos and photos or participate in polls, but the organisers also run several campaigns to engage young Muslims. The campaign "Faith through your lens" was a photography competition on how they perceive religious beliefs, and the "Reelhood" campaign collected their views on the key issues they faced as young Muslims in Britain, which were then presented on the website.[43] The emphasis on helping is underlined by the fact that the website organisers also run the Muslim Youth Helpline, an anonymous counselling telephone service specialising in problems of young Muslims who might not feel sufficiently understood or supported by regular helplines.[44]

Muxlim, finally, is a website that enhances "Muslim Lifestyle" by collecting and reporting about any Islamic products around the globe, from clothing lines to comics, music, news and businesses.[45] It was partly based in the UK, but founded by a young Finnish-Egyptian business man who is very active on a global scale. As with the successful British glossy magazine Emel,[46] the focus is on Islamic lifestyle independent of age group, but the website's design and many of its featured topics and companies appeal especially to young people, in particular to the more affluent with an international orientation.

Islam 2.0

The different media products available to young Muslims in the West cater to a variety of demands and desires, and, echoing Mandaville, demonstrate the plurality of Islam (Mandaville 2001: 183). Some of them mainly report about and promote a certain genre, like hip-hop in the Platform Magazine or comedy at A

---

43 MuslimYouthNet campaigns: http://www.muslimyouth.net/campaigns.
44 Muslim Youth Helpline: http://www.myh.org.uk.
45 Muxlim: http://muxlim.com.
46 Emel Magazine: http://www.emel.com.

part ça tout va bien. Local or global community news, also about Muslim life-styles, are shared through Unity FM, Waymo or Muxlim. In the first instance, they can contribute to enhancing Muslim community feeling. At the same time, some seek to educate, as in the case of the Revival youth magazine, religious programmes on Unity FM, the control and therefore absence of contents on Waymo, or the demonstration of Islamic humour by A part ça tout va bien. This also implies different levels of consumption and participation. Indeed, some media products are there to be consumed, but do not invite participation, particu-larly the magazines. They can anticipate a new lifestyle or identity and hope for it to be picked up, or promote currents they observe and support. Others, like Waymo and MuslimYouthNet, supply a framework that lives by user generated content. This also prescribes a desired identity to a certain extent, by employing a particular design, mottos, images and by having an eye on the uploaded con-tent. But there is enormous opportunity for participation in new media and web 2.0 facilities, with ideas flowing both ways and the ever-changing "final" prod-uct made by many parties. At the same time, there is room for offline involve-ment and media training, provided for instance by Gazelle Media and Muslim-YouthNet, the results of which are then again displayed online.

Belonging to the *ummah* is often invoked as being facilitated by the use of global media and the world wide web, and Mandaville also speaks of the internet as an opportunity for the marginalised to find like-minded people, which leads to a new form of "imagined community" or to "reimagined Islam" (Mandaville 2001: 183). I would argue, however, that even the new media involvement re-mains rather local, and despite the global connectivity actually strengthens a community feeling on a local level. Waymo, for example, supports the develop-ment of a German Islam, and indeed the reference to anything German – lan-guage, local events, customs, politics – is significant, and is not exceeded by the almost obligatory care for Palestinians and other Muslims far away. The online space is not so far removed from the actual space in which the user interacts, but perhaps acts more as a filter of the environment to find like-minded counterparts. In terms of visibility, this is very different from fashion and even performing arts and therefore relies less on coincidental interaction with the public. If a user knows where to look online, however, a large presence of Islamic media and lifestyle products becomes publicly available.

Some authors have interpreted the presence and influence of new media as causing a substantial change in Islam itself. Mandaville claims that they enable new interpretations that contribute to a "remaking of Islam" (Mandaville 2001: 184). Saminaz Zaman sees new religious authorities on the horizon due to the internet, because many users search for religious advice online (Zaman 2008).

This can take the explicit form of online fatwas, that Cesari also points to in her concept of "virtual Islam" (Cesari 2004: 111), or appear less strongly in the playful education of Waymo or The Revival's website. Zaman also points out that the internet "stimulates nostalgia as much as newness" (Zaman 2008: 470), if used to listen to the call for prayer or Quranic recitations, which warns against overestimating the potential of new media. The examples presented, however, show that Islamic youth culture is expressed through media old and new, but that the medium is in most cases more than its literal meaning of just conveying a content. Youth specific media create a space for young Muslims to interact with each other and with Islam, for instance by learning about it or forming an opinion and possibly an identity based on elements of Islam. The internet based media products invite participation in other and sometimes more direct ways than the other genres of Islamic youth culture, but there is also a high degree of interconnectedness between the genres. While media offer their own spaces of exchange and means of expression, they are at the same time often used as a means of distributing and promoting Islamic fashion styles, comedy and music.

C. Conclusion: Defining Islamic Youth Culture

The collection of artefacts includes Islamic youth cultural manifestations in music, comedy, fashion and media. It is a movement among the more religious of Europe's young Muslims. Some products may appeal to those who do not see Islam as their primary identity, but nonetheless as part of it, while other products require a very strong religious identification.

Some of the musicians or companies are interconnected with each other across the genres, as for instance Waymo and Styleislam, Poetic Pilgrimage and Tawheed, both the pioneers Ammar114 and Mecca2Medina with many rappers or young Islamic activists, or A part ça tout va bien with other French Islamic organisations. Others seem entirely unaware of similar activities to their own or prefer promoting their idea just by themselves. Neither is there a close transnational connection despite very similar occurrences in Germany, France and in the United Kingdom. On top of that, the level of professionalism varies greatly, from quality culture to well-meant attempts.

This could raise a valid objection: does this phenomenon even represent one unified culture? What justifies studying it as one culture? There are a number of reasons for doing so, I would argue. First, there are several recurring themes and similarities across many of the artefacts. They play with coolness and an unexpected image of Islam, and a lot of them refer to the same basic religious principles, invoking the Prophet Mohammed, the idea of unity, the words and sign of the *shahada*, a commitment to the *hijab* and prayer gestures, all translated into a language of youth. Nearly all artefacts also teach about Islam or Muslims and seem to be concerned with religious transmission. Second, they share a similar framework and correspond to a certain idea of what the subcultural product should be composed of. It is often emphasised that the message is more important than the music or the fashion itself. More importantly, one of the central categories is the notion of *halal*. Whether or not something is permissible is the factor that decides whether it gets integrated into this youth culture or not; Samia's sex-free comedy, Ammar114's moral rap or Elenany's stylishly covering clothing are such examples. In a nutshell, "*halal* fun" well summarises the underlying notion of this youth culture that opposes two adverse concepts: on the one hand that of having fun without any moral barriers and without dedication to God, and on the other hand the concept of being purely religious without any generation-specific means of expression. At the same time, the concept of *halal* does not have fully determined boundaries. While there seems to be a basic consensus about certain things being off-limit, other things are very much open to debate – like music or certain kinds of music, or ways of dressing. In some cases, Islamic youth culture also challenges the boundaries of what is permissible, which involves active religious knowledge and interpretation on the part of the producers and the consumers.

It appears justified to conceive the phenomenon as *Islamic youth culture* in the singular form. The variations in genre, space or people involved do not differ to such a great extent that they would outweigh the commonalities or make it reasonable to speak of several Islamic youth cultures. It seems more sensible to perceive the various manifestations as characteristics and specifications of one youth culture. Most importantly, Islamic youth culture must not be understood as the youth culture of all young Muslims, but only of those who actually participate in it. Indisputably, young Muslims have the choice to engage in many youth cultures, with Islamic youth culture being only one option.

The artefacts furthermore reveal a noteworthy relationship between form and substance. Clearly, this youth culture is both Islamic and Western, or German, French and British, respectively. At first sight it would seem that the artefacts bear a Western form that gets filled with Islamic contents. On closer inspection, however, this is only true on the surface. In fact, it has become evident from the examples that the substance is also made up of the experience of living Islam in the West: much of the fashion and media deals with strengthening young Muslims' self-confidence in a minority context, for instance, or rappers address the negative image of Islam in the media. At the same time, while much of the form is Western – for example: style, music production, beats, performances, urban hip-hop culture, media formats – this is not entirely the case. The form also borrows from Islamic design traditions, phrases and settings such as a family festival or a gender-segregated audience. It is therefore premature to equate the form with the West and the substance with Islam. Rather the blend goes both ways, or in fact, the elements of style and substance are strongly entangled.

That not all of the producers seem aware of a larger movement is also reflected in the absence of a name for it. Ascriptions from outside, like Pop Islam (Gerlach 2006), are rejected, but few alternatives are offered. As for music, the use of Islam in the name is mostly avoided except for the American website Muslimhiphop.com. This may be due to the contested permissibility of music in Islam, thus none of the artists wants to claim, by talking about their works as being Islamic music, that this is something inherent in Islam or even brought about by it. Another possibility is that the producers do not perceive their artefacts as being primarily Islamic – some people argue that Islam is a way of life, and thus they could claim that their product is just an expression of who they are. While this is a compelling amendment, I do not fully share this view. Already from a descriptive perspective, the artefacts appear as deeply imbued with clear Islamic references, underlined by the presence and absence of certain themes and some proselytising elements. It is therefore plausible to mention this important integral part and to speak indeed of an *Islamic* youth culture.

In order to come up with a definition, it is also worth mentioning what does *not* form part of this youth culture. There are many ethnicity-based cultures without any religious references, such as Turkish-German hip-hop or Arab-French media products, which differ greatly from Islamic youth culture in terms of expressions, behaviour and aims. Neither does Islamic youth culture describe the cultural traits of every young Muslim, especially if they are very pious, but not involved in anything subcultural. Yet another cultural phenomenon are young Muslims who display religiosity in some contexts like the family, the mosque or during Ramadan, but who adopt a non-religious behaviour in other settings with the peer group, such as partying, clubbing and alcohol consumption.

Surprisingly, a transnational consciousness remains limited in Islamic youth culture. The obvious global flows of Islamic beliefs and practices and of youth cultures are certainly acknowledged. But there is little awareness of similar scenes in other countries and hardly any exchange. Moreover, relations with the Islamic world are insubstantial, so that Styleislam's expansion to Turkey and Saudi Arabia remains an intriguing exception. This highlights how important the focus on the local environment is. There is a strong discussion with and also commitment to the country in which the youth culture takes place, even if very similar trends are happening in the neighbouring countries.

The ephemeral nature of the examples is telling of the fact that this youth culture is still in the making, and is constantly being remade, but it can also be observed that Islamic youth culture follows some rules. Quotations from other youth cultures, subcultures and styles, pieces of religious beliefs and practices, cultural traditions and experiences of the contemporary social world coalesce into this youth culture that manifests itself in hitherto unexpected expressions in the performing arts, fashion and various media. This also involves a commitment to keeping on this side of the *halal-haram* divide, while at the same time reinterpreting this fine line. Moral values, at times conservative, also play a major role in the various messages expressed in style.

Following the presentation of artefacts, the next chapter will explore in what way young Muslims consume and interact with them. Subsequently, the spotlight will be on the producers' ideas and aims.

IV. Living Islamic Youth Culture:
Observations Among Consumers

A. INTRODUCTION

The examples and artefacts of the previous chapter have given an extensive insight into Islamic youth culture, but their mere existence does not yet make a statement about what role they play in everyday life. They do not reveal how, in what settings and by whom they are consumed and if consumption is what Islamic youth culture is all about. This requires participation and observation in the field in order to shed light on the way Islamic youth culture is lived.

The data were gathered in a systematic, but in a non-prestructured way to allow for the greatest possible openness and to avoid premature conclusions, and was continuously summarised in descriptive field notes. In the subsequent analysis I then generated concepts to give the data an analytic structure. This happened on two levels: first, I looked for thematic clusters in the empirical findings, and second, matched them with supporting subcultural theories. As a result, the phenomenon is grasped as a youth culture by reconstructing its constituent parts. I thus conceptualised the structure that would best represent those elements: as an interplay of style, idea and action.

Style includes any findings related to fashion and accessories, language and body language, music, as well as visibility in general. Idea comprises notions of community, gender, generation, education, values and morality. Action refers to rituals, festivals, concerts, social work, leisure activities, actors, organisations and social interaction.

Definitions of youth and subculture have above all emphasised style as being a key component (Lindner 1981; Hebdige 1993; Scherr 2009). Style is "intentional communication", for example, through dress, which should be interpreted as a meaningful choice (Hebdige 1993: 100–101), as it endows an "alternative identity" to members of a subculture and plays with being different (ibid.: 89).

Scherr points out that style goes beyond the visible and comprises, besides fashion, also language, body language and music (Scherr 2009: 183).

Most theories, however, agree not to limit a subculture to style, and emphasise the importance of the idea behind the style. Brake interprets subcultures as a "counter-concept" to a more mainstream culture and as a strategy to solve collectively experienced difficulties (Brake 1981: 23–25), therefore giving them an intentional meaning. Hebdige calls this "ideology" (Hebdige 1987: 89). Scherr also points to a substantive dimension of youth cultures by referring to their intention of demarcation or political or cultural alternative (Scherr 2009: 187). This is what I refer to as the "idea" of a subculture.

An idea, then, needs to be put into practice. It determines the style, but it also requires actions to be able to convey a message. While Scherr includes a readiness for action in his definition of youth culture (Scherr 2009: 188), Hebdige claims that "differences are reflected not only in the objects of subcultural style, but in the signifying practices which represent those objects and render them meaningful" (Hebdige 1993: 127). I thus included action as the third main component of youth culture.

Breaking the phenomenon down into its components does not mean isolating them from each other. Even if not every event or participant in Islamic youth culture combines all of these elements, they rarely stand on their own. For instance, an Islamic youth cultural style would hardly be adopted without the person's support for the idea. Also, there are overlaps between the elements – for instance, when young people use their own language to talk about Islam, this is not only expressing a style, but also reveals a demand that is part of the idea. Instead of arranging the following account along the tripartite structure of Style–Idea–Action, alternative options could have been a structure by place (countries or cities), people or chronology of events. I think, however, that this analytic framework complements the interpretation of fieldwork observations well, and the close look at the components of Islamic youth culture helps to understand how it works and what it tries to achieve.

The observations made in this chapter certainly depend to a considerable extent on the researcher. A Muslim or a male researcher or simply another person might have observed and participated in different events or noticed other things at the same events, and thus could have come to divergent conclusions. I have therefore tried to give evidence of my interpretations in the form of numerous examples from the field, but the reader is also invited to form an opinion of his or her own.

B. A SUBCULTURE IN PRACTICE

A group of girls are sitting at the breakfast table. They rose at 5 a.m. for morning prayer and subsequent Quran recitation and will join small groups of recreational activities and debates after breakfast. They are participating in a youth camp for Muslim girls and young women in Germany. Sarah, 29, and Juman, 17, both of Tunisian background, start talking about men. Juman is wearing a well-matched pink and black outfit: black cap, pink head-scarf, black cardigan, pink shirt, black long skirt. Sarah has put on a simple, white head-scarf, which she is only wearing for the occasion of the youth meeting, as she does not usually veil in her everyday life. Juman complains that some "brothers" do not lower their gaze when they talk to her: "Dann denk ich immer, 'Senk doch den Blick, Mann, echt, das ist voll unangenehm!'."[1] The four other girls at the table agree, adding that there's nothing to see anyway if the woman is veiled. Sarah answers that – *masha'allah*[2] – Juman is *muharama*, a woman who respects herself. Juman in turn replies *al-hamdulillah*, thank God, and adds that whoever has no respect for themselves or does not show it would get in trouble, and that holds true for both women and men; again, everybody agrees. The topic changes to headscarf styles. A Syrian-German woman claims that only classical styles suit her and indeed she is wearing a restrained ivory-coloured shawl. Nadia, a revert of German and Syrian background, has put on a functional grey stretch shawl, which she, too, does not wear outside the youth camp. A Turkish-German girl is wearing more old-fashioned material with large colourful flower prints. The conversation then drifts off to headscarf policies in Islamic countries – which the girls identify to be stricter, at times, than in Europe.

To explore the style, idea and action of Islamic youth culture as it is acted out, I embarked on a series of field trips from my bases Frankfurt, Marseille and Birmingham. They took place within these cities and beyond, and I mingled with Muslim youths at Islamic festivals, concerts, debates and Friday prayers, among others. The following events ranked among the most fruitful encounters.

The beginning of my field research in Frankfurt coincided with the "Day of Open Mosque", which has taken place annually on 3 October in Germany since 1996. Also being the Day of German Unity since the reunification in 1990, this day has been deliberately chosen by Germany's Muslims to open their Mosques and invite the public for guided tours, tea and question-and-answer sessions

---

1 "That always makes me think, 'Lower your gaze man, really, that's so uncomfortable!'."

2 "What God has willed"; phrase added to any compliment to prevent pride and bad luck.

about Islam. The three mosques I visited that day already revealed some structures I would find throughout the field research, and I encountered many people, who later helped me gain further access to the field. The first mosque offered a women's breakfast; many non-Muslims from within the neighbourhood and surrounding churches had followed the invitation, which included a guided tour through the mosque and some explanations about Islamic practice. I met Hibah, a young architecture student, about whom I had read in a local news article that focussed on Islamic youth work and hip-hop. She introduced me to her friend Barika, a gender sociologist, with whom she joked about all Muslims being terrorists and all non-Muslims infidels, which they found extremely funny – comic relief in a tense everyday environment. Although it was included in the open day's programme, I was practically the only visitor in the second mosque, which was located away from the centre in a more impoverished area. After attending a prayer, I met a group of girls of around 17 years old, who incorporated me into their group. I followed their mutual teasing and chats about fashion, make-up, the driving licence, and about religion – the latter expressed through remarks like a communal decision to stop using swearwords as they considered this an unislamic behaviour, or expressing respect for an elderly cleaning lady, who they were convinced would gain many points in reward for her efforts and go to paradise. I found out that they were travelling to an Islamic festival in Leverkusen the next day and signed up to join them for the bus ride and the event. The third mosque was in yet another part of town and hosted many visitors, primarily Catholic retirees while I was there. We were served tea, and I met doctoral student Alima, who was asked during the guided tour whether she studied theology, to which she replied to everyone's amusement: "No, law, but that's almost the same." She and young mother Hafiza felt "too old" for Islamic youth culture, but I ran into both of them many times again during my field research.

One such occasion was an Eid al-Fitr celebration at the end of Ramadan, where I was also introduced to Ammar114 and had conversations with converts about religious biographies, or a *sadaqa* (charity) event, both of which featured youth entertainment and took place in local town halls in different parts of Frankfurt. An important mosque was the *Islamischer Info-Service (IIS)*, which was much frequented by young Muslims and therefore became a meeting place for anyone involved in Islam and youth work in the city.

Two major and insightful events were held outside Frankfurt. The youth camps of the *Muslimische Jugend in Deutschland (MJD)* were very popular and gathered high numbers of participants. One was the annual *Muslimisches Mädchen Meeting (MuMM)*, the Muslim Girls' Meeting, a four-day camp for around 200 girls from all parts of Germany, taking place in a remote village near Trier at

Easter 2009. The other event was the large annual MJ-Meeting in Bad Orb near Frankfurt, which was attended by nearly 1,000 young Muslims over several days on the Pentecost weekend in 2009.[3] The young people I encountered in these settings were approximately 13 to 29 years old and of Turkish and Arab background, and some had also converted.

The 2006 publication by journalist Julia Gerlach on the topic of "Pop Islam" also acted as a gate keeper in several instances. She had interviewed some of the people I met, and due to our overlapping interests, many drew a connection and voiced their opinion about Gerlach without my prompting them. Many criticised her approach or felt inadequately portrayed, while others had a more generous view. Whether or not people liked her book, it was well-known and facilitated starting a conversation.

In Marseille, I visited many mosques and Friday prayers, and studied the mosques' neighbourhoods. Islamic book shops and restaurants were often linked with an Islamic centre. At a *Mawlid*, a festival commemorating the Prophet's birth, I met some of my interviewees again, who used the event to sell their fashion. Indeed, the audience, especially the young people, had dressed up for the event, which did not otherwise cater for young Muslims, for example, in terms of music. The focus was less on entertainment than on religious education, and several female organisers were wearing a tag saying dawah, identifying them as "missionaries". Their task was to proselytise among those young people of Muslim background who did not practise their religion as strictly or at all, although this was kept traditional and not done using any youth language or styles.

I also visited several concerts by Islamic artists that, in contrast to German events, were not integrated into religious festivals, but took place in a commercial setting, using concert halls and requiring prebooked tickets. Observations at music stores confirmed a recognisable commercial success. Each interview setting gave additional insights into the interviewees' everyday life, whereby all of them kept it separate from mosques or prayer, unlike their counterparts in the other countries.

In Birmingham, I attended a panel debate on "Islam, Hip Hop and Social Change", hosted by local and London Muslim artists at The Drum, a black cultural centre. Several of my interviewees were among the panel members and debaters, as the event gathered many key figures of Islamic youth culture, including some from outside the music scene. A large gathering of Islamic societies from all the British universities took place at Birmingham University and was accompanied by an exhibition of several social initiatives by young Mus-

---

3   The coincidence with Christian holidays is owed to the school holidays. Both camps take place annually at this time.

lims. At an Eid Mela in one of Birmingham's parks I was able to witness an annual celebration of the city's south Asian population, a mainly culturally inspired, but also partly religious celebration with many musical acts. Birmingham's Islamic radio station Unity FM was another place to meet and talk to young Muslims, who worked there as radio presenters or volunteers.

Because many of the interviews took me to London, I also visited mosques and Friday prayers there. In 2008, several British Islamic institutions hosted the large-scale exhibition "Islam Expo" at a London exhibition centre. The event exhibited Islam around the topics of art, history, politics, health and lifestyle, music, theatre and sports. Islamic youth culture in its various genres formed an integral part of the exhibition. With fashion and music shows and booths hosted by representatives from the Islamic media, many of my interviewees were present at the event. Although smaller and more intimate settings usually provided a better opportunity for asking questions, these large events were useful for studying the relationship between producers and consumers, to observe interviewees outside the interview situation and to see the youth cultural artefacts being used.

The vignette above with the girls at the breakfast table comprises in a nutshell some of the main characteristics of Islamic youth culture and its styles, ideas and actions. The elaborate fashion among veiling women is as important for style as language, illustrated here in the use of German – even despite a shared Arab background – and the extensive use of Islamic expressions (*masha'allah, al-hamdulillah*). The strong opinion on gender roles and "appropriate" behaviour reveals parts of the idea of this youth culture, and the setting is a youth camp organised by the *Muslimische Jugend in Deutschland (MJD)*, which forms a significant part of the action.

1. Style

A youth culture that wants to stand out, attract, provoke or convey an attitude needs a visibility that contributes to its specific style. The first thing that comes to mind are fashion and accessories, but also an idiosyncratic way of communication, expressed through a particular language and body language, and the preference and consumption of a music genre form part of a style.

Fashion and other visible accessories are thus among the main components of subcultural style, and no less so in Islamic youth culture. The choice among religious Muslim girls to wear a headscarf is certainly first and foremost a religious one, but then it also becomes integrated into fashion, which in turn facilitates taking the religious decision to wear it. In everyday situations, but in par-

ticular for special occasions, many of the young women I spent time with carefully chose outfits with the headscarf matching the dress, shoes and accessories.
The headscarf was often artistically tied in different layers and colours, which
seemed as important as binding it tight to avoid showing a single hair. Many
wore a short dress over trousers, serving again the dual purpose of concealing
the body contours, and to be able to wear the same dresses as their non-Muslim
peers. The "layered look" copies a trend that became generally popular several
years ago, wearing skirts with trousers, and imitates the layers of cloth of the
hijab. These outfits are not ready-made products, but the women's own combinations of what is available in high street shops. Prêt-à-porter Muslim fashion is
still rare, and I did not encounter many Ünicité or Elenany products in the field.
Styleislam was much more active in showing a presence at festivals and youth
camps. They displayed their large advertisement banner (fig. 7 in Chapter III) at
festivals in Leverkusen and at the Muslim Girls' Meeting, and hosted a sizable
booth at the large MJD Meeting, at which they also designed a T-shirt for each
of the nearly one thousand participants. Some of my informants wore a Styleislam shirt in their profile picture on social networks, and a girl praying at the IIS
mosque pinned her headscarf with a lime-green Styleislam button saying *"I love
my Prophet"*. The brand was well-known to young Muslims, especially in the
surroundings of the MJD, with which Styleislam has established close relations.
Their items seem popular in situations where young people present themselves in
front of their peers, especially in Islamic settings, and in some cases an Islamic
outfit becomes the desired, almost mainstream attire: in the vignette above, two
of the girls were only wearing the *hijab* for the occasion of the Muslim Girls'
Meeting to give it a try, as they explained, but anticipated group pressure may
have played a role as well.

Certainly not all young women dressed in an eye-catching way, and some rather preferred to dress more inconspicuously or "modestly". While in some cases
this was simply rooted in a lack of interest in fashion, others linked this to their
school of thought. Strolling through a shopping centre with a Salafi-informed
woman, she pointed out a fashion shop for young people as one of her favour-
ites, but lamented that the coats were too short: they only came down to her
knees, while she felt obliged to wear one that comes down to the ankles. She also
preferred grey and brown colours, which in her interpretation of the Quran were
the "recommended" colours for female dress. While this may have been her personal decision, her interpretation or the Salafist's more generally did not seem to
leave much room for individual choice and variety in terms of exegis. Others
who did not carefully choose their outfit were traditional and elderly women and
occasionally Turkish-German girls from a traditional background, whose floral

triangular *hijab* made a rather old-fashioned appearance among the colourful and matching styles of many MJD girls. Face-veiling *niqabs* were hardly ever visible at any of the events.

As for men, the sartorial equivalent to the headscarf – Islamic street wear – has not spread quite as widely as the success of some clothing companies might suggest, at least in public. Streetscapes in European cities show young Muslim men dressing in average Western clothing, and what still seems more common than a piece of Islamic clothing is growing a beard in any shape or size. It has become popular to adopt the Prophet's way of life as laid out in the *Sunna*, but as a side effect a beard is also considered stylish. One interviewee, who otherwise supported Salafi views, was pleased to see that bearded men increasingly featured in fashion advertisements, such as those of H&M clothing stores. To his mind they copied the Islamic style, and he did not agree to my objection that beards were not so new in the European context either. Be that as it may, what was remarkable was his impression that a minority no longer just sought acceptance, but were already setting a trend.

Thus, the meanings of the headscarf, the beard and other Islamic fashion items are manifold. As a fashion, it offers variety and self-confidence, and serves to support the larger trend of Islamic youth cultural expression. But the fashion does not only have the purpose of making this idea more visible; it is also part of the idea of showing a person's belief. Moreover, fashion is almost always gender-specific, and the *hijab* and the beard in particular underline and enforce distinct gender roles. While these are displayed in public, Islamic fashion products are less visible to the general public, but celebrated in Islamic settings, where they are interconnected with and mutually enforcing other activities of Muslim youth organisations. Displaying different appearances in various settings also underlines the fact that style is not completely fixed, which should remind the observer not to essentialise and reduce its representatives to one style. After Friday prayer at a mosque in Marseille, for instance, a traditionally clad man took off his *djellaba* only a few meters down the street, and turned into a business man, ready to return to work.

Another important feature of style is language and jargon. What is striking first of all is how young Muslims insist on living Islam in the respective national languages of Germany, France or Britain. Most of them know at least colloquial Arabic, Turkish or Urdu and may also study Quranic Arabic, but they have grown up speaking German, French or English and have the desire to talk about their religion in this language. If religion is supposed to make any sense to them, they demand, it must be transmitted in their language. Thanks to its German-language Friday sermons, Frankfurt's most popular mosque among youths is the

one at the *Islamischer Info-Service (IIS)*. It is also the policy of the MJD to conduct its local youth groups entirely in German. A team leader explained to me
that this would help the kids to learn how to respond to questions about their
religion in the national language and also to integrate people of both Turkish and
Arab background. The girls in her group seemed to welcome this approach, since
the first thing they told me about their group was: *"We meet at the mosque every
Friday and talk about Islam. In German."* And another one shouted: *"We've got
a nice religion, haven't we?"* Pride and legitimacy-seeking often take turns
among the young Muslims, and using the German language is certainly a means
of acquiring the majority's acceptance more easily. This is a debate that has tak-
en place in the 1980s and 1990s in Britain (Lewis 1994). At meetings like the
one held by the Islamic university societies in Birmingham, the use of English
was self-evident and beyond debate. The meeting included Muslims of all backgrounds, also converts, and everyone was British. Certainly, this was even more
underlined by the fact that the societies were part of the British university system. At the Birmingham Eid Mela, which is a cultural rather than a chiefly religious festival, there were more languages present besides English, such as in
music performances by Asian musicians.

The use of jargon, then, possibly creates a demarcation or at least underlines
a feeling of togetherness, besides being an expression of religiosity. Among the
religious youths, there was extensive use of the popular Islamic phrases *in-
sha'allah* (God willing), *alhamdulillah* (thank God), *jazakallah* (may God reward you), *subhanallah* (God is glorious) and *masha'allah* (what God willed;
compliment). In Islamic countries it is very common to use them in nearly every
sentence, with or without the deeper meaning that everything were dependent on
God's will. In a non-Muslim context it becomes imbued with a stronger religious
meaning. In a lecture on personality development at the Muslim Girls' Meeting,
the speaker recommended, among other things, the repeated use of these phrases
in order to enhance one's faith and to remind oneself constantly of Allah. From
her own experience of using them extensively herself, she was able to share that
this was not always easy and that other women have teased her for doing so;
when she added that these women had been wearing the veil and were actively
involved in MJD youth work, the audience murmured with indignation. For others, however, the use of religious phrases might primarily feed a sense of belonging to a faith or a group. When talking to non-Muslims, the phrase was either
used in translation or omitted completely; thus, it also worked as a linguistic
marker of difference. This use of phrases is certainly not confined to young people, but was enforced in group settings of festivals and youth camps, and may be
appealing for its group affiliation. Finally, language also comprises youth lan-

guage. This is not only reflected in actual linguistic articulations, such as the abbreviated *jaz* for *jazakallah*, but entails any stylistic expression. The artefacts presented in the previous chapter have illustrated this.

Body language often expresses a view on gender roles, as alluded to in the anecdote of the breakfast table conversation. Some of the very pious men and women I encountered indeed lowered their gaze when talking to each other, and some male speakers decided to address only the male part of a segregated audience with their body language. At a talk by the Frankfurt Islamic society, a woman, who had taken a seat in the men's section, accused the speaker of deliberately ignoring the female audience by only directing looks and gestures towards the men. This was the only criticism I encountered of this, at least in the German environment, rather common practice.

Finally, another major component of style is music. Any festival included musical performances, which were only rarely in a traditional style and usually featured Poetic Pilgrimage, Pearls of Islam, Ammar114, Amantu and some less well-known groups. Of course, this is neither the only type of music young Muslims listen to, nor their only interaction with Islam. In a conversation about their music preferences, the young people on the bus to the Leverkusen Islam festival told me that at least some of them listened to all kinds of music genres. But they said they were also huge fans of Ammar114, whereupon a team leader reminded them that they should not be attending the festival only to see him, but mainly to learn from the more serious lectures. Still, the Islamic artists were well-known to and hugely popular with the youth. The reason may be that this type of music relates to familiar things like their own and their family's religion and to the musical preferences of the peer group, which in turn provides them with something – a style, perhaps – of their own: a special twist to regular mainstream music, and a generation-specific component within Islamic practice.

2. Idea

A youth culture is not usually held together just by style, but also very strongly by a substantial idea. Islam, broadly, is the key idea of this movement, but as it is a religion of multiple components, interpretations and currents, it would be oversimplified to content oneself with that. Also, there are some notions that go beyond religion.

Looking at it more in detail, religion informs Islamic youth culture in terms of many different concepts, including values, morality, community awareness and social commitment. As indicated by the artefacts, the notion of *halal* was also very palpable in the field. A popular "hang out place" in Marseille, for instance, was the Halal Fried Chicken fast food restaurant opposite a Salafist mosque. The Mosquée as-Sunna was linked to a bookshop that served as a gathering place for middle-aged men after prayer. The Halal Fried Chicken shop – or "HFC", alluding to its popular American counterpart – was the equivalent venue for youth and families. It shut down during lunchtime on Fridays, to allow the owner to attend Friday prayer, and when it reopened, it filled with young people who either worked or had lunch there. The mosque is known to be frequented by Salafists and indeed the common garment for men was a long, usually white *djellaba* and a white crocheted hat. For women it was the black *chador*, with a few wearing the face veil[4] or gloves; no sign of young and sportive Islamic street wear. Salafists do not generally embrace Islamic youth culture, mainly because of their rejection of music and related hip-hop culture. However, the Islamic adaptation of a fast-food chain seemed clearly acceptable in the Salafi-dominated environment, despite showing no other relationship with youth culture. This underlines the presence of different Islamic interpretations, but also that Islamic youth culture favours non-Salafi currents. The example also shows that "*halal*-ness" does not have invariable boundaries, but that it depends on one's viewpoint. In Islamic youth culture, *halal* is also an important notion, but while it includes subcultural forms, it is more rigid with regard to gender relationships.

Salafism is hardly ever present within Islamic youth culture, whose existence is often rejected or denied by Salafists. At one occasion, I was supposed to interview a young rapper from London, who was accompanied by his elder cousin. The shy interviewee did not dare say much about his activity, as the cousin had taken over the conversation. Declaring himself a Salafist, the cousin even denied that my research topic existed: because music was not permissible, he claimed that there was not a single Muslim who produced music, despite his own family member being a prime example (only after I had separated the two was I able to conduct an interview with the young rapper). At an interview with one of the fashion producers in Germany, I was given recorded lectures by Salafist preacher Pierre Vogel; the interviewee did not see a conflict between the Salafist worldview and his own activity, because he did not consider his street wear production to be part of a larger movement that automatically included and affirmed music or other subcultural manifestations.

The predominant conservative attitude within Islamic youth culture came to the fore particularly in the practice of gender segregation at several events. Fes-

---

4 This was observed in 2009; whether it changed after the niqab ban was implemented could not be verified.

tivals usually had separate seating areas for men and women, with married couples either sitting together in the men's area or separately, the children going back and forth between the two. At the MJD meeting, a moral code was implemented to instruct the youth and increase their awareness of gender and conduct. Girls and boys stayed in separate houses, and the girls covered the windows with paper to create female-only spaces in which they could take off their headscarves. At night, everyone gathered in a large hall for some cultural performances; girls sitting on one side and boys on the other side of the aisle. The girls were allowed to clap only, while boys were supposed to express their applause by cheering and *Allahu akbar* calls; girls were not allowed to shout louder than the boys or at all, nor to show their excitement about the male musicians – otherwise they would get a reminder from the team leaders the next morning. Another example was a situation on the bus that took a group of young Muslims from a Frankfurt mosque to the Islam festival in Leverkusen. The bus itself was segregated, with the girls most naturally taking a seat in the back of the bus. Throughout the trip the youths entertained each other by singing songs, telling jokes, giving talks, all about religious and other topics, using the microphone at the front of the bus. But because it was at the front, the girls were not allowed to use it to perform as well – and they did not object. Apart from the questionable impact on gender development and the role that both men and women are expected to fulfil, this practice is also based on the assumption that homosexuality does not exist, because if it did, it would render the carefully established gender segregation obsolete.

This could, however, mainly be observed in the German context, where this was common practice at MJD events and beyond. Neither in France nor in Britain was the segregation that dominant; among the network of black British Muslim artists, who had for instance organised the panel debate in Birmingham, the view was upheld that interaction between the sexes was unproblematic if the women were veiled. This shows that different interpretations converge in Islamic youth culture, but that some can be especially strong in one national setting at a certain time, and also that conservative currents are prevalent.

Other core values of Islamic youth culture include various forms of social engagement, such as youth work, political activism, interfaith dialogue, charity, personal development and education. At the panel debate "Islam, Hip-Hop and Social Change" in Birmingham, the participants were convinced that their contribution to rap music also contributed to community cohesion and interfaith dialogue by openly addressing topics that Muslims had an urge to discuss, especially after 9/11 and 7/7 and as citizens in the West. Rappers Mecca2Medina, Lowkey, Poetic Pilgrimage and Cambridge PhD student "Sheikh" Michael

Mumisa discussed once more the permissibility of music. Mumisa has acted as the legitimising voice for Muslim rappers on several occasions, since as an Islamic scholar he claims that no proof has been given of music being forbidden, and the panel agreed that if they kept to certain (self-imposed) rules, such as respectful language, rap was just another means of expressing one's faith. They were thus concerned with no less than reinterpreting Islam and solving inter-generational and inter-cultural differences within Islam.

The MJD was very concerned with the education and personal development of young Muslims in Germany, not only in order to enhance their religiosity, but also to provide them with skills and confidence for the job market and to make them become active citizens in German society. Any encounter with Islamic youth culture was therefore accompanied by youth work of various kinds; fun and education alternated constantly. The German name of the Muslim Girls' Meeting – "MuMM" – is more than just an abbreviation, as the word also stands for drive, courage, decisiveness. These qualities were to be imparted to the female participants during the meeting. The lecture on personality development encouraged the 13- to 29-year-old girls and women to reflect upon their strengths and weaknesses and their aspirations; the suggested strategies for amelioration were based both on psychological guidebooks and on Islam. Part of the entertainment on the bus ride to Leverkusen and the train journey to the Muslim Girls' Meeting was quizzing the youngsters on what they had learned at school, and the MJD team leaders also confirmed that supporting the children in their school education was part of their work. The current generation of young adults and parents-to-be seems to want to leave mistakes of the past behind, when many immigrant parents were not able or willing to assist in their children's education and perhaps focussed more on the transmission of religious or cultural traditions. This generation emphasises that religious education should not be an obstacle to general education, addressing both Muslim families and wider society. They seek to even out any potential disadvantages of the children's backgrounds, and moreover, aim to promote the image of well-educated Muslims as a means of countering such prejudices, which eventually also enhances the image of Islam itself.

Charity work also forms part of many events of and around Islamic youth culture. As one of the five pillars of Islam, *zakat*, or alms-giving, is an obligatory act, complemented by *sadaqa*, a voluntary donation. Many of the producers of Islamic fashion or music donate part of their earnings, and every festival makes a collection, which is usually made public, so that it becomes part of good practice and of religious education. The recipients are often Muslims, as with the charity organisations Islamic Relief or Muslime Helfen, but charity is not limited to giving money and also includes doing good within society. This idea is also in line with Amr Khaled's organisation Lifemakers, which the Egyptian televangelist founded to encourage young people to serve their society, especially in the non-Muslim countries of Europe. A case in point was a blood donation event by the German Red Cross at the MJD Meeting, whom the organisers had invited and who were pleasantly surprised at the young Muslims' great willingness to give blood.

The relationship between young people, organisers and producers is not straightforward. Young Muslims are consumers of Islamic youth culture and recipients of religious education, and yet they are not just passive, but stand at the centre of the movement, voicing their demands. It is impossible to determine who is responsible for starting it, and there is evidence for both: it could be a top–down approach, an idea implemented by a few leaders who want to change the predominant practice of Islam, or to make young people of Muslim background return to religion. Such leaders could be scholars and imams or members of youth organisations and producers of Islamic youth culture, or some of those acting on behalf of the others. On the other hand it could be a bottom–up movement, with young Muslims at the forefront of living a new Islam, to which leaders and producers react by offering apt subcultural artefacts and forms of youth gatherings that support this spirit. A third, and probably most adequate, option is to reject the hierarchical division because it may not be possible to distinguish participants from leaders other than by a vague age threshold. Many of the producers may be in their thirties and thus up to 15 or 20 years older than their target group, but they may also still count themselves among the participants and followers of Islamic youth culture. Team leaders in youth organisations may until recently have been participants, or have started taking over organisational tasks early on. Also, there are different roles within this movement that people gradually grow into.

Regarding the prevailing morality, it could thus be assumed that it is imposed upon the younger generation by adults, who claim that pre-marital sex is one of the gravest sins in Islam, and that any mixing of the sexes inevitably paves the way for this. The young people for their part, it could then be supposed, would try to circumvent this – after all, adolescence usually brings with it an increased interest in the opposite sex. But instead, they have indeed internalised morality and are promoting it now, also in order to appear in a good light themselves, like the girls in the vignette at the beginning of the chapter. Similarly, a 17-year-old girl on the bus to Leverkusen told me that she was the only Muslim in her class and did not speak to her classmates. They only talked about drinking and clubbing or how many boyfriends they had already had, and they "disgusted" her.

Using such a powerful word as "disgust" hints at a strong moral commitment on her side. Of course, this could be mixed with a self-defence strategy against the prejudices and exclusion she might suffer from in the class, possibly caused by her wearing a headscarf.

More generally, religious transmission emerges as a central idea of Islamic youth culture. Instead of religion being passed on the traditional way via the family or the mosque, here it is transmitted by subcultural artists and their artefacts and by youth workers, all of whom are not much older than the youths themselves. They want to improve or replace traditional methods of religious education that have little relevance to young Muslims, and demonstrate that rather than Islam itself, this is what has lost its relevance. It is a process of adjusting to the demands and lifestyles of the younger generation, who have adapted to their surrounding, and therefore also ask for prayers and religious education in the national language. It is also a matter of providing alternative youth entertainment in a familiar way, such as the youth camps that children know from school trips. Other events are self-organised by people of the same age, like the meeting of Islamic societies at Birmingham University.

The idea of Islamic youth culture thus evidently consists of several beliefs and attitudes, forming one overall vision that cannot just be summarised as "Islam". It becomes visible in style, with the individual person perhaps adopting just parts of it, and takes the form of actions. Part of the idea is also to have a debate, for instance about art in Islam, and to challenge and change common notions – not necessarily in a progressive way, but in a different way.

3. Action

Some youth cultures may place the largest emphasis on style, which very often carries an idea, such as in the case of punk. In other cases, however, the ideas need to be put into practice, and styles need to be celebrated, which requires activities, which then become a third constituent element of the youth culture. One example would be anarchic subcultures and their demonstrative actions in the public sphere.

Also Islamic youth culture is to a great extent based on action. Very often it becomes embedded into religious celebrations and festivals that follow a particular structure. Whether the event celebrates *Eid al-Fitr* at the end of Ramadan, commemorates the Prophet's birth with a *Mawlid*, collects for a charity, or marks the anniversary of an Islamic organisation, it usually caters for all generations and is therefore open to expressions of Islamic youth culture to entertain and incorporate young people. The events I visited usually started with lectures or debates by Islamic scholars and were followed by entertainment shows, including charity auctions or comedy performances. Later in the evening there were music performances by one or two popular religious rappers. In between, the call for prayer regularly gathered people in designated areas. Inside the hall, the seating arrangement was often gender-segregated, while everybody mixed freely outside. Outside the hall booths sold *halal* products, food, religious literature, clothing, including Islamic street wear, religious chants and audio recordings of the Quran, as well as music by the groups performing at the event.

Other significant events that put Islamic youth culture into practice were concerts. At the Islam Expo in London, Mecca2Medina presented an "Urban Youth Stage", where young acts could try out their potential for contemporary Islamic music. It had been advertised as "the place to see the mixing of two formidable cultures – Urban youth and Islamic cultures – creatively coming together as one and in doing so reflecting Britain's vibrant multi-cultural society"[5], and it was highly successful with the large and mainly young audience. The bigger concert at night included international acts like Outlandish, a Danish band with often Islamic lyrics, and other, more traditional singers. Although this was aimed at a younger audience, family members of all generations attended the concert together, as was also the case at any Islamic festival in Frankfurt. At the *sadaqa* celebration, for instance, kids were dancing and singing along near the stage, while the parents and grandparents were bopping to Ammar's rap further back in the audience.

French concerts took place in different settings, as many of the well-known Islamic acts were less closely connected to Islamic organisations, possibly because of their commercial success. The *Mawlid* in Marseille, for instance, had not picked up on the trend of specifically catering for the young members of the audience and instead presented a traditional Syrian band. At a concert by Abd al Malik, a converted rapper from Strasbourg of Congolese background, the audience was not primarily Muslim. Abd al Malik's Sufi messages of peace, respect and his attachment to France also seem to resonate with the "bo-bos", bourgeois-bohèmes, a term used to denote white upper middle-class, middle-aged, well-to-do people with left-wing alternative worldviews and lifestyles; typically the population around the liberal district of Cours Julien in Marseille, where the concert took place. Certainly, the audience would have been different in another district or with more affordable ticket prices (30€), but the success with the wider population does not limit these rappers to Islamic festivals. Similarly, a con-

---

5   Islam Expo 2008: http://www.islamexpo.com/attractions.php?id=1&art=18.

cert by Médine in Paris Montmartre saw a diverse audience, of younger, but by far not only young Muslim men.

Music by French Islamic artists is available at the commercial store FNAC, whereas their British and German colleagues are not successful in selling theirs commercially. Instead, they offer it for download online and only perform at festivals. Much of this music is therefore consumed online; the majority of uploads onto Waymo are music videos of contemporary and Western Islamic musicians. In the settings of concerts and festivals, however, the interaction between producers and consumers, artists and fans, became visible. Unless the musicians were well-known stars, which the majority was not, they mixed freely with the audience. Also, fashion designers and media representatives were present at festivals and presented their ideas or tried to get young Muslims involved, as did the editors of the magazine The Revival or the Muslim Café.

One component of Islamic youth culture that only became apparent during the participant observations and would not have been revealed by the analysis of artefacts and possibly not by the accounts of the producers either, was youth work, which emerged as an important feature and seems to have two main purposes. One is religious education and the transmission of religious knowledge, beliefs and practices, which also takes the form of proselytism or *dawah*. The other purpose is to help young Muslims gain confidence and develop skills, to educate them as citizens and to offer recreational activities. This was best illustrated at youth camps, at which fun and entertainment alternated with education in religion and social skills. The regional or national meetings that last for several days resemble youth trips organised by schools, the Church or scouts associations, and in Germany are mainly organised by the MJD. The organisers offer several activities for the participants to choose from that provide an even mixture of leisure, education and religion. The Muslim Girls' Meeting offered group sessions of theoretical activities (Quran recitation; debates about the headscarf, purification of the heart and women's liberation) and practical activities (tae kwon do, folk dance, drums, theatre, Islamic manga drawing, dyeing prayer mats). The programme also featured lectures on religious and general topics, and – interspersed with the five daily prayers – entertainment such as a barbecue, a campfire, a chamber of horror, early morning exercise and a "Bunter Abend", a German tradition on group trips, denoting an evening of performances offered by the participants.

For the opening of the Muslim Girls' Meeting, the roughly 200 participants gathered in a room, and while people were entering and taking seats, one of the chairwomen recited from the Quran. In her introduction, she presented the programme for the following three days and reminded the girls why they were there:

to learn and to have fun, but above all to please Allah. After this more serious reminder, the organisers went on to stress the fun part of the meeting and to encourage a positive group identity by showing a video of how much the participants had enjoyed the previous year's meeting and by playing some games outside. Here, and during the entire meeting, several small activities were introduced to celebrate the group, such as singing and cheering in conga lines and Mexican waves. In a parade of honking cars, the participants had been picked up from the station and taken to the youth hostel; similarly, religion was celebrated through *Takbir* calls: one person shouts *Takbir* and the audience replies *Allahu akbar* (Allah is great); one shouts *Ashhadu* (I testify) and the crowd replies *La ilaha illa allah* (There is no god but God), which the youths excessively enjoyed over and over again.

Also, on the first day of the Muslim Girls' Meeting, the participants were asked to voice their expectations of the camp. The positive expectations included those typical of any youth camp, like meeting nice people, having fun, but also learning a lot and attending meaningful lectures, while the girls' only worry was that they might not get enough sleep. Indeed, the programme at both the Muslim Girls' Meeting and the large MJD Meeting started around 5 a.m. with morning prayer and ended after the night prayer at 10.30 p.m. on all days, which evoked some reluctant comments from the participants, but team leaders underlined the importance and the beauty of it, in terms of religious practice and group experience. As it happened, nearly every participant at the Muslim Girls' Meeting rose at dawn to join the collective prayer, remarkably including those who could not pray at the time: according to a widespread interpretation, women are not allowed to pray during their period; a belief common to many religions, based on the age-old suspicion of blood standing for impureness, in particular when applied to women. Still, several girls who observed this rule gathered for morning prayer to sit on the side and join in the general atmosphere – a way of inclusion, circumventing the exclusion that religious interpretation imposed on them and that they had also accepted, internalised and self-imposed onto themselves. The early rise was followed by Quran recitation, for which the girls gathered in groups of ten or fifteen on the corridors outside their bedrooms, many still in pyjamas. The team leader started to read out a *sura* in the typical singsong manner of Quranic recitation, after which the girls took turns, reading from their own copies. Some struggled with the Arabic, but all of them had been trained in the language, including the Turkish participants. The team leader pointed out the belief that one would be rewarded for recitation at any time, but even more so in the early morning hours.

What can be observed in a condensed form at youth camps forms an integral part of Islamic youth culture in everyday settings. A light-hearted approach to religion, including fun and entertainment, is emphasised as much as religious rituals. For instance, several interviewees asked to pray before, during or after our interview, some of which therefore took place at mosques or had to be paused or ended for the sake of prayer. Youth work of social and religious dimensions was provided by young adults of Muslim background from youth organisations and mosques, and by producers of Islamic youth culture. Some acted as individuals, while others were part of several networks. Some young people, for instance, had participated in young Muslims' meetings on a European level and had continued networking, which was why I met a few German MJD members again at the British meeting of Islamic societies. Youth work was also undertaken by the Birmingham radio station Unity FM, who integrated many volunteers and educated them not only in radio production, but also in the religious and political issues discussed in the programmes. The fact that the volunteers could choose to play music during their shows was a stimulus for constant debate about different Islamic interpretations and the relationship with youth interests. A much wooed protagonist was Tariq Ramadan, who spoke to young Muslims at the Birmingham meeting of Islamic societies and at the MJD Meeting, among others, and whose deep piety, conservatism and strong commitment to European societies resonated well with the audience.

The Islamic Info Service IIS played a major role in the support and education of young Muslims in Frankfurt, not only due to German-language Friday prayers, but also because of the extended services offered. It hosted a shop that supplied religious books, also especially for young people, including publications by the popular Amr Khaled, and offered counselling support on Thursday nights as well as religious education at the weekends. The IIS was therefore well-known and popular among young Muslims in Frankfurt. Equivalent Islamic book shops in Marseille did not cater for young customers, with the exception of religious children's books, but rather redirected people either to mosques, or, if the customer did not seem very religious, to proselytising centres on the city's outskirts. These bookshops only served as a meeting place for elderly men, while in one case young people were redirected to the Halal Fried Chicken restaurant and the mosque in the vicinity. Mosques usually taught religion in a traditional manner. Generally in France, only the religious youth organisations seemed to adopt an "edutainment" approach and to allow for forms of transmission, learning and social interaction that would reflect the influences of the French environment.

The element of action in Islamic youth culture does indeed reveal a high level of activism. Religious and social engagement, youth work, and a great deal of fun and entertainment complement the ideas and styles found in this youth culture. They reflect to a large extent the forms of education and leisure activities that are common in the respective national contexts.

C. CONCLUSION: A FOCUS ON ACTIVITY

The empirical findings from the participants' observations have confirmed some of the impressions gained from studying the artefacts in the previous chapter: Islamic youth culture places great value on being stylish, on practising Islam in a generation-specific way, on observing religious permissibility, and it adopts many characteristics of the society where it is set.

However, some of the findings are also new and go beyond what the artefacts tell. It has become obvious that the artefacts are not just consumed individually, but that they form part of a wider set of activities, which gives a much more dynamic picture of Islamic youth culture. Youth organisations, rather than traditional mosques, are involved in youth work, including religious transmission, social work, education and fostering good citizenship, as its team leaders are part of the movement themselves. Also, the gender dimension is much more pronounced when Islamic youth culture is actually lived out and gender roles, a desired behaviour and morality come to the fore. At the same time, women are very active members of the movement, both as participants and in a leading capacity.

The preliminary definition of Islamic youth culture, as concluded previously, comprised notions of *halal* and fun, expressed in several genres, as well as a close relationship between substance and style. While the observations have rendered more details of these elements, a comprehensive description should additionally incorporate the element of action. The significant role of youth organisations, youth work and events has only become obvious in the field. Furthermore, from the artefacts it could not be gleaned whether the producers' intentions had any relevance for young Muslims. They do indeed, although it also becomes apparent that young people do not just consume ready-made products of Islamic youth culture without reflection; rather, they choose whatever appeals to them in a certain setting. Moreover, in the field the boundaries between consumers and producers appear less definite – it is not only the producers who are active and provide a youth culture that is then passively consumed, but the youth also contribute significantly to the characteristics of Islamic youth culture, for instance at youth camps, debates and festivals.

It could be held that the movement is just a way of living Islam, rather than a youth culture, a view I have occasionally encountered in the field. While it is fair to hold this opinion personally, the larger perspective implies that much would be lost if this was accepted as a full explanation. The findings in their entirety indicate interacting clusters of styles, ideas and actions, which justify regarding the phenomenon as a youth culture.

Most youth cultures, then, are thought of as being intrinsically rebellious or deviant in demarcation to a perceived mainstream culture. With that in mind, Islamic youth culture strikes the observer as well-behaved, virtuous, compliant and morally conservative. But not every youth culture needs to take a rough, delinquent route or to shut itself off entirely. In some parts, Islamic youth culture adopts, embraces and merges with other cultures, such as religious beliefs, sub-cultural practice, values of social commitment and of morality. In other parts, it performs a demarcation on two levels: first, it sets a statement within a non-Muslim environment by showing pride in being Muslim, and second, it opposes the first generation of immigrants. Members of that generation often follow cultural rather than religious traditions, may be less involved with the society they live in, are not used to unconventional approaches to religious education and especially are not familiar with Western subcultures. Thus, while it is true that Islamic youth culture is more righteous than riotous, it does try to tackle several conflicts.

As much as the findings from France, Britain and Germany overlap and thus underline the similarities of this contemporary European movement, there were also differences in terms of visibility in the public sphere (dominant in Britain), the degree of institutionalisation (much less in France) or in the gender divide (especially in Germany). This reveals how much is dependent on a certain interpretation of Islam that has become popular and prevalent, again depending on who is setting the agenda at a certain point in time. The MJD's emphasis on gender segregation, for instance, has left its mark on current practice among many young German Muslims, while the popularity of Tariq Ramadan may have fostered both an engagement with wider society and a conservative worldview.

Beyond the phenomenon itself, understanding youth culture in terms of its components style, idea and action helps to grasp it in its entirety and context, by going beyond what is immediately visible. Among other things, it reveals who is part of the movement, what they try to achieve and how they achieve it. It is crucial to fathom all of this in detail in order to give a thorough ethnographic account and to be able to draw conclusions about why the youth culture emerges at a certain point in time and in a certain place. The next chapter will address this question further by analysing the producers' perspective and their motivations for engaging in Islamic youth culture.

V. Producing Islamic Youth Culture:
A Typology of Motivations

A. INTRODUCTION

The interviews with the producers were aimed at finding out about the individual meaning Islamic youth culture had for them and about the motivations that prompted them to become engaged in it. The resulting typology outlined in this chapter is meant to provide answers to this research interest by presenting the interview data in a condensed and well-structured form. At the same time it is supposed to convey some of the interview dynamics through verbatim quotations and case studies.

The typology is based on categories that are taken from the codes, which were used to structure and analyse the interviews. The codes themselves have been derived from the research questions, interview questionnaire and the major themes emerging from a first analysis. Of the twelve codes on average, four have shown to be the most influential for the typology: the central motif, the target group, the view on Islamic youth culture and the perception of society. Of course the result is based on the producers' accounts and the way they presented them during the interview; I did not attempt to speculate about any meaning that could not be reconstructed on the basis of the interview transcript. In the end, the analysis has yielded four types of producers and their motivations for creating Islamic youth culture: "Campaigners", "Improvers", "Empowerers" and "Proselytisers".

Central Motif
The concept of the "central motif" is proposed by Jan Kruse (2009). This should not be understood as a simple "motive of action", but rather recurring images, lines of argumentation or thematic statements – a "motif" in a more figurative sense (ibid.: 156). As the interviews often have more than one major theme, the

one that is most relevant as the central motif is the one connected to the participant's main aim and motivation. This was the main interest and research question, and it is therefore what the interviews were directed at: at the beginning of each interview I repeated the same introduction, which included a word on my study as a whole, and that I was interested to hear what the interviewee's experiences in this field were, and why they did what they did (see Appendix A). By introducing my interest in this way, it was clear from the outset that our common task for the following hour or so would be to determine the interviewee's motivation for their activity, thus indicating a direction for our conversation. Once I had identified all the central motifs, I looked for a pattern. At first, they seemed to group into political, social, religious, artistic and economic motifs, but were very unevenly distributed – the vast majority had a social motif, only few an artistic or an economic one. This became more balanced as this category was combined with the other ones.

Table 2: Central motifs

Political motif	Social motif	Proselytising motif	Artistic motif	Other motifs
5 cases	12 cases	9 cases	3 cases	business (2), spiritual (1)

Target Group

Despite the claim that they produce their music, fashion or media products for anyone, the interviewees' primary aim was usually directed at a certain group, which could roughly be divided into the Muslim population, non-Muslims or society at large, and the producer him- or herself. The inward-looking versus outward-orientated standpoint proved to be rather significant, with only very few cases corresponding to both, but even then one of the two was more dominant. Targeting oneself only became apparent in one case where the interviewee understood her music to be an act of spiritual devotion, but because she also wanted to share this notion with others, it was possible to reclassify her motif into the Muslim target group. In order to reduce and condense the groups, such reclassification was also necessary for some of the other cases, whose central motif could be interpreted as having another prominent aim, especially in connection with the target group and after reconsidering some other features of the respective interview. One of the two interviewees with a business motif, for instance, was regrouped with the outward-orientated political group, while the other one was dropped from the sample altogether: his features hardly matched any of the others, which was due to the fact that he had not strictly met the criteria of the sample, as he was only buying and selling, but not creating products of Islamic youth culture and therefore turned out to be much less committed to the idea. This had only come out during the interview and later proved incompatible with the typology. The cross-tabulation of central motif and target group finally led to four new categories.

Table 3: Central motif and target group

Target/Aim	Socio-political aim	Religious-proselytising aim
Outward-orientated	*10 cases*	*3 cases*
Inward-looking	*11 cases*	*7 cases*

Understanding of Islamic Youth Culture

The category of Islamic youth culture deals with the interviewee's definition of Islamic youth culture, which also reveals their personal assessment of and interest in the movement. Although the responses are complex, they usually tend to be either more religiously concerned or more subculturally concerned. For those who are more religiously concerned, the message is much more important than the medium that is used to distribute it. In fact, the medium may be replaceable, while the (religious) message is not. The more subculturally concerned, on the other hand, take their medium very seriously, often in an artistic way, when the message is closely intertwined with the genre itself. Their message is also Islamically inspired in one way or other, but focuses less on Islam itself than on Muslims. This category was then combined with the previous clusters and once more condensed to three distinct groups.

Table 4: Central motif, target group and definition of Islamic youth culture

Socio-political aim, outward-orientated, more subculturally concerned	Socio-political aim, inward-looking, more subculturally concerned	Religious-proselytising aim, both outward-orientated and inward-looking, more religiously concerned
10 cases	13 cases	8 cases

Perception of Society

There is much to say about the participants' perception of and relationship with society. At many points during the interview, they made statements about society, how they feel perceived and how they feel Islam is perceived, they judge public opinion and non-Muslims, in the media and in personal encounters. Pigeonholing the various responses into just two groups, an affirmative and a critical attitude, may seem superficial at first, but shows some convincing results in combination with the other categories. Also, the reasons underlining a positive or negative perception of society are an important source for giving evidence of the decision on types and for characterising them more closely. The reasons given for an affirmative perception, for instance, range from positive personal feedback by non-Muslims to appreciating the tolerant environment in which they can pursue their activity. Negative perceptions are fuelled by anti-Islamic media reports, reactions to the headscarf, sometimes a generally pessimistic attitude towards Western values, but mostly experiences of discrimination and frustration. The classification does not make a statement about whether or not the interviewee is engaged in society; however, this becomes apparent in the final typology.

Final Typology

Combined with the interviewees' perception of society, the previous table – including the central motif, target group and definition of Islamic youth culture – allows the distinction of four different types of motivation among the producers.

Table 5: The four final types

The four types	Affirmative perception of society	Critical perception of society
Socio-political aim, outward-orientated, more subculturally concerned	**Campaigners** *(8 cases)*	**Improvers** *(5 cases)*
Socio-political aim, inward-looking, predominantly more subculturally concerned	**Empowerers** *(10 cases)*	
Religious-proselytising aim, both outward and inward-looking, more rel. concerned		**Proselytisers** *(8 cases)*

The types will be presented in the following sections. By way of introduction, prototypes will highlight the most important features of each type. Subsequently, I will describe the type's characteristics in detail, analysing in what way the four main categories and further features, such as gender, nationality or subcultural genre, have shaped it; a full list of interviewees and these features is available in Appendix B. An explanation of the short term used as each type's name will complete the presentation of this typology.

B. FOUR TYPES OF MOTIVATION

1. Type One: Campaigners

Mona, 29, British rapper[1]

"We always dealt with issues like justice, freedom, unity, peace, love, all these different things and like representing the kind of like underclass and representing those people who did not have a voice. There's no point in me – if I'm doing a piece about what's happening in like I don't know Iraq or something, there's no point in me telling that to the Muslim community. 'Cos they know all about it."

Mona is member of a British female rap duo and 29 years old at the time of interview (2009). She is of Christian Caribbean family background and converted to Islam in 2005. Together with her rap partner, also interviewed in this sample, the group embarked on a musical and spiritual journey three years prior to their conversion, which they also performed together. At first, their aim was to voice the concerns of young, black, British women in their songs, which was later extended to Muslims. The terrorist attacks of 7 July 2005 had a major impact on the duo, as they had converted only days before the incident, and were therefore thrown into an environment where Muslims were in the spotlight. Major support came from the forerunners of the genre, Mecca2Medina, the band that made Islamic hip-hop popular and even acceptable in more conservative Muslim circles, and who pushed Mona and her partner to be one of the first two Muslim female groups to perform on stage.

The central motif of Mona's interview is representation: on the one hand, this is about representing themselves as (black) Muslim women or likeminded people in their audience.

---

1 In the presentation of the prototypes, some details have been changed for reasons of data protection. The names of all interviewees are fictitious.

"Ultimately we believe as [band name] that if someone isn't speaking for you, you have to speak for yourself. You know, looking at Muslim women in particular, you know, like when people are always saying 'Oh, the Muslim woman is this, the Muslim woman is that, the Muslim woman is this', and then you always have Muslim men speaking for Muslim women or someone who is not Muslim saying 'Oh no, the Muslim woman is this or that'. So we feel it's essential for us to represent ourselves. [...] We are just human, we just adhere to a different faith and, you know, so we decide that we wanna speak about being human, about being Muslim, about being black, about being female, about being British, all these different things. So essentially that's what we try to do with our music."

Speaking out for oneself is important to her, as she feels that otherwise it is men or non-Muslims who speak for Muslim women. On the other hand, the motif is about representing those who cannot speak out for themselves, giving a voice to the "oppressed", raising awareness of injustice and conflicts around the globe. The central motif is a political one, not only because of the political topics raised, but also because of the notion of representation. While she treats being Muslim, black, female and British as a special condition, with a need for representation in society, she also tries to level the differences. This striving for normality, emphasising the fact that one is "just human" with a different faith, occurred with many respondents throughout the sample. Almost of equal importance as the political aim is the desire to simply make good music. In the same sentence in which she talks about the aims of representation, she expresses how much the music itself means to her: *"We just wanna make like good music. So all these other different things that we wanna do, like love, peace, community, represent people, represent like the underclass, paint a different picture, and like represent ourselves and those people who feel we represent them – but at the same time, we do wanna make good music."*

Mona's conversion to Islam followed a longer search for spirituality from the age of 14, and coming from a Christian background she says *"I really tried to throw myself into Christianity at one point, but for myself, I just found it wasn't really right for me"*. Islam, however, did not appear right for her either – on the contrary, she openly admits to strong prejudices against it, believing that Islam suppressed women, which would go against her sense of resistance that she derives from her cultural heritage of the black rights movements. Only after reading Malcolm X's autobiography and a book by Moroccan feminist Fatima Memissi, her view changed. What finally convinced Mona and her group partner was the idea of separating Islam and culture, thus attributing all misogynist traditions to culture, disentangled from Islam. Mona's subjective interpretation of Islam is mainly liberal and non-dogmatic. Evidently, she has no understanding of the prohibition of music by more conservative Muslims, but does try to play by the rules sometimes, when she is ready to make concessions such as performing without instruments. Her approach to religion is a rather spiritual one, following notions of peace, love and justice rather than one particular school of thought. A self-ironic remark that this is slightly *"hippie-like"* underlines her non-dogmatic stance.

Islamic youth culture in the UK, the existence of which she affirms, results to her mind from a generational clash or a *"form of schizophrenia"* of the youth, who try to please their parents, but also to fit in with British culture. She thus depicts the movement's development as a display of identity search. If their parents' culture does not satisfy them in terms of identity, young Muslims look to define it themselves. Feeling the urge to tell people about who they are, they come up with Islamic subcultural expressions that differ from traditional forms; it is *"the Islam that they understand in a form that they're able to digest"*.

Being a Muslim in the UK is a *"very unique experience"* for Mona, in a positive way: she feels that in some Islamic countries she would be unable to express herself as a Muslim, while in France she thinks she would not be allowed to wear a headscarf, which leads her to a very positive perception of British society. Despite experiencing some anti-Islamic insults in the street soon after 7/7, Mona emphasises the positive feedback they received from non-Muslims regarding their music. The only other criticism has been voiced by Muslims about the permissibility of music and women performing on stage, and it is voiced strongly (*"how we're leading people to hell fire"*). While the criticism disturbed both of them at the beginning, Mona explains several coping strategies, from ignoring it to writing tracks about it to seeking support from Islamic scholars who speak in favour of music. She also shares the often expressed view that everything depends on one's intentions, and that their music does more good than harm.

A Portrait of the Campaigners

The participants of this type all share a socio-political aim. This covers aspects of representation, as in the case of Mona or of businessman Mansour who founded a Muslim media platform to counter the misrepresentation of Islam in the mainstream media. Another aspect is coexistence, or *vivre ensemble*, which French comedian Hilal expressed as his main motif, while the British rapper Mujab claims to follow the example of Prophet Mohammed to establish peace between various faith groups within society. Others have a more general positive message of life spirit as do three female musicians, Asma from Germany and Soumeya and Selma from the UK, who want to use their music to inspire others to reflect on life and to send out a message of love and positivity. One participant, Nour, employs a much more subtle and deeper engagement with society at large in his media productions on the traits Islam and Western culture share at such levels as abstract art; in fact, he calls for a much more sophisticated way of fusing Islam and the West than most examples of Islamic youth culture, which are boring and superficial to him.

All of the participants of this type are outward-orientated, as their central motif is laid out not only to target Muslims, but wider society. This does not necessarily correspond to the responses when directly asked, since almost everyone claimed to be targeting all members of society, but with this type, the claim is more realistic. The message is often derived from Islam without being purely Islamic, or concerns Muslims in their role as members in society, and the protagonists also strive to appeal to a non-Muslim clientele.

Like Mona, those who correspond to the same type are clearly subculturally concerned when it comes to Islamic youth culture. The medium in which they excel is very important to them, whether comedy, music or media design. Their different messages are often closely connected to the medium, as in the case of Hilal who uses comedy to work against the tense and nervous relationship between Muslims and non-Muslims. It could be argued that the Islamic focus gets lost in treating Muslims rather than Islam in this context, but the message expressed in the central motifs of this type is a multilayered one, often inspired by an Islamic perspective, ethics or history as well as the more cultural side of Islam.

This type is determined by a very positive perception of society, both on the personal level of good feedback from non-Muslims and on the wider level of enjoying a tolerant environment. There is a particularly positive view among the black, British converts in this sample within this and the third type, cherishing the liberal and permissive setting in Britain that allows them to practice their religion and pursue their religious subculture. The impression Mona had of other countries, seeing them as less favourable to her activity than Britain, is typical and offers another dimension to the outward-orientated attitude of this group.

Both Asma and Hilal place their being a human and a citizen higher than their identity as a Muslim, despite their strong religiosity. Hilal condemns any sort of communitarianism; he has possibly internalised one of the major accusations of French Muslims and has the urge to show that he differs from this stereotype. Soumeya is a British second-generation convert and tells me she prefers performing for non-Muslims as they generally appreciate her music more, certainly also because she does not have to justify herself in terms of the permissibility of music. She even deeply criticises her own community for resting on their victim status as perceived terrorists, and although she also claims to suffer from Western prejudices such as against the headscarf or the Prophet Moham-med, she maintains a strongly positive perception of society. The two media participants, Nour and Mansour, give evidence of their positive outlook through their actions – Mansour negotiates with government officials, also of the United States, to improve the *"Muslim media"* situation, while Nour has left the antag-onism behind by looking at cultural commonalities on an abstract level and by working for institutions like the BBC. Integration may be an issue for the partic-ipants of this type when it comes to their audience, but personally they have moved on from the stage where this was a pressing issue to solve.

Altogether, the eight participants corresponding to this type all share a cen-tral motif of a socio-political aim, mainly target a wider society outside the Mus-lim population, are more subculturally than purely religiously orientated and have a positive perception of society. Like Mona, they use their activity to voice political issues and global concerns from a Muslim point of view, both to raise awareness of the topics and to strengthen Muslim representation. Their interpre-tation of Islam is generally non-dogmatic and based on several individual deci-sions, and of all the interviewees they are the most casual with regards to Islam, showing as much concern for societal issues as for their being Muslim. This does not mean, however, that they are any less religious than participants of other types.

Furthermore, there is a striking predominance of British interviewees, an equal number of men and women and a majority of performing artists (rappers) and also media producers, but no-one from the area of fashion. The most com-mon background is black from non-Muslim countries, with only three people from Islamic countries, and therefore half of them are converts, while the other half have been brought up religiously, one of them by converted parents.

Of course, this distribution is not random, but corresponds to and explains some of the type's characteristics. Most remarkably, the positive outlook on so-ciety, one of the decisive factors of this type, is linked to the British dominance. Throughout all the interviews, British participants have spoken most positively about their environment, and despite occasional criticism, have cherished the support and tolerance they have experienced, along with other positive judge-ments of Britain or non-Muslims (see also Type 3). French and German inter-viewees were much more critical and recounted more negative experiences, es-pecially on a structural level (see Types 2 and 4). Although the genres are dis-tributed over all the types, the prevalence of the music sector may be linked to the participants' socio-political aim, especially in connection with the Black heritage. Interviewees were keen to emphasise this, relating to the musical tradi-tions of their parents' cultures, their strong belief in the permissibility of music and the political nature attributed to rap. Activities in the media sector could be a sign of participating in a mainstream field; the absence of fashion underlines the non-Muslim target group – even though there are fashion products by Muslim designers that do not only target Muslims, but represent a form of communication with non-Muslims. As outlined above, neither conversion nor continuous religious upbringing seems to have had a strong effect on the types, although the relatively high number of converts within this type may be connected to a stronger bond with mainstream society.

Summarising this group as "Campaigners" underlines the passionate outspokenness and the involvement in socio-political issues that are common for this type. The name is meant to put the most important features in a nutshell, rather than reduce the type to them or to make all members of this type sound the same. One needs to bear in mind the variety of motifs, including, for example, the spreading of a general positive attitude rather than a concrete political statement. Also, the positive views on society are typical of this group and have various sources, and also the subcultural side of Islamic youth culture is conceived by the members of this type in many ways – and yet in similar ways as opposed to the other types.

2. Type Two: Improvers

Baschir, 24, German comedian

"Man hat das Gefühl, man muss erst mal beweisen, dass man ein ganz normaler Mensch ist. Der ganz normal auch Humor hat, der ganz normal auch mal schlechte Tage hat, und der auch nicht immer superfromm ist, und der auch mal hier und da 'n Fehler sich erlaubt und, sag ich mal, nicht ganz korantreu handelt oder so ähnlich, ja? Und das ist dann so, dass wenn die Leute sehen, wir sind ganz normale Menschen, das ist doch schon etwas."[2]

Baschir is the founder of a comedy and theatre group, or cabaret (*Kleinkunst*) as he prefers, that performs in German. He was born in Germany, is of North African background, in his early twenties and married. In their plays, the group tackle societal issues from a Muslim perspective. They perform at Muslim

---

2   "You've got the feeling that you have to prove first of all that you are just a normal human being. Who has got humour like everyone else, who's also got bad days like everyone else, and who isn't always super pious, and who allows themselves to make a mistake here and there and, I'd say, not acting quite in line with the Quran or so, right? And that's, when people see that we are just normal human beings, that's already something."

festivals all over Germany on a voluntary basis, for example, at weddings or at events of the *Muslimische Jugend in Deutschland*.

While Baschir admits to an influence of Islam on their work, he considers the message to often be universal, such as honesty, doing good, seizing the day or any other human virtues to which Christians, atheists, liberal and conservative Muslims alike would subscribe. The Islamic influence is paired with many references to German and other Western art and comedy – one role model is Loriot, the long-time prototype of German comedy and caricaturist of the German petit bourgeoisie. Other inspirations come from wider popular culture (Spongebob) and American Muslim comedians (Allah made me funny, Ummah Films, Funnymentalists). Baschir also appreciates Turkish-German comedians, but because they emphasise the ethnic rather than the religious, the approach of these "assimilated Muslims", as he calls them, is completely different to his. Adding to the wild mix of influences, he is also a fan of the German language, in particular as used in the poetry of Schiller, and has composed a piece imitating this language.

The central motif of this interviewee is to provide Muslim entertainment as something with which Muslims can identify. At various points during the interview Baschir explains his understanding of how humour works: people laugh about things when they find themselves in the situation or habit that the comedian presents; they also understand other situations, but do not find them particularly funny. In the case of pious Muslims, he says, they do not relate to stories about casual relationships, but would laugh about scenes of engagement and marriage or about a mosque situation. This prompted them to bring "Muslim humour" on stage, which is much appreciated by the audience. Much of this has to do with morality and whether the themes of the comedy are *haram* or instead *"islamkonform"*, in line with Islam.

This aspect meets another main motif of the interview, *"Wir sind ganz normale Menschen"* – we are normal people –, standing for the urge to show German society that Muslims are ordinary people just like them, only adhering to a (different) faith, without being strange or terrorists. The two aims stand in chronological order. Currently, at the beginning, the group are trying to establish Muslim entertainment. The achievement of this would contribute to the second aim in the following stage, showing the normality of Muslims.

A remark of his about humour reveals the problematic nature of this undertaking. He understands humour as a way of dealing with the unbearable. Being considered abnormal – a topic he keeps coming back to – seems to be the unbearable for him and other Muslims, which is why he chooses humour to tackle it. The activity therefore also works as a kind of cathartic process for himself and for the community; and thus both an inward-looking and an outward-orientated perspective form part of the motif. The initial target group consists of Muslims, especially at the beginning, while the group work on establishing the genre. Later, Baschir would like to target an extended audience, but considers this possible only once "Muslim entertainment" has confidently found its place in the entertainment industry. All throughout his explanation, there is a great concern about society and one's place in it.

Baschir's subjective Islam interpretation is determined by taking his faith seriously, in an almost traditional, but not narrow-minded way, which allows him to look at Muslims in a light-hearted way. For example, he rejects the term "Pop Islam" for being misleading; even if he likes pop culture, as a pious person he does not like mixing the terms – "Pop Christianity" would sound just as strange to him. He does, however, support the trend if termed differently, and would simply call it Islam, practised according to the *Zeitgeist*. Muslims have always shaped a society's culture, and therefore he rejects the more conservative opinion that Islam and arts or comedy do not go together. Historic examples are calligraphy or architecture, which are mentioned in the Quran as little as rap or comedy. This links with a separation of Islam and culture as was the case with many interviewees. He identifies as a German with Moroccan roots and Islamic faith.

There is a moralistic approach to his plays, although perhaps not one that is exclusively Islamic, and an acknowledgement of boundaries. His understanding of arts, for instance, is clearly inspired by Islamic principles: a saying by the Prophet, "God is beautiful, and He loves beauty", makes him appreciate arts and aesthetics of any kind, but with a belief in limits. Satire does not allow everything, and for Muslims the boundaries are set by obscene and *haram* issues or anything offensive to people or God. Yet, setting the limits is done on the basis of his own reasoning; he is able to reject controversial issues, such as the prohibition of music, because reading the sources fully convinced him that music and arts are not forbidden. This view also informs Baschir's understanding of Islamic youth culture. If he is more subculturally than religiously concerned, it does not mean that his comedy is not strongly influenced by religion. It rather means that his activity focuses more on Muslims than on Islam itself, and he would speak of Muslim instead of Islamic youth culture, in order to stress that it is made by people and not prescribed by the religion. Religion here takes the role of creating familiarity within the genre and making it relevant to the audience, also by providing a moral framework.

Baschir's perception of society is a negative, but not a pessimistic one. It is mainly determined by his impression of not being considered "normal", neither on a personal basis nor collectively. The group have received positive feedback from non-Muslims, which they highly appreciate, especially because they usually have more negative perceptions due to unfavourable media coverage of Islam. Such an experience is not even always one of discrimination or rejection, but often one of being "other". Baschir recounts an example of where a colleague of his at work accidentally bumped into the room where he was praying and later apologised to him extensively. Baschir was not bothered at all, as such things happen when religion becomes integrated into everyday life, but the matter became special and abnormal precisely because of the exaggerated apology. Comedy is therefore his way of releasing the tension between Muslims and non-Muslims and of suggesting a humorous view to members of his community on issues like practising one's faith in workaday life.

A Portrait of the Improvers

This type's central motif is a socio-political one that is mainly concerned with one's place as a Muslim in society. The participants corresponding to this type seek to improve the current situation, offering various approaches to easing tensions. Some, such as German fashion designer Murat, choose to start a dialogue with wider society. He wants to foster communication in order to fight misunderstanding and prejudice. Muslims and non-Muslims in the West are at odds in his eyes and the relationship between them needs to be improved, which is only possible if people get to know one another. His central motif is *"Dialog ist alles. Dialog ist einfach alles"*[3], and even though he admits the term dialogue is slightly overused, social worker jargon or "multiculti", he firmly believes in it. To him, a T-shirt with a printed slogan is the medium that corresponds to what he aims to achieve, because it evokes a dialogue in the streets between the person wearing it and the random onlooker. Sarah, a female French comedian has the motif *"passer un message, pour un peu 'éduquer', entre guillemets, la population pour que les gens changent de façon de voir"*[4]. Her main aim is to change the perception non-Muslims have of veiled women, adding an educative purpose to her sketches. Other interviewees of this type are more concerned with Muslim youth in terms of identity and participation. Yasemin, who also works at an Islamic fashion label, believes that having an Islamic brand of one's own will have a positive effect on young people's self-esteem. She cares about young Muslims' self-awareness, and wants to help young people feel more confident about themselves as Muslims – also to entice them away from the victim status with which

---

3   "Dialogue is everything. Dialogue is just everything."

4   "Passing on a message in order to 'educate' the population a bit, in quotation marks, so that people change their perspective".

they might have made themselves comfortable. An Islamic brand, she thinks, would boost their self-confidence. Besides strengthening their religiosity, this would eventually relax them and make them more creative, so that they can confidently participate in society. This notion ties in with Baschir's desire for normality, and is made even more explicit by Bouchra, a French fashion designer of sports and swimwear. She has a central motif that concerns the participation of veiled women and providing them with the chance to participate, especially in public leisure activities, one of which is going to the beach, while the other is the participation of veiled women in the Olympic Games. By designing fashionable, sporty clothes that are religiously modest at the same time, she offers a third option to stopping playing sports and going to the beach, or taking off the headscarf (and more) – and thereby makes it possible for Muslim women to take part in both their religion and leisure activities of wider society.

The category of the target group plays a less distinct role than with the other types, since both an inward-looking and an outward-orientated attitude – or indeed a combination of both – are present here. It is not the category that most determines the affiliation to this type; both the central motif and the perception of society are much more significant in this respect. Murat and Sarah, for instance, are both concerned with a dialogue with wider society and with changing misconceptions of Islam, thereby, of course, enhancing the situation for Muslims. Sarah also directly targets Muslims in her comedy plays, for example, by addressing the topic of racism between ethnically different Islamic groups. Although Baschir is more orientated towards Muslims, he also has a message for wider society. Swimwear designer Bouchra caters for Muslims, but also wants to make a statement to allow religious women to participate in sports – directed at very conservative Muslims and at secular French people. Yasemin is perhaps most concerned with helping Muslim youth, and yet the need for an Islamic brand is especially apparent in the non-Muslim environment.

As they are mainly subculturally concerned with their activity, the respondents of this type have chosen their medium carefully and have high artistic standards for themselves. The medium is intrinsically tied to a message that would be quite different if expressed otherwise. T-shirt designer Murat appreciates urban street culture as an authentic expression "from below" and uses urban design to take the dialogue and social interaction again to the street. Religion comes into that as a resource from which he draws conclusions for his activity, claiming that prayer in isolation is meaningless and that exchange is necessary. Yasemin, on the other hand, has a much more pessimistic view of youth culture, especially when it does not serve a deeper purpose, and yet her aim focuses not so much on Islam itself. Being concerned with young Muslims, she acknowledges the subcultural form as meaningful to them. She rejects the term "Pop Islam" on the same grounds as Baschir, for to her Islam is a modern religion and corresponds to the time in which it is practised. Bouchra would be more religiously concerned if her artistic interest and leisure activities did not play such a major role. Although she reduces wider Islamic youth culture to religious education, she does not seem to feel part of it, and so both her type of fashion and Muslim women are her main focuses.

The relationship of this type's participants with society at large is the most demarcating quality from Types 1 and 3. The widely negative perception of society, along with the public perception of Muslims, results from various experiences ranging from negative media reports to deliberate ignorance of Islam to actual discrimination. What is remarkable, however, is that this does not lead the participants to turn away from society – on the contrary, they actively pursue a socio-political aim to enhance the situation. To enhance it *for Muslims* one might argue, but as it does not take place in isolation and rather in order to counter isolation, the aim is clearly to find better solutions for the whole of society.

Both Yasemin and Sarah also put part of the blame on Muslims. As did Baschir, Yasemin also sees her fellow Muslims as tensed up, which she describes copiously (*"Verkrampfung", "Betäubung", "Barriere im Kopf", "sich selbst bremsen", "an Kleinigkeiten aufhalten"*).[5] But the main issue remains the relationship with wider society. Two of the Germans had spent some time in London and elaborated widely on the differences between the two countries. In the UK, they perceived integration as being at its best, for example, with religious symbols like the headscarf or the turban being incorporated into public service uniforms. In Germany, both of them observed much more anti-Muslim sentiment, also from personal experience, based on the negative influence of the media and a lack of knowledge of the "other". While this may be biased such that parts of London can be exceptional compared with the rest of the UK and that the British media are no more favourable towards Muslims than their German counterparts, the main point of interest is that there seems to be a palpable tendency towards Muslims' positive assessment of their environment in Britain. The majority of British interviewees confirm this perspective from the other side. Also, Sarah faces forms of discrimination, as people often take her headscarf to be an indication that she is not very educated or independent. Since only French and Germans are among this type, the link between the perception of society and nationality becomes very apparent.

---

5   "Cramping", "numbness", "barrier in one's head", "hindering oneself", "wasting time on trivial details".

Altogether, and as with the first type, the participants corresponding to the second type have a socio-political aim and are also more subculturally than religiously concerned. However, their determining characteristic is that they have a negative perspective on society. It is worth noting that this does not stop the participants from social or political engagement; on the contrary, it works as an incentive. With five participants it is the smallest group of all the types.

Like Baschir, they seek to make a statement explicitly as practising Muslims, not as secular ones. Releasing tension is one of their shared aims and emphasises the fact that their products target Muslims, non-Muslims or both; in Baschir's case, both target groups are united in his group's twofold aims. Baschir's confidence that what he does is *halal* and meaningful in the contexts of Islam and society is another commonly shared feature. This confidence also allows them to give responsibility to Muslims and yet to demand that wider society shows an interest in what they do.

Most strikingly, only French and German interviewees correspond to this type, which appears as the main reason for the strongly critical stance. They are engaged in fashion and comedy, not in music or the media, and there is no male or female predominance. With no converts in this group, the respondents have either been brought up religiously or reverted to Islam and thus share a background from an Islamic country, Turkey or North-Africa.

The short name "Improvers" emphasises the negative perception of society as an impulse for a socio-political motif to improve the relationship of Muslims and non-Muslims. It does not claim to capture the manifold approaches of how improvement can be achieved or the status that requires amelioration, which is a matter of mutual perceptions of Muslims and non-Muslims, or possibly a lack of any kind of relationship. The term is meant to highlight the most important features that demarcate this type most from the other ones.

3. Type Three: Empowerers

Salima, 25, British fashion designer

"I wanted to make the brand relevant to Muslims so that they would understand it [...] I didn't see how this traditional art would make sense to Muslims now."

Salima is a young, London-based fashion designer and founder of her own label. Of Arab background and born in the UK, she describes her brand as *"Islamic in spirit"*, but relevant for young Muslims in the West and today. The relevance lies in the subcultural.

The close connection of British and Islamic traits recurs throughout the interview. The incentive for Salima to start her fashion line was a lack of clothes that *"fulfilled all the requirements (*=halal*) and were stylish at the same time"*. She even found Islamic street wear unsatisfying for being too masculine and using too little Islamic design.

The form of her final product is very much influenced by Islamic shapes, which again carry Islamic philosophical concepts. Her design is also influenced by growing up in Britain and adapting it to the British environment, not only in shape, but also in substance. She praises, for instance, the freedom of expression she enjoys in Britain and claims that this has found its way into the brand itself. In terms of graphics, her style makes traditional Islamic art and London urbanity meet. Salima's target group are young women with an aspirational attitude, the *"independent-minded Muslim market"*. There are also non-Muslims among her customers, who appreciate the sophisticated cultural London mix, but notions of identity are strongly at play in the fashion and thus appeal more widely to Muslims.

Salima's central motif is to create a brand that is *"Islamic in spirit and relevant to the youth"*, telling of a deep discussion of what it means to be British and Muslim. She perceives a great divide between Muslims and non-Muslims in Britain, but tries to make sense of the two, the British and the Islamic, in her designs. Solving this is an artistic issue for her, inspired by questions of identity – concerning herself and her customers. She acknowledges that her design is marked by growing up in British culture, therefore *"part of myself is gonna appeal to the non-Muslims anyway"*. As for the Islamic elements, she incorporates both graphics and ideas, for example, by relating repetitive patterns to the Islamic philosophy of perfection through repetition. The link between the British and the Islamic is the notion of relevance. Traditional art and ideas, including religious rules around *halal* clothing, are pointless in Salima's opinion, if they do not relate to people on a day-to-day level. If the clothes fit their environment, as in this case, if they have a London-specific *"urban feel"* to it, the concepts conveyed are made relevant to young Muslims in the here and now. Salima offers a solution to like-minded fellow Muslims, not just on the obvious level of helping frustrated Muslim women find modest and pretty clothing, but also and especially by refusing to apologise neither for Islamic culture nor for being British, and by standing by it.

Expressing an optimistic view on youth culture in general, Salima's concern with the subcultural side of her activity exceeds a religious concern. She understands youth culture as the belief in the ability to make a change and displays this passion in her own activity. At the same time, she has a very positive and engaging attitude towards Islam, which she joyfully refers to as *"such a happy religion"*. She derives this from her interpretation that there is no need for force or extremes in Islam, and thus "normal" Muslims should be role models. Any more extreme interpretations are spread by radicalists, whom she despises for making Islam miserable and oppressive and causing people to turn away from it. Because it is impossible for her to distinguish enjoyable elements of Islam from non-enjoyable ones, she does not see the need for terms like "Pop Islam". She puts forward a healthy and balanced view between letting go of one's ego without ceasing to be a person when practising Islam, as well as living a halal life, but also upholding one's Western identity. Of the problems she distinguishes for Muslims living in Britain, she traces most of them back to inner-Muslim issues. She despises men for not fulfilling their role as leaders of the community and family, thereby worsening the situation of Muslims. Certainly, in this way she criticises certain people who act within a system, but not the system of strict gender roles itself. A relaxed interpretation in one area does not necessarily lead to a non-traditional view in another, or only to a certain extent.

Salima started practising Islam at the age of 19 as a result of her own choice. She recalls going on a pilgrimage with her family as being her religious turning point, but because she was probably brought up in a religious way, it did not represent a complete U-turn, as with similar cases of "reversion". It did, however, make her actively decide in favour of Islam and choose the right interpretation for her, regarding it as a source of personal happiness that in no way conflicts with a (subcultural) life in Britain.

Although ambivalence marks Salima's perception of society, she has a mainly positive perception of it. She mentions a few factors that contribute to a divide between Muslims and non-Muslims in British society, for instance, a different and mutually exclusive way of socialising (pub versus the family) or a lack of knowledge about each other. However, personally, she has only had positive comments about her work, speaks highly of the freedom she enjoys in the UK and has a strong opinion on British politics, which she feels greatly concern her as a citizen. Above all, she deliberately weaves her Britishness into her Islam-inspired fashion in order to make it relevant to young Muslims.

A Portrait of the Empowerers

The central motifs of members of this type express a social aim. Most of them have an interest in the empowerment and identity of young Muslims, and some interviewees do so in a very direct way. The most prominent activist on the German side is Hamid, a founder of an online platform, whose central motif is: *"Wir müssen den Jugendlichen so 'n bisschen 'n Tool geben, wo sie ihre eigene*

Kultur entwickeln können und die auch austauschen können.[6] By attracting the more religious part of young Muslims and giving them a space to create and exchange a subculture, he seeks to empower them to actively shape an identity that is very often imposed on them by various parties. A very similar motif is expressed by Mahmoud, co-editor of a Muslim youth magazine, who wants to *"help in the development of a new identity"*, the "new identity" alluding to a fusion of British and Islamic traits to be proud of. Working at a helpline and webspace for Muslim youth, Rasha's motif is also about empowerment. She emphasises the young people's ownership of the website's user-generated content, does not want to provide solutions but rather empower them to take their own decisions, and places them at the centre of her narrative. Like Hamid, she aims to give them a space and to assist, but then leaves them plenty of rope – in contrast to Salima, who stays less in the background with her fashion, but who also advocates living with a British-Muslim identity.

Contributing to a similar aim, but with a different twist, two respondents mainly seek to promote creativity. Ibrahim has almost retired from his career as an Islamic rapper on the British scene, but uses his involvement in the scene now to promote Islamic youth culture on many levels. Timothy, who has published an Islamic music magazine and established an artists' network, voices *"expressing creativity"* as his topmost aim: by displaying the creativity of which Muslims are capable, his aim is not only to change the image of Muslims, but even more so, he wants to reflect this back to them to enhance self-esteem, especially in young people. Similarly, Ibrahim aims to show that Islam can form part of a "cool" way of life, which for him might work as a way to evoke pride in young people in being Muslim.

Fashionista Jamila almost takes this a step further with her motif *"It's just nice to be able to feel like everyone else"*. Longing for normality like Baschir (Type 2), she wants to leave any differences behind, but unlike him, she directs that at more conservative Muslims rather than society at large. Also, she does not wait for Islamic fashion or youth culture to happen in the future, but rather explains retrospectively why it occurred, and therefore makes a statement that normality had better be accepted by those who are still sceptical.

Apart from the identity-based cluster of motifs, some interviewees of this type rather focus on the religious to improve what they regard as their community. French musician Kamal wants to use his songs to open young Muslims' hearts to make them more interested in learning about religion. What sounds like proselytising at first is more an attempt at fixing a generation clash; with

---

6   "We kind of need to provide a tool for the youth where they can develop and also exchange their own culture."

mosques providing religious education in Arabic and young people speaking only French, he is not surprised that the youth feel that Islam is not for them. He does not blame them, but rather the elders if they are against the French influence and language. Mediating between the two parties and making French Islam acceptable within his own community is what he strives for.

A similar motif is expressed by Iqbal, who works at a Muslim radio station. Trying to cater for all ages, he finds himself mediating between older, more traditional members of the Muslim community and the youth, *"to try to get a balance between the two"*. The imbalance lies in the music and permissibility debate, which as a radio station they inevitably have to face. It creates an ongoing dispute, sometimes only implicitly, but a more open conflict at other times. Elderly Muslims on the one hand request the station to only broadcast lectures and Quran recitation in order to get an Islamic message out to the community; young people, on the other hand, claim that such a message must be presented in a form that relates to youth. Interestingly, the station has not been able to agree on one policy towards music, for example allowing certain types of music or lyrics and not others. The current state is an unwritten law: any music can be played, but people seem to have a sense of an invisible boundary. Most of the time, the music is *nashid* or Islamic rap, and if "Western" music is played, Iqbal interprets this as *"checking the boundaries"*. Boundary in this context must be understood as the line where the *halal* ends and the *haram* begins – certainly always down to subjective interpretation. Iqbal appears to stand on the youth's side and that of the boundary-flexing broadcasters. However, he also tries to make concessions towards the traditionalists for the sake of broadcasting for the whole community, and therefore establishing a balance between the conflicting ideologies of the audiences, as well as broadcasters, is to him *"the whole idea of the station"*.

Finally, spoken word artist Rehana has the most personal approach to contributing to the wellbeing of Muslims. Drawing on the Qawwali[7] Sufi tradition, she understands her music as an *"act of devotion"*, using it as a spiritual search for the self, but then also wants to pass the experience on and *"promote this good energy, promote this love, promote this kind of positiveness of the music, of using music to get to Allah"*. Although this carries a proselytising element, the emphasis is on sharing a message of love and positivity, on overcoming the prohibition of music and thereby improving the situation for (young) Muslims.

Overall, central motifs within this type focus on strengthening young people's sense of themselves as Muslims in a non-Muslim environment, whether by encouraging them to craft an identity and to display creativity, by bridging a

---

7   Qawwali is devotional Sufi music from South Asia; *qaul* stands for an utterance of the Prophet.

generation gap and advocating the perspective of youth, or by disseminating spiritual positivity.

As a common and distinct feature, the respondents of this type all target Muslims, and youth in particular. They do so in different ways and with different motifs, but tailor these to the needs they perceive among Muslims. Some respondents do not consider themselves part of their target group and employ a slightly top–down approach, such as Hamid, Mahmoud and Rasha, but also those who mediate between generations, Kamal and Iqbal. Others share their demands of those targeted and thus form part of the target group, like fashion-orientated Salima and Jamila, and especially Rehana in her spiritual practice. Again others are also personally involved in the scene and passionately promote Muslim arts and music, not least to make it acceptable among more traditional Muslims, as do Timothy and Ibrahim. Overall, this type's inward-looking orientation towards Muslims does not represent a turning away from others, but stands for an urge to help younger Muslims feel as much at ease with society as they do.

Like Salima, the respondents of this type are passionate about the medium of their activity, but they also feel strongly about their message. The emphasis on the subcultural is accompanied by a concern for young Muslims and is used to reach out to them. As with the other types, the messages can be Islamically inspired, but instead of an Islamic message as such, the ideas focus on identity-related issues with regard to Muslims and how these can be subculturally expressed. The medium is therefore again closely linked to the message and also to the respondent, and is rarely interchangeable with a different means of expression.

Much the same as the first type, but in contrast to the other two, the Empowerers are strongly characterised by a very positive outlook on society and an affirmative relationship with it. This may for a large part be owing to the fact that, again, most participants of this type are from the British sample, which underlines once more the connection between the national environment and the attitude towards society. The positive attitude mainly stems from a grateful acknowledgement of freedom and tolerance towards their activity, as with the first type. Rehana even *"feel[s] blessed"* for that, and has experienced no difficulties with non-Muslims, just with Muslims, who *"have, to be honest, a little bit of a problem"*. Maybe this is partly why these respondents turn to Muslims as their main target group, as they see a need for development in parts of their community. Personally, Mahmoud also stresses a very good perception of society at large, but in his area of northern England he witnesses the difficulties of less educated or disadvantaged young Muslims, who stay rather isolated and reject British culture. This is precisely what he wants to change, believing that a positive identification with Britain is possible. Others also emphasise a good relationship with Christians or mention support from non-Muslims with regard to their activity. This is not to say that they lack a critical attitude; like Salima, they may even articulate an ambivalent relationship, especially when it comes to media reportage, but on the whole their engagement with society results in a positive outlook that they strive to pass on to younger Muslims.

With ten interviewees, the Empowerers type has the most representatives. They follow a social aim, but other than Types 1 and 2, they are only inward-looking in the sense of strongly caring about Muslims. They are subculturally orientated, but slightly less than the first type, as the message and the medium are equally important to them. They also tend to focus more on Muslims than on Islam itself. Their very positive outlook on society is another striking feature that shows that a focus on a community does not imply isolation or demarcation from wider society.

Salima displayed a strong personal connection with her European home country, which is also found as a matter of course in the other interviewees of this type. They, too, uphold a close relationship between their British (or French or German) and Islamic traits and regard subculture as a way of showing young-er Muslims the relevance of Islam to their lives in these countries. Often, the subcultural product is also that of a very personal identity debate, and the pro-ducer becomes part of his or her own target group, as in the case of Salima. Hav-ing found a sensible solution for themselves, they offer it to younger Muslims.

The participants corresponding to this type are balanced in gender with slightly more men than women, so there does not seem to be a gender-based preference for dealing with community issues. Half of the participants are en-gaged in media, while the rest are active in the music or fashion arena. The prominence of the media is likely to result from another trait of this type: the emphasis on involving young people in their activity, for which web 2.0 facili-ties offer a wealth of opportunities, as well as a radio station and a youth maga-zine that both depend heavily on young volunteers.

Even more than the first, this type is dominated by British participants, with only one German and one French representative. Again, this strongly accounts for this type's positive outlook on society, as they repeatedly point out the liberty Britain provides for them, happily identify with being British or express that they could not picture living in any other country, including in the Islamic world. Like Salima, this is said without being uncritical, but with an articulate commit-ment to British society. A variety of backgrounds comprise Arab countries of origin, followed by the Caribbean and Pakistan, as well as Nigerian and Indian backgrounds. More distinctly, the most common personal history with Islam is that of a continuous religious upbringing, with only two converts and one revert, a fact that certainly influences the focus on engagement within and the development of the Muslim population.

A desire to empower young Muslims is shared by all respondents of this type; thus, the label "Empowerers" focuses on this motif. As outlined above, this is does not limit the respondents' view to their immediate environment – on the contrary, they enjoy a positive relationship with wider society – but their engagement appears most useful if catering for Muslim youth. As a short name, it does not capture all the nuances and different approaches combined in this type, but is only able to accentuate the shared general motivation.

4. Type Four: Proselytisers

Jabir, 29, French rapper

"Quand je fais réfléchir les gens, j'suis, ma mission c'est ça. Par exemple, chez les musulmans y'a certains musulmans qui sont trop loin dans la religion, c'est bien – c'est pas trop loin, mais ils se, ils se sont un peu coupé du monde. Alors que normalement la religion c'est une lumière qu'on doit partager aux gens, c'est pas une lumière que tu gardes pour toi."[8]

Of Arab background, Jabir has spent his whole life in southern France. He started rapping at a young age, like most of his peers. Coincidentally or not, he mentions his "entry" into religion right after that, around the age of 13. His growing religiosity gradually began to influence his lyrics.

Without saying so explicitly, it becomes very clear that Jabir's central motif is making *dawah* among (young) Muslims. Repeatedly he expresses his desire to be a mediator between religious books and young people, or even between God and the people, in order to pass on religious knowledge and to facilitate the relationship. Corresponding to the concept of *dawah* and the idea of "invitation", he does not strive to advertise Islam and convert people directly, but to invite them to think about it and eventually to take the decision themselves, after hearing from him about the benefits of the Islamic faith. Jabir is someone who likes comparisons: he equates what he has to offer to the produce of a *boulangerie*; a

---

8   "When I make people reflect, I am, that's my mission. For example, among Muslims there are certain Muslims who are too far into religion, in fact – it's not too far, but they have shut themselves a bit away from the world. Whereas usually religion is a light one must share with the people, it's not a light that you keep to yourself."

bakery does not need to advertise either, because people will always come and buy bread. It is worth noting that he chooses a basic foodstuff for his comparison, a necessity that people will eventually need and seek. Another time, he likens religion to light – the old metaphor – with the aim of sharing the light rather than keeping it to oneself. Further comments underline his motif of *dawah*, such as expecting recompense at the "Last Judgement", or in fact punishment if he fails to fulfil his duty of passing on his religious knowledge.

He explicitly targets non-practising Muslims and youth in particular, who do not normally read and therefore have to be educated differently about religion. One reason he gives for this focus is that he wants to present young people with a completely different lifestyle to the rough street life of the *banlieues*, with better values than burning cars, or in other words, make them realise that approaching God would result in leaving behind one's problems, alcohol, drugs and a life in and out of prisons behind: *"Quand tu te rapproches de Dieux avec la réflexion, tous ces problèmes, tous ces fléaux, l'alcool, le shit, la prison et tout ça, tu t'en éloignes"*[9], is something he deals with in his songs, and he stresses that reflection and realisation are eventually much more effective than simply banning, for example, alcohol. He thus targets a potentially delinquent group of non-religious young Muslims to open up more positive and religiously inspired life choices to them.

In terms of his subjective interpretation, Islam mainly means values to him – in his case quite conservative ones. For example, his view that there should only be relationships within marriage goes in hand with an emphasis on virginity, which he also deals with in a song, and the clash of values he sees with the West where sex is too prevalent and to which Islam is a counter-current. Like many others, he also understands religion as imbuing all parts of life, and no longer as being confined to the house or mosque. Open to debating his religion with anyone, he qualifies this view after second thoughts, excluding those who doubt the existence of God.

Overall, Jabir holds rather conservative moral values and otherwise maintains a quite literal belief. The fact that he is a rapper only superficially challenges this traditional perspective, because he regards music purely as a means to an end: *"La musique, c'est rien, c'est une passerelle. Pour moi le plus important y'a le Coran, y'a ma religion, c'est plus important. La musique, faut que tu t'en*

---

9   "When you move closer to God through reflection, all these problems, all these troubles, alcohol, drugs, prison and all that, you move away from that."

serves juste pour que ce soit un déclic"[10]; – music must only serve the purpose of evoking a morally positive reaction. Even though he does not seem to have a conception of the phenomenon of Islamic youth culture as a whole, he gives a short definition, picking up on my examples of music and fashion, which reveal his take on this kind of activities, *"utilis[er] la culture pour promouvir l'Islam"*.[11] This meets with the central motif and is underlined by yet another comparison in which he equates his music to a metro, tram or bus to get from one point to another – a highly utilitarian approach. Yet, he receives his share of criticism for using music, but he puts it down to irrelevant extremists. He is confident that if music is used as a vehicle for a religious message or *dawah*, it is permissible.

Finally, Jabir's perception of society is not a positive one. Frustrated by the stigma of being Arab and Muslim, he feels that non-Muslims are only interested in the violent *banlieues*, paired with a disinterest in Islam as a religion, while the media present an extreme picture. At the same time, he has a few prejudices himself, judging Western values as negative and in opposition to Islamic ones. Altogether, he seems less engaged with wider society, as his main interest lies in targeting Muslim youth.

Contrasting this prototype, the presentation of a second respondent of the fourth type will highlight an important difference, which shows the two varieties within this type: while the first targets young people of Muslim background, the second is concerned with informing non-Muslims about Islam.

Ridvan, 25, German T-shirt designer

"Es ist eine schöne Religion, man kann mit uns leben, man kann auch mit uns arbeiten, man kann mit uns ein' Kaffee trinken gehen, man kann – es heißt nicht, Deutschland und Islam, Parallelgesellschaften. Man kann zusammen leben. Auf jeden Fall, und das ist – ich hoffe, dass wir auch ein Stück dazu beitragen. Ich denke mal, zum Beispiel bei so einem Interview, wie wir es jetzt grade führen, trägt man auch schon mit dazu bei, ja? Das heißt, wenn irgendwann, *inshallah*, deine Doktorarbeit fertig ist, [...] da werden sicherlich Dinge drinstehen, wo man sagt, 'Ach, wirklich? So? Der mit dem Bart ist gar nicht böse. Die ham wirklich irgendwo 'ne eigene Moderichtung, aber sie ist durchaus auch mit unsrer vereinbar. Ja, der Islam ist ja vielleicht auch was für uns, ja vielleicht ist das 'ne Religion, die mich auch anspricht'. Vielleicht kommen Leute auch dadurch erst in Kontakt mit dem Islam. Das ist natürlich auch – das nennt man im Islamischen *dawah* heißt das, also das

---

10 "Music, that's nothing, it's a footbridge. For me the most important thing is that there's the Quran, there's my religion, that's most important. Music, you've got to use it only as a trigger."

11 "Using culture to promote Islam."

heißt Religionsarbeit, den Islam präsentieren auf die schönste Art und Weise. Wir wünschen natürlich auch jedem Nicht-Muslimen, dass er den Islam kennenlernt, dass er sich damit beschäftigt, um natürlich aus islamischer Theologie, um zu sagen, dein ewiges Seelenheil ist nur mithilfe des Islam zu retten."[12]

Ridvan runs a little T-shirt business that prints Islamic symbols and slogans on shirts. He is of Albanian background and of German nationality, a fervent revert to Islam, and a university student; he works in a team with two other colleagues of a similar background. Compared with all other interviewees, Ridvan holds some of the strongest views in terms of a literal and conservative understanding of religion. Despite this, he constantly performs a religious self-positioning throughout the interview, displaying himself as more liberal than actual radicals.

His narrative is that he wants to build bridges and create dialogue to abolish prejudices among Muslims and non-Muslims. While this may be part of the answer, several explicit statements of his suggest a different main motivation, that of *dawah*, in his case targeting only non-Muslims. When asked how he defines building bridges, he first conceptualises it as overcoming the wall that the media have erected between Muslims and non-Muslims, but then adds that eventually a non-Muslim, engaged in dialogue with him, might find out that Islam is the right thing for him or her. His central motif is to present Islam in the "most beautiful way", and he explicitly defines it as *dawah*, prompting him to actively inform about Islam on any possible occasion, whether inviting for discussion via T-shirt slogans or even openly during our interview. One of the reasons why Ridvan wants to inform about Islam is a belief in the superiority of Islam – which also undermines his motif of wanting to build bridges between equal partners – show-

---

12 "It is a beautiful religion, you can live with us, you can work with us, you can have a coffee with us, you can – it's not Germany and Islam, parallel societies, you can't live together. Definitely, and that is – I hope we also contribute something to this. I think, for example at an interview like we're doing now, one also contributes to it, right? That is, when at some point, *inshallah*, your PhD thesis is done, [...] it will surely include things that make people say 'Oh, really? Well? The guy with the beard is not evil. They really have some sort of fashion style of their own, but it is compatible to ours. Well, Islam might also be something for us, perhaps it's a religion that also appeals to me'. That way, people might first be exposed to Islam. Of course that's also – in Islam that's called *dawah*, religious work, presenting Islam in the most beautiful way. We certainly also wish every non-Muslim would get to know Islam, concern themselves with it, because from the perspective of Islamic theology your eternal salvation can only come about by means of Islam."

ing, for example, in the statement that salvation can only be obtained through Islam, which also holds true for non-Muslims.

His subjective view of Islam is determined by a verbatim interpretation of the sources and the duty of dawah, and not surprisingly, he is a fan of radical preacher Pierre Vogel. For a man, he comments surprisingly often on gender issues, defending women's rights, but only in order to cement clear-cut gender roles and be apologetic about prescriptions that could also be interpreted otherwise. For instance, he quotes the Prophet's instruction not to shake hands with women and appreciates how Pierre Vogel interprets this case: it does not imply inferiority on the women's side, he says, but focuses on the benefits for the community. If you do not shake hands, you do not give kiss on the cheek either, and so there is nothing that can lead to fornication, the mortal sin. Even if the rationale behind the argument is rather unconvincing, it is a telling example of Ridvan's dealing with scripture. His very literal understanding of religious requirements is, however, accompanied by a deliberate self-presentation as more liberal than others. For instance, while he would not print the name of Allah on a shirt, as it might be taken on a visit to the toilet, there are others – in his view: extremists – who call his activity haram for making money with Islam. He may be right in a way; his examples reveal once again the extent of variety of what Muslims classify as *haram* or not. Also, he does not cross the line to violent extremism, which he despises, but rather remains concerned with values and with the moral and theological eminence of Islam.

As a revert to Islam, having discovered Islam for himself a few years ago, Ridvan describes Islam as the most beautiful thing that ever happened to him; the turning point came when he realised that he believed in heaven and hell – which already suggests a strong presence of religiosity – and that he would be destined for hell if he did not live in line with the Quran. His initial overzealousness decreased, but he is still very passionate, and yet at times apologetic about his faith.

General youth culture does not meet his approval for being dull, uninspiring and mostly *haram*, which he extends not only to music, but also to extravagant looks in men and women alike. He endorses Islamic youth culture as long as it remains modest and if it has a charitable dimension – clearly prioritising religious over subcultural aspects.

His relationship towards society appears ambivalent at first. On the one hand, he emphasises (or rather: pays lip service to) bridge building, while on the other hand he looks down on society in a culturally pessimistic way. Characterising German society as selfish, disregarding any rules and its own religious foundations, he finally displays a highly critical perception of society at large. Of course he has a solution at hand, both for society and for each individual's salvation.

A Portrait of the Proselytisers

The common central motif shared by respondents of this type is a religions one, educating about the Islamic faith with the goal of persuading others. *Dawah*, or proselytisation, is undertaken for various reasons, above all for the conviction that Islam offers a better way of life, whether for its life-saving qualities in the case of disadvantaged youth or the alleged moral benefits for society at large. The latter view is expressed by three German interviewees[13]. Apart from Ridvan, there is a designer, Samir, who wants to set boundaries through the work he does, not by including certain (religious) topics, but by excluding any – in his view – immoral ones. By omitting nudity and also homosexuality, he believes in making a statement for wider society, on which he focuses. In the third interview of this kind, the respondents describe their motif as *"die Aufmerksamkeit wieder auf Werte zu lenken, die wirklich Bestand haben"*[14], again displaying a preferred framework of values to a society that increasingly ignores such values.

More concerned about Muslim youth on the edge of street crime than about non-Muslim society, other interviewees use *dawah* to offer a more promising future to them. German rapper Adel strives to show young people what Islam stands for, and that is for him, a lifesaver: *"[Ich] wollte einfach auch Jugendlichen in meiner Lage sagen, egal wie tief du vielleicht gesunken bist, [...] Gott vergibt jedem und du kannst was aus dir machen, wenn du willst"*[15]. He even regards it as his duty to make *dawah* and to show what Islam is about. Similarly, British rapper Ahmad presents Islam as a way out of street crime, although and in contrast to Adel, he has barely managed the step himself. Having taken part in a street worker project called "Divorced from the streets and married to Islam", this title also circumscribes his central motif. Given his personal experience of youth street crime, he and his band members want to draw young people away from it by presenting the benefits of a good, moral, religious life – proselytisation for the sake of crime prevention. Nabil, a French businessman in the fashion sector, may have less dramatic circumstances in mind, but also wants to con-

---

13 To be precise, there were four interviewees, as one of them insisted on being interviewed together with his business partner; as they shared most views, they would both be classified as the fourth type.

14 "[...] directing awareness back to values that really endure."

15 "[I] also just wanted to tell young people in my situation, no matter how low you may have got, [...] God forgives everyone and you can always make something of yourself."

vince young people that they can have a better lifestyle; his idea is to create a community around (divine) unity and (Islamic) values. The negative alternative, especially in sports fashion, is adhering to capitalist brands and values. Because he uses youth cultural codes, he hopes to persuade them to accept another value system and is confident that he is offering not only a youth culture, but a complete way of life. Finally, there is Rami, another German singer, who is much more spiritual in his motif, *"den Weg zu Gott leicht machen"*.[16] In his songs, he teaches young Muslims how to get closer to God, but again, based on the assumption that they would otherwise drift towards a purely materialist life, possibly bordering on delinquency. Thus, all respondents of this type think of Islam as the solution to the problems they perceive in their target groups.

Corresponding to the two streams within the central motif, the target group of this type is twofold. Three interviewees mainly target non-Muslims through products like T-shirt slogans and design that are visible in public settings. They display an attitude of moral superiority, and although they vary in their degree of open proselytisation, they are convinced that Islamic values and morality would be the better alternative for the whole of society. But just as important are the five interviewees who target young Muslims. Especially in the cases of Adel, Ahmad and Rami, who have a history of street gang membership and drugs, they know very well to whom they are preaching. Talking from experience, they know with what young, non-practising and predominantly male Muslims spend their adolescence, and therefore, the interviewees act as role-models, trying to point the Muslim youths in the direction that saved them. Therefore, there is an important difference between the target groups within this type; however, creating two completely different types here would not be justified for reasons of similarity in many other respects, especially with regard to the motif.

All respondents of this type are united by their approach towards Islamic youth culture, which is much more religiously than subculturally concerned. The religious message, or helping others with religion, is the top priority. Some of them are even sceptical about Islamic youth culture and only accept it if it serves more than just fun or business and, of course, only if it is *halal*. Subculture seems to be a means to the end of making *dawah*, as pinpointed by Jabir. The genre of expression is therefore not the greatest passion of these interviewees, not even of the rappers, who have ceased to listen to music after becoming more serious about their activity. An exception may be Adel; although no longer consuming music either, he cherishes the genre highly for its subcultural connotations in voicing people's rights and therefore remains closely committed to rap. The fourth type is the only one with all respondents emphasising the

---

16 "Facilitating the way to God".

religious side of this youth culture rather than the subcultural – only two other interviewees would have a similar view, but are unrelated otherwise – and they are more hesitant than others to welcome the new movement.

The participants of this type have a negative perception of society for various reasons. However, as opposed to the second type, this does not work as an incentive to engage on a social or political level and instead makes them look for religious solutions, finding that an Islamic lifestyle is the solution to many problems. These problems might be seen as society's own, like for instance the predominant moral standard, or as the difficulties of young Muslims in that society, both of which are understood as the lack of guidance such that Islam could provide. Hence, the solution must be passed on, resulting in the respondent's proselytising attitude. Among the negative experiences with society are media reports, personal interaction with media representatives, as well as a lack of media support, feelings of discrimination, but also an excess of liberty, temptations and laissez-faireism. Many respondents do report positive personal relationships with non-Muslims or non-practising Muslims, but since the issues are interpreted as structural and overarching, they believe there is much preaching to do on a broad level.

Altogether, the fourth type puts forward a religious aim as the central motif. The eight participants of the fourth type believe that their target groups would benefit greatly from leading a more Islamic life. This results partly from their own experience, but also from their critical perception of society. Unlike Type 2, where the negative view worked as an incentive for improvement on a social or political level, the fourth type looks for a religious solution and the dissemination thereof – a proselytising mission.

The target group is an interesting feature, because there is an important difference between those targeting non-Muslims and others targeting young people, who are born Muslim, but do not practise. Both are represented in this type, as all of them offer Islam as the solution to any problems. Yet, it is important to note the difference in target groups, since the ones who have non-Muslims in mind propose a very literal understanding of the religious scripts, and allude to a superiority of Islam over other faiths and convictions. Those who target young Muslims do so more in order to provide life support, for example, to young Muslims involved in street crime. With religion placed at the centre of the activity, the message becomes more important than the medium, which may in some cases even be replaceable. Unlike the majority of interviewees, the ones corresponding to this type are more religiously than subculturally motivated in their activity.

As with the two prototypes Ridvan and Jabir, there is a strong expression of cultural pessimism in most of the interviews. Moral values are seen as being under threat by the liberal laissez-faire attitudes in large parts of society, and while these no longer exist today, they have in the past – but also in other cultural systems, at which point Islam is referenced. For example, Ali criticises the fact that German families no longer care for their elders as they used to do, instead "deporting" them to homes for the aged; in the Islamic world the elderly are still revered and cherished. Many of these interviews centre on values, giving the impression that values matter more for these participants than for others. Yet, that is not quite true; like most people, all interviewees in the sample have a value system in which they believe, whereas the ones corresponding to this type are keen to emphasise it much more and to establish a lack of values in their target groups in order to indicate a need. At the same time, many respondents are aware that some of their statements could be perceived as extreme, and are – like Ridvan – keen to point to more extremist views for contrast.

Strikingly, all participants of this type are male. Aside from former street gang membership, which accounts for a male dominance, it seems more likely for men to proselytise. Half of them are musicians, others are mainly in fashion, but hardly anyone overemphasises their genre. The distribution of nationality stands out once more, with more than half of the participants being German, then French, and one British exception. Again, this accounts for the critical view of society, but may also be related to the proselytising motif. Otherwise, there is a mix of Arab, Bosnian and African backgrounds. The majority was educated continuously in Islam, while – perhaps counter-intuitively – only three converted or reverted, so this does not serve as an explanation for an increased urge to pass a conversion experience on to others.

The name of this type highlights the proselytising aim of this group's religious motif. Although many other interviewees have a similar desire to pass on a message, it is much more pronounced with this type. The label "Proselytisers" is certainly somewhat sketchy, as it does not make a distinction between the two subgroups, one of which targets young non-practising Muslims and the other one society at large. Also, the proselytising element must be kept in mind as the search for a religious solution to problems resulting from negative experiences in society and a critical perspective towards it. While some respondents of other types are also inclined to inform about and spread their religion, they subscribe to different aims and approaches from the interviewees of this type; hence, this short name concentrates on what is less conspicuous with the other types.

C. CONCLUSION: PATTERNS OF A MUSLIM-EUROPEAN CULTURE

There are many characteristics that producers of Islamic youth culture have in common because they are held together by contributing to a very specific sub-culture. With other traits, however, the interviewees differ strongly and have very individual opinions, but they do form distinguished clusters, depending on the perspective and questions applied from the outside. In this chapter, I have presented a typology of motivations, taking into account the most significant characteristics of the question of why someone would engage in producing Islamic youth culture. Focusing the interview analysis on the respondents' central motifs, target groups, understanding of Islamic youth culture and perception of society led to four different types: The Campaigners are the most outgoing and try to make a statement on socio-political issues from a Muslim perspective. The Improvers turn a critical perception of society into an incentive for social engagement and improvement. Starting from a more positive point of origin again, the Empowerers help young Muslims develop a positive Muslim-European identity, and finally, the Proselytisers make a religious offer to anyone struggling with other existent value systems in society.

These results show that there are four broad answers to the problem of why Islamic youth culture is created, each of which consist of many facets. Both individual and contextual aspects play a significant role – the influences of the producers' biographies, of subculture, religion and society on their activities are therefore manifold and closely connected to the context of the European home country, as the presentation of data in this chapter has demonstrated in detail. In an attempt not only to present the rich data from the interviews, but also to reduce their complexity at the same time, I have developed this typology that structures the data and pinpoints the most important features, while maintaining the dynamics of the participants' accounts. It also permits drawing some general conclusions on the entire sample and possibly on similar cases beyond it.

Unexpectedly, individual experience with Islam – whether a person converted, reverted, or was brought up religiously – did not have a significant influence on their motivation, neither in terms of central motif or target group, nor with regard to their view of society. It was therefore not included in the main categories that shaped the types, but was instead added to the description at the end. Nationality appeared to be more a meaningful factor, while ethnic background again played a more marginal role. In order to explore this in more depth, it will be beneficial to interpret these findings in the light of related studies. In the following chapter I will therefore discuss how the types established in this chapter and the previous findings tie in with the wider literature and what conclusions can be drawn for the phenomenon itself and for further research in this field and beyond.

VI. Beyond the Findings

A. A CONSERVATIVE AVANT-GARDE

The ethnographic expedition into Islamic youth culture has given insights into the nature of this phenomenon and revealed its many characteristics in detail. While it provides an answer to some of the initial research questions, it does not yet sufficiently shed light on the reasons and the context on a more general level, and thus the findings need to be evaluated and interpreted in the light of the literature. In turn, this also helps to evaluate the relevance of the theories. The aim of this chapter is therefore an overall discussion of the phenomenon of Islamic youth culture in Europe, which first entails clarifying any questions that remain from the empirical investigation, how it connects to the theory and what further implications the findings have. Then, this chapter will link back to the theory and discuss how the empirical results support, extend or amend the theories outlined in Chapter II, and what can be learned from this research for the study of similar cultural phenomena.

Islamic youth culture has emerged as a cultural practice of young, religious, European Muslims to express and live their faith in subcultural ways. A strong commitment to piety and religious permissibility is cherished alongside fun and entertainment. Islamic concepts continue to recur in subcultural expressions from the performing arts, fashion and media across Germany, France and the UK. The subcultural artefacts require a relatively high degree of religious identification and thus appeal mainly to those who identify primarily as Muslim. The artefacts also form part of a wider set of activities, often set up by youth organisations like youth camps, or religious festivals for all generations, and keep within firm moral boundaries. Despite a high degree of diversity and not necessarily subscribing to a larger movement, many traits are shared across the participants of Islamic youth culture. This includes recurring notions from the Islamic and the subcultural realm, presenting Islam in a cool and unexpected way and in a juvenile language. Producers and consumers also share a set of ideas, which is revealed by the emphasis placed on the message of a subcultural artefact – a song, a piece of fashion – and by the returning theme of the *halal*, of what is religiously permissible. A separate look at the producers, furthermore, helped to identify the aims connected to the provision of Islamic youth cultural artefacts. The presented typology demonstrates four different approaches to becoming active in Islamic youth culture: campaigning, improving, empowering and prose-lytising, all of which possess further characteristics and reveal a certain percep-tion of society.

A Hybrid Creation

Islamic youth culture is a hybrid form, made up of elements from three different spheres – the subcultural, the Islamic and the European national contexts. While at first sight it looked as if the subcultural sphere was providing the form and Islam was contributing the substance, this simple binary form had to be revised based on the ethnographic findings. The form is more than the outer neutral shell of rap or pop music, a youth magazine, a social network, a comedy show or a street wear outfit. It also carries values and histories, and thus substantive mean-ings (Therborn 2011), including, in the case of hip-hop for instance, an aspect of voicing social injustice, but also sexuality and violence, or, in the case of social networks, notions of exchange, participation and the dissemination of different opinions. Furthermore, as the findings from the participant observation suggest, the form does not only refer to a subcultural genre, but also relates to a style and a set of actions that are used to display and live out the youth culture, and doing so is again a substantive choice. For instance, part of the idea is promoting a good school education, claiming generation-specific spaces and being, in parts, a little rebellious. The substance is once more determined by a Western experience as it reflects the attitudes of Muslims living in the West, a circumstance that in-evitably has lead to different Islamic practices or at least tells of particular social conditions they face and thus address in the subculture. The Islamic contribution, therefore, influences much of the substantial content – a variety of theological beliefs and spirituality that also inform ideas about community, conduct and morality – but not all of it. The form also carries Islamic traits, with the incorpo-ration of Arabic phrases, traditional designs, calligraphy; in one case a rapper even argued that rap was poetry, which resembled that of poets around the Prophet Mohammed writing favourable texts about Islam. Hebdige's concept of "bricolage" aptly describes the practice as applied to the artefacts; known objects are stripped of their context and provided with a new meaning (Hebdige 1993) – here, sports labels and other symbols used in Islamic fashion could be thought of in this way. This practice certainly involves more than a bit of "handicraft" or *bricolage*, as the attachment of a new meaning has further aims and implications that are perhaps more intriguing than the process of manufacturing a piece of style.

Hybridity, therefore, well describes the process of borrowing and exchanging from different cultures – if the subtleties are taken into account. More than just combining a religion with subculture, several different traits are taken from both, while others are rejected, and are then put together to form a new culture. In the early twenty-first century, it is still young, but with time and if it can become established, the hybrid nature of the subculture will no longer be perceived; this also constitutes a process of "normalisation" of young Muslims in Europe. It is important to acknowledge the intentionality connected with it (Werbner 1997). As it is not the most obvious combination – because youth culture has no "need" of religion, and Islam has no need of an affinity to youth culture – they are intentionally combined rather than flowing together because they appear in very similar settings or are consumed on the same occasions by the same people. Where two languages are spoken by the same people in the same place, it is very likely that the languages will start mixing. Here, the mixture was less probable at first. That Islamic youth culture is indeed driven by a high degree of intentionality has been revealed in detail by the typology of motivations, which has shown that the choice of creating a hybrid youth culture has four major sets of intentions. The case of Islamic youth culture, therefore, supports an understanding of hybridity as an intentional blending of cultures, and this concept has informed the search for the idea behind the movement.

What facilitates the hybrid combination is a practice that has been observed with many young Muslims in Europe, that is the disentangling of religion and culture (Tietze 2001; Roy 2006). This allows for religious principles of a "pure" Islam to be adopted and traditions and unjust behaviour to be rejected by attributing them to culture, while keeping the (sub)culture one grew up in: German, French or British. One example is the rejection of misogynist behaviour or so-called honour killings on the basis that they can merely be justified on cultural grounds, but not at all with Islam (in some cases this carries a slightly apologetic tone, since the distinct gender roles in Islam at least would have to be questioned in this context). In the case of converts, a culture such as the Caribbean one is often retained and combined with the religion of Islam, but not with the culture of any Islamic country. This practice became apparent in many instances during the field research and is also significant for most of the members of all types.

The Role of the European Home Country

The hybridity concept ties in with the relationship of the local and the global, because the motivations of the producers have revealed a strong connection to local situations in their adoption of globally flowing cultures. Not only could Islamic youth culture be regarded as a local (urban Western European) variety of Islamic practice, but within this youth culture there are also differences between countries. One striking finding of the typology was that the British respondents appeared to have a much more positive view of society than their French and German counterparts. Studies on the attitudes of British, French and German Muslims on their European home country support this impression to some extent. Penn and Lambert show that British Muslim teenagers tend to be less radical, are more successful at school and face less discrimination than their peers in France and Germany (Penn/Lambert 2009), which is likely to result in a more positive assessment of their surroundings. The Gallup Coexist Index 2009 looks at Muslim integration in these countries in more detail (Gallup 2009); investigating the correlation of religiosity and national identity, the study finds that both are high with European Muslims: 52% of French Muslims, 40% of German Muslims and as many as 77% of British Muslims identify "very strongly" or "extremely strongly" with their country. In fact, in some cases country identity is even higher among Muslims than among the general public – 8% higher in Germany and 27% higher in the UK (ibid.: 19). Other survey questions indicate that European Muslims show a similarly high confidence in institutions as the general public, for instance, German Muslims expressing a particularly high level of confidence in the judicial system and the national government (again higher than the general public), but very little confidence in the media. Indeed, the media were mentioned during the interviews as a source of frustration, especially among the German producers of Islamic youth culture, as they are thought to both represent and influence the (widely negative) public opinion of Islam.[1]

A 2006 survey by the Pew Global Attitudes Project also found that Germans expressed a much more negative view of Muslims than people in France and the UK, where the majority held positive opinions (Pew Research Centre 2006). That the situation of Muslims in Europe is a delicate one was once more revealed by a study conducted on behalf of the Friedrich-Ebert-Stiftung (Zick et al. 2011). Finding strong Islamophobic tendencies in many European countries, the survey shows that Germans particularly strongly disagree with the statement that

---

1   On the other hand, the Gallup survey also found that while European Muslims are generally suffering more than the general public in terms of satisfaction with their lives and future expectations, German Muslims appeared more thriving than the general public (ibid.: 25–27).

Muslim culture fits into the country well (83%, as opposed to 61% in the UK and 50% in France). Around 45% of German and British respondents agree that there are too many Muslims in their countries, with 36% in France (ibid.: 60–63, 171–172). The differences among France, Britain and Germany vary between survey and for different questions, and the French case is perhaps the least clear, but the compilers of the Gallup Coexist Index come to the conclusion that "British Muslims are more likely than all populations surveyed to identify strongly with their nation, and to express stronger confidence in its democratic institutions while maintaining a high degree of religious identity" (Gallup 2009: 24). It is therefore not surprising that most British participants among the sample are concentrated in the two types that express a very positive view of the society they live in, and that some of them were involved in the "Proud to be British" campaign by British Muslims.

Surveys like these certainly do not make a statement about how Muslims then *deal* with their either positive or negative view of society – and society's view of them – and what that prompts them to do. My typology goes beyond a mere expression of attitudes, because it highlights different approaches to activism. Research on Muslims in Western societies often focuses on political participation in elections or parties, or on Muslim organisations, but hardly ever on other forms of social commitment or volunteering. The typology shows that Islamic youth culture is also, among other things, a form of social commitment that is in many ways concerned with the relationship between Muslims and non-Muslims: The Campaigners are spreading a positive message, also about Islam, to wider society in order to promote the idea of diversity and of living together in a pluralist society. The Improvers tackle stereotypes of non-Muslims and Muslims' feeling of self-consciousness, while the Empowerers convey their positivity to young Muslims to increase their participation and activeness. The Proselytisers point to a different solution, but in the case of targeting young Muslims at least, this is done to try to keep them away from a potentially criminal path; in the case of targeting non-Muslims, this is more a matter of playing two value systems off against each other. For all types it cannot be denied that the producers spend much energy on locating themselves and Islam in society.

Further country differences include the fact that Islamic youth culture is much more visible, present and available in the UK, but much less so in Germany and in France in particular. The primary explanations seem to be the respective migration histories and models of integration in the three countries. Because a substantial Muslim population has been around in the UK since 1948, British-born Muslim youths have started earlier to experiment with culture than their French and German counterparts – the first examples emerged in the UK in the

1990s, at least a decade earlier than in the other two countries. On top of that, the British model of integration favours a pluralist and multicultural society in which immigrants and their children are encouraged to maintain their cultural and religious identities while engaging in society. Despite recent denials of multiculturalism by the Conservative Party,[2] the model has been very influential and marked in Britain, especially in comparison to other countries. The French assimilationist model also allows for full participation and French citizenship, but demands cultural assimilation to a large extent; the strong *laïcité* is certainly less tolerant of religion being celebrated in the public sphere than is the case in other countries. The German model has for decades been the least open to granting immigrants citizenship rights, discouraging them to participate visibly in society. The difference in the integration models appears to be one factor that affects both the development and visibility of Islamic youth culture and the producers' attitudes towards society at large.

A Diversity of Backgrounds

A striking observation among the producers' backgrounds is the low number of South Asians in the British and Turks in the German sample. The migratory backgrounds in the whole sample are diverse, with slightly over a third accounted for by people of Arab background, just under a third by people of Caribbean, African or other black and non-Islamic backgrounds, and the rest by other Muslims from various countries, including only two or three each from Pakistan, Turkey and Bosnia. The German producers are the most diverse, while a North African background dominates in France and a black heritage in Britain. Compared with the statistical distribution of these groups among the Muslim population of each country, this implies that Islamic youth culture is not necessarily produced by "mainstream" Muslims – one would expect people of Turkish background in Germany, indeed of North African, but also black West African heritage in France, and Pakistani or Bangladeshi origin in Britain. Two explanations might account for this. One has to do with ethnicity-based subcultural preferences and religiosity, the other with conversion biographies. Both deal with the fact that the producers of Islamic youth culture are a rather specific group, differing from the ethnic distribution within one country and among France, Britain and Germany.

The first explanation, regarding subcultural preferences, is connected to multiple identifications. Not all religious Muslims would engage in subculture, but it does require a high degree of religiosity, for instance, to produce lyrics entirely

---

2   See the speech by the British Prime Minister on Islamic radicalisation in February 2011: http://www.number10.gov.uk/news/pms-speech-at-munich-security-conference.

centred on Islam. Someone of Muslim background who chooses a subcultural career may do so to express part of his or her identity, an identity that could emphasise the ethnic or the religious background or any other trait. It is not self-evident that Muslimness is placed higher than any other of one's identities. To illustrate this for the case of young Turkish Germans, a person might choose to be identified primarily as Turkish and engage in Turkish-German hip-hop, *or* as Muslim, and perform Islamic music. As the Bertelsmann Religion Monitor suggests, around 40% of German Muslims consider themselves highly religious (Bertelsmann Stiftung 2008: 45), while another study has found that around 14% of German Turks identify themselves as being highly religious; another 53% would still classify themselves as religious, but do not give religion the highest importance (Zentrum für Türkeistudien 2009: 61). While such surveys of self-attribution always face methodological difficulties, there is a tendency that indicates a slightly lower religiosity of Turks (with possibly a higher identification with Turkishness or anything else), so that more Muslims of other backgrounds would account for the highly religious.

Those who do engage in this sector place a higher emphasis on religion than on culture. This makes the youth culture attractive for others who have the same priorities, instead of providing a predominantly Turkish or Pakistani cultural space. Corresponding to the producers, the audience of a performance may not be looking for a national or ethnicity-based gathering, but an *ummah*-based one. It therefore stands to reason that Islamic youth culture does reflect a statistical distribution – indeed not that of migrational background, but one of religiosity.

The second explanation of why the producers' ethnic background differs from what would be expected is linked to conversion. Many of the artists in Islamic youth culture have converted to Islam and therefore bring a variety of backgrounds with them. However, that only shifts the question to why converts are so dominant in this context. One reason might be their previous career, especially in the music genre, where there are several converts. Musicians often stop performing when they convert, but resume soon after, albeit with a different spin. Converted producers of all genres had been active in their subcultural field before conversion and thus seem to have fewer reservations about engaging in it than other Muslims. Another reason is that converts are often very engaged in their new faith community and would like to communicate their newly acquired knowledge, consciousness and also their own conversion experience, to other Muslims and to non-Muslims, for which Islamic youth culture offers a stage.

An important case in point in this context is that nearly all converts in this sample come from a black ethnic background, and most are in the UK. Reasons for the conversion of black people to Islam are as complex as with any other conversion, but some answers have been supplied by Mattias Gardell's extensive treatment of the black Nation of Islam movement in the United States (Gardell 1996), Monika Wohlrab-Sahr's conversion typology, including Afro-American converts to Islam (Wohlrab-Sahr 1999) and Richard Reddie's investigation into black British converts to Islam (Reddie 2009).

In the dissemination of Nation of Islam beliefs, Gardell draws an important connection to hip-hop. He assumes this musical genre to have "populari[sed] the message of black militant Islam" and equates hip-hop to reggae in that the latter spread Rastafarianism in the 1970s in the same way that hip-hop expanded black Islam in the 1980s and 1990s (Gardell 1996: 295). Identifying rap as the genre with the largest political influence in the 1990s, Gardell reveals how rap lyrics very often, though implicitly, make allusions to teachings of the Nation of Islam (ibid.: 294–296).

For the British context, Reddie partly attributes the reasons for conversion among young blacks to the formation of "Nation of Islam (UK)" in the 1990s, including the influence of Malcolm X's autobiographical book and film (Reddie 2009: 152–153). He also acknowledges the significant role played by hip-hop, with popular black US rappers converting to Islam, the impact of which multiplied through the understanding of hip-hop as a holistic way of life and the use of the lyrics to spread a message or to "educate and to indoctrinate", although he does not limit this to Nation of Islam ideas, but refers to any black Muslim beliefs (ibid.: 212, also 195–196, 206–212). Like Gardell, he draws a parallel with the Rastafarian movement, not emphasising the music, but the countercultural aspect: "There are clear resemblances between the subversive approach of the Rasta movement in Britain during its heyday and the current countercultural positioning of Islam" (ibid.: 8). In a similar way, this "subversive approach" is supported by Wohlrab-Sahr's third type of convert, whom she characterises as a symbolic emigrant or symbolic fighter. Consciously or not, the converts of this type take part in the historic polarisation of the Western versus the Islamic world and think of Islam as an imaginary principle contrasting with their own problematic situation (Wohlrab-Sahr 1999: 350–354). As also Mandaville underlines (Mandaville 2009a: 166), the geopolitical situation favours identification with Islam as the religion of the "oppressed", and while this appeals to many (young) people, it may play a stronger role in contexts where black consciousness and reflection on black history are evoked.

What Kind of Youth Culture?

The phenomenon in question is partly a form of social involvement and even a devotional practice, but it is also clearly a youth culture. It can be problematic to look at a very expressive, outgoing youth culture and to draw conclusions from it about the majority of young Muslims in Europe, as has been criticised in the case of some subcultural research (G. Clarke 1990). However, I do believe that it is possible to locate the phenomenon in a larger context and to regard it as typical of the relations of at least some young Muslims and society. Also, an exceptional form – such as a youth culture – can be an only slightly exaggerated way of expressing a situation, which is also experienced, but not communicated, by many other young people. The way Islamic youth culture was integrated into different settings, like festivals and organisations, shows that it has an influence beyond its immediate followers.

As a youth culture, it has developed its own style, expresses a distinct set of ideas and takes on several forms of action. This raises further questions about who initiates this. I have chosen to distinguish between consumers and producers to emphasise the latter's role as the key figures of action, which begs the question of whether this youth culture is a top–down or a bottom–up movement, at least where Islamic youth culture is targeted at young Muslims rather than wider society. It could be argued that some producers preconceive an identity they want the young people to adopt, but it could also be the case that they pick up on an already existing trend, make it more visible and spread it further. Or that it is an offer that appeals to those young Muslims who are looking to combine their faith and European youth culture and who adopt the idea, usurp and develop it further, until it becomes a "chicken or egg" issue of whether the idea was there first or whether it was put forward because it reflected an existing state. Also, the "producers" are a special case in this respect. Contrary to some of the subcultural research that found consumers to change and finish an industrial product of pop culture (Chambers 1985), the producers here are located on a meso-level between commercialised youth culture and the final consumption: producers of Islamic youth culture use and modify industrial products like sports labels, give them an Islamic touch and transform them into something new for their consumers, for young Muslims. This makes them part of the whole movement. For example, if performing artists choose to ban anything *haram* from their songs and sketches, this is not just done to please the customers, but it is also the only way that the artists themselves want to perform. On the other hand, the Empowerers are guiding young Muslims towards something they have identified to be beneficial to them, which in fact the Proselytisers do as well. It could therefore be said that both approaches are part of Islamic youth culture, but that the bottom–up element is stronger, not least because the producers are part of the scene rather than outside of it. Standing outside the scene would involve a completely different approach; one could imagine such an approach to be taken by influential actors from abroad, or by imams, who do not really subscribe to youth culture themselves, but who make use of its benefits. Neither is the case here – Islamic youth culture is clearly produced by people who have been relating to the same issues as their target groups for an extended period of time, usually in their own youth. I therefore cannot verify Gerlach's thesis that Egyptian televangelist Amr Khaled is responsible for the movement in Europe (Gerlach 2006), not even to a minor extent. Neither was there any evidence for Boubekeur's impression that economic interests drive Islamic youth culture (Boubekeur 2005); instead, a wide range of other explanations have been found.

It is unusual for a youth culture to be more conservative in moral terms than most of their peers or wider society. But this does not mean that it is not a youth culture, because youth cultures are neither defined by a particular ideology, nor by being particularly provocative, rebellious or against social (or moral) norms. Of course, there is an element of this in many familiar youth cultures, since part of their ideology is to be a counterculture against a perceived mainstream norm, but this is not an essential feature. Second, some of Islamic youth culture's innovative claims challenge other mainstream views, those of both elderly Muslims and wider society. It is novel in the way that it challenges traditional forms of living and teaching Islam, which the elder migrants may not approve of, and at the same time it extends the boundaries of popular art forms into the religious realm, something that secular society is less used to.

At the same time, Islamic youth culture is morally conservative; gender-segregated events or sex-free lyrics and comedy are just a few examples. I would attribute this to the way Islam is currently interpreted and practised, especially in Europe. The Gallup Coexist Index found moral conservatism to be the most significant area, in fact the only area in which European Muslims' opinion diverged from that of the general public (Gallup 2009: 30–35). For instance, the question whether sex between an unmarried couple was morally acceptable was answered largely positively by the general public (France 90%, Germany 88%, UK 82%) in contrast to Muslims in these countries (French Muslims 48%, German Muslims 27%, British Muslims 3%); similarly for the issue of homosexual acts (France 78%, Germany 68%, UK 58% versus French Muslims 35%, German Muslims 19%, British Muslims 0%). The poll also shows quite significant differences among opinions on all sides in the three countries, which are far from being unified on further questions on other moral issues, and that the tendencies of Muslim opinions seem to be at least slightly influenced by the views of the general public in the respective societies; but the contrast is still much greater. The authors therefore support the results of a study on the ostensible "clashes" between people in Islamic countries and the West that found any diverging values to be more a matter of "eros than demos", emphasising that there is a wide-spread consensus on democracy and governance, but a strong disagreement about issues of sexuality and gender between European Muslims and the general public in their countries (Inglehart/Norris 2003: 65; Gallup 2009: 30). The findings on Islamic youth culture support these assumptions, as there is also a strong sense of morality paired with a significant affirmation of common social and political values among its participants. In fact, perhaps a conservative practice is particularly enforced in this context in order to maintain religious legitimacy, because youth culture is otherwise often associated with an adolescent interest in sexuality and flirtation.

Because of its innovative and at the same time conventional nature, I would conceptualise the movement of Islamic youth culture as "conservative avant-garde". It has traits of both conservative ideology and vanguard ideas, which makes it a blend less obviously classified as a particular political, social or religious current. The term, however, although capturing much of the movement's character, is perilous: it is much too easily understood as the usual and over-used dichotomy of "Islam = conservative" versus "Western = modern". This is not meant here. Islamic youth culture does indeed follow a conservative morale, which is informed by a wide-spread interpretation of Islam. But Islam also informs this youth culture in many other ways, not least through an emphasis on education and social commitment, along with concepts of religious practice and spirituality. The vanguard or novel ideas emerge not only from the youth cultural practises, but also from living Islam in Europe; avant-garde is meant to denote the spirit of trying out new directions, not referring strictly to the artistic sense of the word. As it is not the case that Islam contributes only the substance to a form that is purely Western, this youth culture is not just "Pop plus Islam". The same is true for the conservative avant-garde, which is influenced by the contradictory, or perhaps hybrid nature of this connection on many levels.

Wensierski's concept of the "selectively modern" may be a useful concept for clarification (Wensierski 2007). The participants in Islamic youth culture may be liberal and youth-focussed about some issues, but morally stricter about others; this is what Wensierski refers to as an individually crafted biography whereby young Muslims carefully select and adopt features of their Western surroundings and others from their Islamic background. Indeed, the commitment to Islamic youth culture is also an active process of making choices and of selecting what is considered compatible with one's religious stance. Yet such a concept of liberal versus anti-modern characteristics bears the danger of a judgemental dichotomy. With the term "conservative avant-garde" I do not seek to imply a judgement, of the sort that a conservative Islam is "saved" or enhanced by the West – any assessment, if at all needed, lies in the eyes of the be-holder, or rather in his or her preferred political and world view. Instead, I would like to highlight with this term the simultaneous occurrence of conservative and innovative traits and the seeming contradiction to point to a deliberate and active choice that has the ability to puzzle Muslims, non-Muslims and participants in other subcultures. Islamic youth culture reflects the Islamic interpretations prevalent at this time in Western Europe, including black British Muslim thought and conservative orthodox teachings, but it also contributes to new perspectives and practices.

"Euro-Islam"

In the findings of this study, there have been several answers to the question of why Islamic youth culture emerges, as especially explained by the typology. It is worth asking further why it appears at this point in time and in this place, and thus to extend into the context of European Islam. Some interviewees have re-jected the idea of calling their way of practicing religion "Pop Islam", and in-stead insisted that it was a matter of interpreting Islam according to the *Zeitgeist*, adjusting it to the time and place in which one lives; for them, this also under-lined the modernity of Islam. It is rather apposite, but also tries to present this practice as normal and unspecific, instead of focusing on its intriguing specifici-ties and wider consequences. One such consequence regards the understanding of youth culture, which becomes part of religious transmission. As several au-thors have emphasised for the case of Christianity, families and religious institu-tions no longer succeed in religious transmission (Collins-Mayo/Dandelion 2010). In the case of European Muslims, this may be because some parents are less religious than their children (Cesari 1998b; Khosrokhavar 1998) or that they and the imams hold on to traditional forms of Islam and of teaching, which are refused by the younger generation (Lewis 1994; Mandaville 2003). The produc-ers of Islamic youth culture take over a mediating role between the two – and with them youth culture itself. Not many youth cultures have a strong affiliation with religion; it is more common to find largely hedonistic or political ones. But all of them have an idea, fairly strongly felt and expressed, and this idea can be informed by religion, as laid out in Chapter IV. The fusion of youth culture and religion differs, however, from the concept presented by Collins-Mayo and Beaudoin, because Islamic youth culture is not produced by mosques, imams or any other institution like the Church, and nor are the youth cultural artefacts a parody of religious symbols, underlining an ambiguous relationship with religion as in Beaudoin's "virtual faith" (Beaudoin 1998). Some, like the T-shirt slogans or the comedy may play with puns and jokes, yet this humorous approach never ridicules, but rather tells of a straightforward, highly affirmative relationship with Islam.

The more significant consequence of the development of Islamic youth culture in Europe is that it has contributed to a concept of youth in Islam. It is the outcome of Muslims having permanently settled in Europe and therefore unsurprisingly having adopted Western traits, of which a Euro-American youth culture is only one aspect. Over the centuries, this happened in many places where Islam had spread, and led to local variations in Islamic practice – in early twenty-first century Europe, this is now the incorporation of a distinct youth sphere within the religion, including youth-specific forms of religious artefacts, expressions, dissemination, teaching styles and languages. Islamic youth culture recognises the life period between childhood and adulthood as having a particular meaning for the religious person. This has rather significant theological implications. The decision by Muslim European scholars to think of Europe as the *dar al-ahd*, the territory of agreement where Muslims can live in peace in a non-Muslim environment, was already a step towards locating Islam in Europe, encouraging engagement with wider society, but also, as Mandaville (2003) has pointed out, a move by the younger generation towards individual choice and interpretation of religious sources. Islamic youth culture has contributed to this by providing a concrete manifestation of the concept and taken it further by making it available on a broader basis through a popular form. It may not even make an explicit reference to the *dar al-ahd* concept, but it is an expression of the fact that this idea has become reality and is lived out, particularly by young Muslims. The internal Islamic debates that are fought around the issues of music and art illustrate the way solutions are found in diverging interpretations and confidently stated, for instance by musicians, against the mainstream opinion of current Islamic scholarship. In fact, there is no reason why this should not be possible in the field of gender roles, sexuality and morality as well, but at the moment this does not seem to be the case within the movement.

The findings, furthermore, support Lübcke's impression that Islamic youth culture is mainly practised by well-educated young Muslims of both sexes (Lübcke 2007), and I admit that it may not resonate with all Muslims. However, the striving and active young people are likely to make their voices heard and play a role in society, which is why their current activities and opinions are particularly insightful.

It cannot be claimed that Islamic youth culture is free from reactions to the geopolitical situation – it is certainly concerned with a collective response to securitisation policies, radicalisation and stereotyping after the 9/11 and 7/7 attacks. In that way, the assumptions of subcultural theory, as suggested in CCCS research, are still valid, though in a very different context: reacting to structural changes in society is at least part of the answer to why the movement is happening at this time and in this place. It is also a location of self for young Muslims in Europe. This identification process includes controlling again the practice of being placed into categories by others – what Tarlo (2010) referred to as a process of managing the heightened visibility after 9/11. One means of doing this is making oneself particularly visible through fashion and showing one's pride in being Muslim; another method is meeting tensions with comic relief – a slogan, a witty song or through comedy itself.

The formation of a European Islam thus has a lot of potential for diversity within Islam and also for the relationship with non-Muslims. Just as the reasons for the emergence of Islamic youth culture are linked to the context in which it takes place, the movement has social and political implications for society as a whole. The participants of Type 1 for instance, the Campaigners, supply a Muslim point of view on socio-political issues, while maintaining a positive attitude towards society. In this way, they contribute to a diversity of opinion and remind wider society of representation and pluralism. The Improvers provoke a dialogue with the aim of enhancing negative relations between Muslims and non-Muslims. The Empowerers, with their focus on helping and empowering young Muslims, also do so in relation to wider society, as it would not be nearly as necessary outside the non-Muslim environment. Their support makes young people participate by acting in a self-determined way and by feeling at ease with their identification as German, French or British Muslims. Those of the Proselytisers who target young Muslims do so with the intention of preventing them from being led into drugs and street crime, with the help of religion, in order to live a "decent" life within society, instead of on the edge. Activities around Islamic youth culture emphasise education, and the involvement in the community of a youth culture, the widely positive identification with the European home country, as well as the partly conservative, but not extremist interpretations, may contribute to a counterweight to Islamic extremism. Islamic youth culture must therefore also be understood as a vehicle of integration into the nations of Europe, a vehicle that is not provided by the French, British or German state, but developed by young Muslim Europeans.

All of this sounds very smooth. Yet Islamic youth culture does give rise to some controversial issues as well. Among the Proselytisers there are a few who suggest the superiority of Islam to other faiths and convictions, especially among those who target non-Muslims. The few interviewees of this subgroup expressed other extreme views in addition to their assumed superiority of Islam, like homophobic statements or a very literal understanding of the sources and gender behavioural norms set in stone. This is only a small subgroup, and proselytising is not problematic or unique as such, but there is at least a small opportunity here for extremist views to sneak into this youth culture, which is otherwise rather immune to extremists. Furthermore, there was a palpable frustration in many interviews, sometimes even among those who expressed a generally positive view of society, revealing a deep divide between many Muslims and non-Muslims, which is obviously not going to be solved by a bit of fun youth culture. Also, Islamic youth culture does not reach out to every young Muslim, and even if the movement is growing, the observer needs to be aware of its limitations.

B. ISLAMIC YOUTH CULTURE IN THE CONTEXT OF RESEARCH

The discussion of the phenomenon suggests that some theories have supported and furthered its understanding, while others were unable to do so, in which case the empirical study of Islamic youth culture may help to contribute to the theories and eventually the research into other, similar cultures.

Authors of the theoretical literature have provided insufficient tools for understanding and explaining the nature of cultural phenomena like Islamic youth culture, the reasons why they occur and the implications for both empirical and the theoretical aspects. In particular, the empirical study presented here makes contributions to youth cultural theories, for instance, in that the nature of a youth culture is not fully understood by mainly looking at the style as its most visible feature. Nor is it sufficient to just identify an idea or a few activities that tie a group of young people together, especially if the connection is loose as in the case of scenes and lifestyles. The concept of studying its style, idea and action has proven to be exceedingly apt, allowing for a comprehensive understanding of the nature of a youth culture. The involvement of both women and ethnic minorities, then, has not only been demonstrated, but also provides evidence of the fact that youth cultures today cannot be thought of *without* these groups and their contribution to creating and disseminating youth cultures. Any subcultural theory, where the practice of cultural fusion or the role of young women is widely ignored, is no longer an appropriate analytical instrument. Furthermore, the investigation of Islamic youth culture has amended the concept of industry–consumer relationships. It is not always simply the case that the consumers as participants in a youth culture finish an industrial product to use it for their own purpose. Instead, if, as in the present case, a meso-level of producers emerges, the relationship becomes more complex, as the participants of a youth culture have to be distinguished as producers and consumers, with different roles and levels of activity, in order to grasp what is being negotiated through the youth culture and how this is done.

In the search for the origins of and reasons for youth culture, subcultural theory has almost exclusively mentioned class. The concept of class has always been and will most likely continue to be one of the essential sociological keys in the profound study of culture, even though the classical Birmingham School of the CCCS may have had too narrow a focus on this notion. In the context of this research, the focus is not primarily on class, nor is it more specifically on the working class, but some of the findings raise the valid question to what extent Islamic youth culture in Europe is a phenomenon of middle class youth. This study cannot give a comprehensive answer, but the findings include many indications that the phenomenon may be primarily a middle class culture. This is indicated, for example, by a generally high level of education among the participants and an emphasis on education by youth organisations like the *Muslimische Jugend in Deutschland*, who conduct their meetings entirely in German, play knowledge quizzes with the young people as a pastime and encourage learning. Prices of Islamic street wear and concert tickets tend to be quite expensive, and participation in new media requires regular internet access. Also, a producer in a Manchester suburb found that the London rappers were far too sophisticated for the young, working class Muslims in his vicinity.

Apart from the class aspect, religion has proven to a large extent to be at the origin of this youth culture, and therefore needs to be considered within youth cultural theory. Another such origin consists of global cultural flows, which must be taken into account by theories on youth culture. From the perspective of the sociology of religion, there has not been an adequate response clarifying the reasons for religion's affiliation with youth culture, at least in the case of Islam. Instead, a number of reasons have emerged to serve as a link between religion and subculture, for instance, hybrid cultural encounters: both Islam and youth culture have become globalised and are travelling to different places. Another link is religious transmission, not from an institution above, but from the young people within the religious community. Identification processes also play a role, when young Muslims, for example, escape the categories used to describe them, and regain control of these ascriptions by taking Islamic interpretation and subcultural expression into their own hands.

Hybridity theories have explained several things about the process of how Islamic youth culture emerges, but often the concepts focus more on the *how* than on the *why* in this process, and therefore do not provide explanations why disparate frameworks such as Islam and youth culture should go together well.

The theories often propound power relations as the reason for hybrid creation – sometimes, it seems, before empirical research is undertaken. While this may be true in many instances and may even have some limited relevance to Islamic youth culture, this explanation is insufficient. Reasons are located both on a global level (both geopolitics of Muslims in the spotlight and global cultural flows), and on a local level regarding identification and the location of self. Here, the micro perspective on the key actors' motivations has revealed further answers; hence, the combination of hybridity theory with the reconstructive methodology, and the development of types has been fruitful in uncovering a detailed and systematic understanding of the reasons.

Not a theory as such, research on Islam in Europe has combined many fields of study and approaches for an exploration of this recent historic phenomenon, mainly resulting from migration. But among the countless studies, too little research has so far been conducted on Islamic youth culture in the three European countries with the largest Muslim minorities. Little is known in the literature about the details of its nature, about its participants and key figures, aims and approaches. This is why the choice of an ethnography was a rewarding methodology to be applied in this field of research. The field also profits from the other theories; one theoretical amendment, for instance, stems from the fact that youth cultural theories have recognised "youth" as a meaningful category to describe a significant life phase. Supported by empirical evidence in a Muslim context, this will have to be taken into account for studies on Islam, in order to understand how Islam develops in non-Muslim settings and what the role played by young people – in contrast to that of scholars – is in the promotion of the religion. The phenomenon reveals that youth cultural theory *can* be transferred to Islam.

Despite the shortcomings of the theories in explaining Islamic youth culture entirely, each theory has contributed significantly to a more thorough understanding. As has been demonstrated throughout the discussion, the theories do overlap in many aspects. But although they complement each other, they have not been used in combination to explain an empirical phenomenon. For complex cultural phenomena, however, it is necessary to combine them in order not to miss some of the most important facets. Otherwise, in the case of Islamic youth culture, this would mean studying the phenomenon only as a youth culture, and thus missing out on the religious beliefs and practices, or as a religion, but failing to see the hybrid fusions between religion and culture, or as a reaction to circumstances in a non-Muslim environment, but ignoring global cultural encounters. The investigation of Islamic youth cultures presents a sound case study, using a combination of theories from youth culture, hybridity and research on Islam in Europe. Integrated with empirical research and a carefully chosen, multilayered methodology, this combined theoretical approach provides a rounded picture of the nature and origins of a culture, explains the process of how and the reasons why it emerges, as well as who is involved in it, and sheds light on the issues negotiated against the background of global and local contexts. Although Islamic youth culture is a rather particular phenomenon, its study allows for general concepts to be abstracted from it and to be transferred to other cultural occurrences of similar complexity.

VII. Conclusion

To recapitulate what has been laid out and discussed in detail in the preceding chapters, I will use the conclusion to extract five main theses gained from the findings. The research into Islamic youth culture has uncovered a plethora of details and characteristics, but the following summaries will call to mind the most significant outcomes. I will finish with an outlook on potential research directions that could start from the point where this research ends.

A Hybrid Mix

Three different spheres fuse into Islamic youth culture: global youth culture, Islam and the cultural and political contexts of France, Britain and Germany. Not all of these in their entirety, but only elements of each, are combined. The makers of Islamic youth culture place every element under scrutiny to decide which will be adopted, adapted or rejected. What they adopt from a Western, globalised youth culture are forms of rap, clothing style, stand-up comedy, new and conventional media products and the corresponding substantive notions, for example "coolness", lightness, youthfulness; some forms also carry notions of social criticism, the urge to disseminate a message, but also superficiality. As a religion, Islam contributes to this youth culture first of all a strong religiosity, and then a range of beliefs and practices, some of which are particularly prevalent, including a sense of community or the principle of the *halal* and *haram* (even though the dividing line between the two can sometimes be negotiated). Islamic youth culture, then, also adopts many features from the European country in which it is set, such as the language, methods of teaching and learning, experiences of living in a non-Muslim place and local youth cultural traits.

The process of selecting and combining these elements is part of the hybrid blend that constitutes Islamic youth culture. Together, the dissimilar features form artefacts of music and comedy, fashion and media, such as Ammar114's lyrics dedicated to Allah, Samia's headscarf puns, Elenany's minaret coat or the

Waymo youth platform offering a space for the exchange of young, German Muslim culture. The artefacts are consumed in a variety of settings, including Islamic festivals and youth camps, where an extensive youth culture develops. As is often the case with hybrid creations, it is an intentional mix, because several aims and motivations are connected with it. It is therefore much more than just an end in itself, which the usually hedonistic character of youth cultures might wrongly suggest. The remaining theses capture these wider implications.

Four Different Types of Motivations

In my study, I have focussed specifically on the producers of Islamic youth culture – on music acts, fashion designers, media producers etc. Conducting in-depth qualitative interviews has revealed patterns of the producers' aims, motivations and attitudes, which paints a diverse picture of the reasons why people engage in this youth culture. The most insightful categories were the central motif (a major recurring theme in the interview), the target group (Muslims or non-Muslims), the producers' understanding of Islamic youth culture (more religiously or more subculturally concerned) and their perception of society (affirmative or critical).

This has resulted in distinguishing four different types among the producers. The first, which I have called the Campaigners, have a socio-political central motif, such as the representation of Muslims in society or peaceful coexistence. They are outwardly orientated, meaning that the messages they seek to convey via youth culture are mainly targeted at non-Muslims. Although they are no less religious than other participants, their concern with Islamic youth culture has a strong subcultural focus, as their activity is also very important to them as a genre. Finally, they stand out as having a very positive perception of society, based on positive feedback from non-Muslims and an appreciation of the tolerant environment – an impression that was particularly voiced by the British participants.

The participants of the second type, the Improvers, also share a socio-political motif. They are concerned with participation, finding one's place in society as a Muslim and creating a dialogue with non-Muslims. Their target group is mixed. Their genre is again very important to them and the message is closely connected to the medium they use, especially fashion design and comedy, thus their understanding of Islamic youth culture is more subculturally than purely religiously informed. What distinguishes them most from the first type is that they have a very critical perception of society and have become disenchanted with Muslim/non-Muslim relations in the past few years. However, this has not caused them to resign, but instead to become active and improve the situation through the subcultural artefacts they offer – food for thought in a T-shirt slogan or a thought-provoking comedy sketch.

The Empowerers share a social aim as their central motif, dealing with the identity and empowerment of young Muslims, who also comprise their target group. They seek to encourage young Muslims to craft an identity based on Islam and their European home country, and help to bridge a generation gap among European Muslims by advocating the perspective of youth. The subcultural genre is important, but no more than the social and Islamically inspired message itself. The more inward-looking focus is not the result of a disinterest in society; in fact, the contrary is true and they express a very positive view of society.

The fourth type, the Proselytisers, have a religious and proselytising motif, as they regard religion as the main solution to any problems. There are two subgroups within this type, distinguished by their target groups: one targets young Muslims who do not practise their religion very strictly, and the other one targets non-Muslims. The first group aims to solve individual problems such as drug taking by promoting Islam as a lifesaver, while the second group tackles societal issues, which they perceive to result from a decay of morals. This type's understanding of Islamic youth culture is therefore more religiously than subculturally determined, and the genre is often little more than a vehicle for the message. The Proselytisers also share a critical perception of society, resulting from negative experiences they have had, or, in the case of the second subgroup, from the belief that an Islamic way of life is preferable to that of a Western society.

Influence of Youth Culture on Islamic Practice

Islamic youth culture may be an exceptional cultural practice that does not relate to all young Muslims in Europe, but it still gives a valuable insight into important issues and circumstances with which many of them are concerned. It is indeed a multidimensional youth culture that has its own styles, ideas and actions. I have called the movement "conservative avant-garde", because it is morally rather conservative while at the same time it proposes new approaches to living and teaching Islam and makes new contributions to youth culture. The conservative character is largely due to the way in which mainstream Islam is practised in Europe today, as more conservative views of moral issues are held than in the general population. But this influence is not the only trait that Islam brings to this youth culture; thus, the term "conservative avant-garde" does not refer to a judgemental dichotomy of an alleged Islamic traditionalism versus Western modernity: Islam for instance also contributes spirituality and a focus on education as well as on social commitment. But moral conservatism is unusual in a youth culture and therefore noteworthy.

Apart from being a youth culture, the phenomenon is also an Islamic practice and contributes to the manifestation of a European Islam. It is often used as a form of religious transmission, which cannot only be observed in the lyrics of songs, but also at meetings of Muslim youth organisations. Moreover, this has contributed to a concept of youth in Islam; young people play a particular role in the development of the religion, as their practice locates Islam in Europe, encourages engagement with the non-Muslim society and emphasises individual interpretation – illustrated, for instance, by the debate of whether or not music should be allowed from a religious perspective. Before the youth movement started to develop, Muslim European scholars came to agree that Islam could exist peacefully in Europe if Muslims participated in society. Without explicitly referring to this – and probably without this having been the scholars' intention – Islamic youth culture is almost a natural manifestation of this idea and a way of popularising it.

Strong Affiliation with the European Home Country

As the artefacts, participant observations among consumers and the typology of producers' motivations have shown, Islamic youth culture is closely connected to the national context in which it takes place. It quotes cultural references from local musicians, comedians or clothing styles, uses the national language and typical forms of organisations, including legal associations, youth camps and scouts groups. Religion and culture are disentangled to live a "pure" Islam free from cultural traditions, which makes space for new cultures to be adopted – subculture as well as French, British or German characteristics. This is not a contradiction, as there is no general urge to keep Islam and culture separate, but rather to leave behind the cultural background of Islamic countries.

Moreover, the reasons why Islamic youth culture emerged have a strong reference to being a Muslim in Europe, as each of the four types has shown. They all deal with Muslim/non-Muslim relations in one way or other, whether they try to improve them through dialogue or hope to strengthen young Muslims' self-confidence in this context. Also, this results to a large extent from the post-9/11 and 7/7 environment to which Islamic youth culture is perhaps not a unified, but still a collective response, because it deals with regaining control over labels, categories and stigmata ascribed to Muslims by others. The fact that the British respondents usually had a much more positive perception of society than their French and German counterparts illustrates the great influence that the national context has, depending on the integration models and citizenship, media and public opinion in the respective countries.

As much as Islamic youth culture deals with locating oneself as a Muslim in Europe, it is not confined to this alone, but is equally concerned with the implications for wider society. Its strong social component is also aimed at facilitating life for all members of a pluralistic society. The inclusion of many European traits into this youth culture makes it a vehicle of integration, which is all the more successful since it is not suggested to young Muslims from an outsider, but developed by themselves with a strong desire for participation.

Intertwinement of the Global and the Local

One of the endeavours of cultural sociology is to explore cultural practices and to search for their origins and reasons for coming into being. In this study, I have provided an extensive ethnography of a contemporary religious youth culture and shed light on the complex circumstances of its emergence. Some of the findings are transferable to other examples, such as the understanding of a subculture through its artefacts and its styles, ideas and actions. Also, the types can be applied to other cases of cultural production, not directly, because every respondent has an individual story, but in the way they have been generated from categories that were significant for the topic. The combination of youth cultural theory with religion and hybridity can similarly be relevant in the contexts of other religions or other minority–majority settings.

Moreover, findings on both the theoretical and the empirical levels have uncovered a peculiar relationship between the global and the local. Elements of a global religion, globalised youth culture, migration history and the geopolitical situation strongly prevail in Islamic youth culture, although the producers have given very personal and biographical circumstances as the reasons for having started their activity. Islamic youth culture refers to global ideas like the Islamic *ummah* and makes explicit references to internationally known youth cultures, but even more so it is concerned with making them relevant to everyday life and to the local context in which they take place. The global influences are subject to local constraints, for example, to policies on how far religion should reach into the public sphere. Most importantly, the appropriation of global cultural flows typically has a local purpose, in this case the need to improve relations among different groups in society or the situation of young people. A distinct local practice of combining global influences results from this: the interpretation of a global given takes place on a local level and has an independent relevance there. Despite or precisely because of that it is insightful to adopt a global perspective alongside an understanding on a micro-level of a cultural phenomenon like Islamic youth culture to detect the global–local intertwining.

Outlook of Future Research

The research into Islamic youth culture opens up further research directions into various fields. The findings raised several points of discussion that might need further clarification. There was an impression that class plays a role, and it would be worth pursuing to what extent Islamic youth culture is a middle class phenomenon and possibly excludes working class youth. With its ethnographic approach, the focus of this study was not to provide numbers and proportions, but it would be intriguing to conduct a more quantitative survey and find out about the size of the movement in relation to other youth movements and to the remainder of young Muslims, who do not participate here. A compelling follow-up study could also look into the paths taken by both consumers and producers of Islamic youth culture after their youth. In fact, the producers are on average a few years beyond their youth, and while they still make youth culture today, they may move on to something else in the future. It could be rewarding to follow the movement for an extended period of time and to investigate the changes it will have undergone in ten, twenty or thirty years' time.

Stepping outside the context of France, Britain and Germany, further studies could look at other countries – examples of Islamic youth culture have also started to appear in the Netherlands and Belgium, Northern and Southern Europe, the United States, Canada and Australia. Another issue is the perception of European Islamic youth culture in Islamic countries, and research could be carried out into the conditions under which it might appear in those countries. Although the phenomenon has shown a strong affiliation to the European environment, the development of a religious youth culture in Islamic countries is certainly possible, where the producers' motivations, for instance, would look rather different.

Going beyond the concrete case study, this research could be taken further by trying the theoretical and methodological approaches with different case studies. Future studies could consider similar youth cultures in other parts of the world, based on different religions in minority contexts, or take a close look at cultural practices that also draw on a hybrid mix of elements from global and local, religious and political, as well as from youth cultural spheres.

Appendix

A. INTERVIEW QUESTIONNAIRE

The interview questionnaire was used in Germany, France and the UK in the respective language. Below is the English version.

At the beginning of each interview
- Test recording device.
- Mention informed consent and possibility of stopping any time.
- Introduction: "Before we start the actual interview I would like to explain to you once more what my study is about. I am looking at Islamic youth culture in the UK (France/Germany), and I'm particularly interested in who contributes to it in what way. So I'd like to learn about your experience in this field and why you do what you do. During our conversation I'll ask you a couple of open questions. It would be great if you could tell me everything that you feel is important in this respect, and I won't interrupt you. Ok?"

Table 6: Interview questionnaire

Question #1		
You produce young, Islamic music (fashion, media etc.). How did you develop this idea? Tell me a little bit about it.		
Substantive aspects	*Questions to keep going*	*Follow-up questions*
Initial idea	Substantive questions	Could you describe to me a very typical piece of your work (or music/ fashion etc.)? Why is it
Ties with biography	And then?	
Motivation	Is there anything else that	

| Wider aims | gave you the idea?

Anything else? | typical?

What do you want to achieve through your music (fashion)? |

Question #2

What influences does your music (fashion etc.) reflect?

Substantive aspects	Questions to keep going	Follow-up questions
Influences Sources of inspiration, "Western" and Islamic	Substantive questions What else? Are there any other influences? Anything else?	Where do you turn to for new ideas and inspirations? And apart from that, are there any other influences on your work? Your experience of being a Muslim in the UK (F/G), what role does it play for what you do? How did you personally experience growing up in a secular society?

Question #3

What does youth culture mean for you? / How would you define youth culture?

Substantive aspects	Questions to keep going	Follow-up questions
Subjective definition of youth culture Definition and label of Islamic youth culture	Substantive questions What else do you connect with youth culture? Is there anything else?	Do you think there is a specific Islamic youth culture in the UK? Have you heard of the term "Pop Islam"? What

		do you think of it? Can you think of a better name for this trend?

Question #4

Who do you produce your music (fashion etc.) for? What's your target group?

Substantive aspects	*Questions to keep going*	*Follow-up questions*
Target group Relationship with young people Assessment of the trend Taking an outsider's view	Substantive questions For who else? Can you think of anyone else? Are there any other reasons?	What kind of people are your fans/customers? What do you think makes your music/fashion so popular? And Islamic youth culture in general? Why do we need a specifically Islamic youth culture?

Question #5

Have you ever experienced any criticism of what you do? Are there people who reject your music (fashion etc.)?

Substantive aspects	*Questions to keep going*	*Follow-up questions*
Problems Contradictions Obstacles Strategies of coping, reassurance of self Strengthening of own idea	Substantive questions Can you give me an example? What happened exactly? What did you do then? Any other similar situations?	What is the situation on the Muslim side? And what about the non-Muslim side? What kind of problems do you fight and how?

Question #6

Who do you think are the key figures in Islamic youth culture, here in the UK (France/Germany), in Europe or on a global scale?

Substantive aspects	Questions to keep going	Follow-up questions
Bigger framework Locating oneself in framework Awareness of international trends Transnationalism	Substantive questions Who else? Can you think of anyone else? Are there any other key figures?	What other people do you know in your field who contribute to this trend? What's your opinion on Amr Khaled? Is he influential on Islamic youth culture in the UK (France/Germany)? Do you know of any other similar trends in other European countries?

At the end of the interview

"Well, this is all I've wanted to ask you. Is there anything that you would like to add, anything that is important to you and that we haven't talked about yet? [...] Thank you very much!"

- Stop recording.
- Ask interviewee to sign informed consent form and to fill in short questionaire.
- Be open for any further "off the record" conversation.

B. LIST OF INTERVIEWEES

Table 7: List of interviewees

#	Fictional name	Sex	Genre	Country	Ethnic back-ground	Conversion	Age	Interview date
Type 1: Campaigners								
A7	Asma	F	Performing arts/Music	Germany		Yes	29	27/11/2008
B1	Hilal	M	Media	France		No	27	07/02/2009
C3	Soumeya	F	Performing arts/Music	UK	3 Jamaica,	No (parents Y)	20	03/07/2009
C6	Mona	F	Performing arts/Music	UK	2 other black,	Yes	29	13/07/2009
C7	Selma	F	Performing arts/Music	UK	1 Morocco,	Yes	27	13/07/2009
C10	Mansour	M	Media	UK	1 Egypt,	No	24	10/08/2009
C14	Mujab	M	Performing arts/Music	UK	1 Pakistan	Yes	30+	10/12/2009
C15	Nour	M	Media	UK		No	42	19/01/2010
Total	*8*	*4 F,* *4 M*	*5 music, 3 media*	*6 UK,* *1 G, 1 F*		*4 continuous upbringing,* *4 converted*		
Type 2: Improvers								
A3	Murat	M	Fashion	Germany		No	33	15/10/2008
A6	Baschir	M	Perf. arts/Comedy	Germany		No	24	26/11/2008

A10	Yasemin	F	Fashion	Germany	2 Turkey,	Reversion	29	05/12/2008
B2	Bouchra	F	Fashion	France	2 Tunisia,	Reversion	40	12/02/2009
B6	Sarah	F	Perf. arts/Comedy	France	1 Morocco	No	28	01/04/2009
Total	*5*	*3 F, 2 M*	*3 fashion, 2 comedy*	*3 G, 2 F*		*3 continuous upbringing, 2 reverted*		

Type 3: Empowerers

A5	Hamid	M	Media	Germany		No	27	14/11/2008
B3	Kamal	M	Performing arts/Music	France		No	31	14/02/2009
C1	Salima	F	Fashion	UK	4 Arab	Reversion	25	29/06/2009
C2	Timothy	M	Media	UK	2 Caribbean	Yes	28	02/07/2009
C4	Rehana	F	Performing arts/Music	UK	2 Pakistan	No (parents Y)	22	03/07/2009
C5	Ibrahim	M	Performing arts/Music	UK	1 Nigeria	Yes	35	03/07/2009
C9	Iqbal	M	Media	UK	1 Indian-East	No	28	18/07/2009
C11	Jamila	F	Fashion	UK	African	No	20	13/08/2009
C12	Mahmoud	M	Media	UK		No	32	01/09/2009
C13	Rasha	F	Media	UK		No	30	09/09/2009
Total	*10*	*6 M, 4 F*	*5 media, 3 music, 2 fashion*	*8 UK, 1 G, 1 F*		*7 continuous upbringing, 2 converted, 1 reverted*		

Type 4: Proselytisers

A1	Adel	M	Performing arts/Music	Germany		Yes	28	11/10/2008
A2	Ali (+Baschir)	M	Fashion	Germany	2 Morocco	No	30+	14/10/2008
A4	Samir	M	Media	Germany	2 Bosnia	No	30+	04/11/2008
A8	Ridvan	M	Fashion	Germany	2 other Arab	Reversion	25	04/12/2008
A9	Rami	M	Performing arts/Music	Germany	1 Nigeria	Reversion	32	04/12/2008
B5	Jabir	M	Performing arts/Music	France	1 Ethiopia	No	29	20/03/2009
B7	Nabil	M	Fashion	France		No	40	01/04/2009
C8	Ahmad	M	Performing arts/Music	UK		No	18	14/07/2009
Total	8	all M	4 music, 3 fashion, 1 media	5 G, 2 F, 1 UK		5 continuous upbringing, 2 reverted, 1 converted		

Total of all interviews

32 *(32 interviews conducted, but only 31 suitable for typology)*		*21 M, 11 F*	*14 Performing arts, 9 Fashion, 9 Media*	*15 UK, 10 G, 7 F*	*13 Arab, 10 black African/Caribbean, 4 Pakistan/India, 2 Turkey, 2 Bosnia, 1 French*	*19 born and raised Muslim, 8 converted, 5 reverted (nearly all Sunni Muslims)*	*Average age 26, between 18 and 42*	

C. LETTER OF FIRST CONTACT

Dear [...],

My name is Maruta Herding and I am a sociology PhD student at the University of Cambridge. My PhD thesis deals with Islamic youth culture in Western Europe and I would like to invite you to participate in an interview as part of the study.

I am conducting interviews with producers of music, fashion and media that are designed by and for young British Muslims. I am particularly interested in the various expressions of and reasons for the development of Islamic youth culture. Therefore I would be keen to listen to your experience in contributing to Islamic youth culture in this country. This topic has been neglected in research and I believe that the public, academic research and also the Islamic community in general could profit from knowing more about this growing cultural sector. Furthermore, I would like to underline the academic nature of this study that seeks to explore Islamic youth culture further without implying a judgement.

During the interviews I usually pose open questions and the interviewee can talk about anything they feel is important to them regarding Islamic youth culture. I would like to conduct individual interviews and I am happy either to talk with just one of you or each of you in individual sessions. The conversation will normally take about one hour and will be audio recorded with your permission. All data are of course treated anonymously and confidentially and I will send you the recording or the transcribed text of your interview if you are interested.

I carry my project out at the Department of Sociology in Cambridge and it is funded by the Economic and Social Research Council (ESRC) of the UK. I have already conducted many interviews with Muslim artists in Germany and France and will now start my fieldwork in the UK. Of course I am ready to travel anywhere in the UK to spare you any inconvenience.

I would be grateful if you considered participating in an interview. If you are willing to do so, please let me know when you are free in the next couple of days/weeks. Also, if you would like to know more about the project, please do not hesitate to contact me. I look forward to hearing from you.

Thank you and kind regards,
Maruta Herding

Maruta Herding | University of Cambridge | Department of Sociology
Free School Lane | Cambridge CB2 3RQ | United Kingdom

D. CONSENT FORM

This research project was approved by the relevant Ethics Committee of the University of Cambridge prior to the beginning of my field research. I have obtained and kept the signed consent forms of all interviewees.

Informed consent

I, _____, herewith give my consent that my interview with Maruta Herding may be recorded and transcribed as part of a study on Islamic youth culture in Britain.

I have been informed that I could withdraw from the interview at any point without justification and that I could also withdraw my consent any time after the interview. I was assured that everything I say will be treated confidentially and that all personal references will be made anonymous in the transcript.

I further agree that parts of this interview may be published and used for teaching under the condition that they are made anonymous.

Date:

Signature:

E. LIST OF CODES

This is a list of the twelve most important categories I used to code each interview. The interview quotes corresponding to each of these categories were then summarised in short memos, so that a document of twelve memos would constitute a comprehensive overview of the whole interview.

Activity	The interviewee's personal description of his or her activity in Islamic youth culture, including the origins and development of the initial idea
Central motif	Any recurring images, themes, structures, positions or symbolic figures, eventually representing the main theme of the interview
Free motifs	Any other important themes the interviewee emphasised
Personal Islamic experience	The role of Islam in the interviewee's biography and changes to this role over time
Subjective Islam definition	The interviewee's subjective definition and interpretation of Islam
Perception of society	Statements about and judgement of society and the image of Islam in society, view of the interviewee's own role as a Muslim in society and perceptions by others
Youth culture	Subjective definition and evaluation of youth culture in a general sense
Islamic youth culture	Definition, opinion and evaluation of Islamic youth culture, opinion on term Pop-Islam or other terms to describe the movement, locating oneself within the movement
Aims	The aims and objectives the interviewee envisages and hopes to achieve through his or her activity
Criticism	Any criticism the interviewee has received for his or her involvement in Islamic youth culture, both from Muslims and non-Muslims
Incentives	All kings of input, inspiration and motivation to pursue the activity

F. GLOSSARY

Al-hamdulillah	"Thank God"; phrase expressing gratitude and relief
Banlieue	French suburban area
Chador	Black full body veil
Dar al-ahd	Territory of contract or agreement, where a Muslim minority can live in peace*
Dar al-harb	"House of war", used to denote non-Muslim territories*
Dar al-islam	"House of Islam", or territory of peace*
Dawah	"Invitation" to Islam, proselytism
Djellaba	Traditional, loose-fitting North African robe, worn by men and women
Dua	Invocation
Eid ul-Fitr	Three day celebration of breaking of the fast, marking the end of Ramadan
Hadith	"Tradition", the account of Prophet Mohammed's sayings and deeds; the second important source in Islam after the Quran*
Halal	Religiously permissible; the term is mostly used for food, but may also refers to behaviour and attitude
Haram	Religiously forbidden; usually refers to certain kinds of food like pork, alcohol, extramarital relationships and more, depending on particular interpretations
Hijab	Islamic female headscarf
Iman	Faith
Ijtihad	Interpretation and exegesis by the believer
Insha'allah	"If God is willing", hopefully; phrase added to any expected future event
Jazakallah	Or Jazakallahu khayran: "May God reward you (in goodness)"; phrase used to express gratitude, indicating that it cannot be repaid sufficiently by the speaker and in this life
Masha'allah	"What God has willed"; phrase added to a positive event in the past or to a compliment to prevent pride and bad luck
Mawlid	Celebration to commemorate the Prophet's birth

Nashid	Traditional form of religious chant with calm melodies and lyrics to praise Allah and the Prophet
Niqab	Islamic face veil
Quran	The Islamic scripture, containing the revelations recited by the Prophet Mohammed and preserved in a fixed, written form*
Salafism	A neo-orthodox brand of Islamic reformism, aiming to regenerate Islam by a return to the tradition represented by the "pious forefathers"*
Salam	Peace, Islamic greeting
Sadaqa	Voluntary or spontaneous charity as opposed to *zakat*, the obligatory alms
Shahada	Islamic Statement of faith: "I testify there is no god but God and Mohammed is his Prophet."
Shii Islam	Heterodox Islam; major sectarian branch apart from Sunni Islam; special recognition of the family of the Prophet*
Subhanallah	"God is glorious", literally God is void [of all evil]
Sufism	Islamic mysticism
Sunna	Standard or practice approved by the Prophet; orthodoxy; particularly important in Sunni Islam*
Sunni Islam	Orthodox Islam; largest sectarian branch in Islam*
Sura	One of the 114 independent units of the Quran*
Takbir	Takbir is the verbal noun of kabir (great) and stands for expressing the phrase *Allahu akbar* (God is great); in a group, if one person shouts *takbir*, the group's reply is *Allahu akbar*
Tawhid	Unity or oneness of God, also expressed by the gesture of an index finger pointing upwards while proclaiming the *shahada*
Ummah	Religious community of all people sharing the same faith, usually the Muslim community
Zakat	Alms giving; one of the five pillars or constituent practices of Islam

*Source: Bearman et al. (2011).

A simplified, reader-friendly transliteration of Arabic was used in this book.

Bibliography

BOOKS AND ARTICLES

ABDEL-SAMAD, HAMED 2010. Mein Abschied vom Himmel: Aus dem Leben eines Muslims in Deutschland, München: Knaur.

ABDULLAH, MUHAMMAD S. 1981. Geschichte des Islams in Deutschland, Köln: Styria.

AITSISELMI, FARID (ed.) 2000. Black, Blanc, Beur: Youth Language and Identity in France, Bradford: Interface – Bradford Studies in Language, Culture and Society.

AL KANZ 18/09/2007. Unicitewear, street wear islamique. Available at: http://www.al-kanz.org/2007/09/18/interview-unicitewear-street-wear-islamique [accessed 05/07/2011].

AL-AZMEH, AZIZ & EFFIE FOKAS (eds.) 2007. Islam in Europe: Diversity, Identity and Influence, Cambridge: Cambridge University Press.

AL-HAMARNEH, ALA & JÖRN THIELMANN (eds.) 2008. Islam and Muslims in Germany, Leiden: Brill.

ALI, AYAAN HIRSI 2008. Infidel: My Life, New York: Pocket Books.

ALI, ABDULLAH YUSUF 1998. The Holy Qur'an: Meanings and Commentary (English and Arabic Edition), Kansas City, MO/Beirut/Jeddah: Manar International, Ouloom Al Qur'an, Dar Al Qiblah.

ALLEN, CHRIS 2010. Islamophobia, Farnham: Ashgate.

ALLIEVI, STEFANO 1999. Les convertis à l'islam. Les nouveaux musulmans d'Europe, Paris: L'Harmattan.

ALLIEVI, STEFANO 2009. Conflicts over Mosques in Europe: Policy Issues and Trends, London: Alliance Publishing Trust.

ALLIEVI, STEFANO & JØRGEN S. NIELSEN (eds.) 2003. Muslim Networks and Transnational Communities in and across Europe, Leiden: Brill.

AMANN, KLAUS & STEFAN HIRSCHAUER 1997. Die Befremdung der eigenen Kultur: Ein Programm. In: K. Amann & S. Hirschauer (eds.) Die Befremdung der eigenen Kultur: Zur ethnographischen Herausforderung soziologischer Empirie. Frankfurt a.M.: Suhrkamp, 7–52.

AMANN, KLAUS & STEFAN HIRSCHAUER (eds.) 1997. Die Befremdung der eigenen Kultur: Zur ethnographischen Herausforderung soziologischer Empirie, Frankfurt a.M.: Suhrkamp.

AMIR-MOAZAMI, SCHIRIN 2007. Politisierte Religion: Der Kopftuchstreit in Deutschland und Frankreich, Bielefeld: transcript.

AMIRAUX, VALÉRIE 2006. Speaking as a Muslim: Avoiding Religion in French Public Space. In: G. Jonker & V. Amiraux (eds.) Politics of Visibility: Young Muslims in European Public Spaces. Bielefeld: transcript, 21–52.

AMIRAUX, VALÉRIE & GERDIEN JONKER 2006. Talking about Visibility – Actors, Politics, Forms of Engagement. In: G. Jonker & V. Amiraux (eds.) Politics of Visibility: Young Muslims in European Public Spaces. Bielefeld: transcript, 9–20.

AMIT-TALAI, VERED 1995. Conclusion: The "Multi" Cultural of Youth. In: V. Amit-Talai & H. Wulff (eds.) Youth Cultures: A Cross Cultural Perspective. London: Routledge, 223–233.

AMIT-TALAI, VERED & HELENA WULFF (eds.) 1995. Youth Cultures: A Cross Cultural Perspective, London.

ANDROUTSOPOULOS, JANNIS (ed.) 2003. HipHop: Globale Kultur – lokale Praktiken, Bielefeld: transcript.

ANSARI, HUMAYUN 2004. The Infidel Within: The History of Muslims in Britain, 1800 to the Present, London: Hurst & Co.

ASSEMBLÉE NATIONALE 2010. Rapport d'information n° 2262 (au nom de la mission d'information sur la pratique du port du voile intégral sure le territoire national). Available at: http://www.assemblee-nationale.fr/13/pdf/rap-info/i2262.pdf [accessed 06/09/2011].

BAKER, HOUSTON A. JR. 1991 (Autumn). Hybridity, the Rap Race, and Pedagogy for the 1990s. Black Music Research Journal, 11 (2), 217–228.

BASIT, TEHMINA N. 1997. Eastern Values, Western Milieu: Identities and Aspirations of Adolescent British Muslim Girls, Aldershot: Ashgate.

BAUMANN, GERD 1996. Contesting Culture: Discourses of Identity in Multi-Ethnic London, Cambridge: Cambridge University Press.

BAX, DANIEL 2006. Die deutsch-türkische Musikszene zwischen Türkpop und Deutschrap. Available at: http://www.migration-boell.de/web/integration/47_916.asp [accessed 24/06/2010].

BAYAT, ASEF 2002 (July). Piety, Priviledge and Egyptian Youth. ISIM Newsletter, 10, 23.

BAYAT, ASEF 2007. Islamism and the Politics of Fun. Public Culture, 19 (3), 433–459.

BBC 18/07/2010. Damian Green Says Burka Ban Would Be "Un-British". Available at: http://www.bbc.co.uk/news/uk-10674973 [accessed 06/09/2011].

BEARMAN, PETER, THIERRY BIANQUIS, CLIFFORD E. BOSWORTH, EMERI VAN DONZEL & WOLFHART P. HEINRICHS (eds.) 2011. Encyclopaedia of Islam, Second Edition, Leiden: Brill.

BEAUDOIN, TOM 1998. Virtual Faith: The Irreverent Spiritual Quest of Generation X, San Francisco, CA: Jossey-Bass.

BECKFORD, JAMES A. & SOPHIE GILLIAT 1998. Religion in Prison: Equal Rites in a Multi-Faith Society, Cambridge: Cambridge University Press.

BELL, ROBERT R. 1965. Die Teilkultur der Jugendlichen. In: L. v. Friedeburg (ed.) Jugend in der modernen Gesellschaft. Köln: Kiepenheuer & Witsch.

BENNETT, ANDY 2000. Popular Music and Youth Culture: Music, Identity, and Place, Basingstoke: Macmillan.

BENNETT, ANDY 2003. HipHop am Main: Die Lokalisierung von Rap-Musik und HipHop-Kultur. In: J. Androutsopoulos (ed.) HipHop: Globale Kultur – lokale Praktiken. Bielefeld: transcript, 26–42.

BERG, BRUCE 2009. Qualitative Research Methods for the Social Sciences, Boston, MA: Allyn & Bacon.

BERHIL, MOHAMMED 2003. Les jeunes en France entre Islam et modernité, Paris: Publibook.

BERLINER ZEITUNG 08/03/2008. Ernsthaft glauben und dabei locker bleiben. Das neue Label Styleislam designt Shirts mit islamischen Botschaften, by Michaela Schlagenwerth. Available at: http://www.berlinonline.de/berliner-zeitung/archiv/.bin/dump.fcgi/2008/0308/none/0006/index.html [accessed 05/07/2011].

BERLINER ZEITUNG 30/04/2007. Wie soll ich leben? Islam wie Butter, by Rana Göroglu. Available at: http://www.berlinonline.de/berliner-zeitung/spe zial/dossiers/wie_soll_ich_leben/77059/index.php [accessed 27/08/2010].

BERTELSMANN STIFTUNG 2008. Religion Monitor 2008: Muslim Religiousness in Germany. Overview of Religious Attitudes and Practices. Available at: http://www.bertelsmann-stiftung.de/bst/en/media/xcms_bst_dm s_25866__2.pdf [accessed 24/06/2010].

BHABHA, HOMI K. 1990. The Third Space: Interview with Homi Bhabha. In: J. Rutherford (ed.) Identity: Community, Culture, Difference. London: Lawrence & Wishart, 207–221.

BHABHA, HOMI K. 1996. Culture's In-Between. In: S. Hall & P. Du Gay (eds.) Questions of Cultural Identity. London: Sage, 53–60.

BHABHA, HOMI K. 2004. The Location of Culture, London/New York: Routledge.

BLUMER, HERBERT 1967. Symbolic Interactionism: Perspective and Method, Englewood Cliffs, NJ: Prentice Hall.

BODENSTEIN, MARK 2010. Organisational Developments towards Legal and Political Recognition of Muslims in Germany. In: A. Kreienbrink & M. Bodenstein (eds.) Muslim Organisations and the State – European Perspectives. 55–68.

BOHNSACK, RALF 2010. Rekonstruktive Sozialforschung, Opladen: Barbara Budrich.

BOHNSACK, RALF & WINFRIED MAROTZKI (eds.) 1998. Biographieforschung und Kulturanalyse: Transdisziplinäre Zugänge qualitativer Forschung, Opladen: Leske + Budrich.

BOUBEKEUR, AMEL 2005 (Autumn). Cool and Competitive: Muslim Culture in the West. ISIM Review, 16, 12–13.

BOUCHER, MANUEL 1999. Rap, expression des lascars: Significations et enjeux du rap dans la société française, Paris: L'Harmattan.

BOUGAREL, XAVIER & NATHALIE CLAYER (eds.) 2001. Le nouvel islam balkanique. Les musulmans, acteurs de post-communisme, Paris: Maisonneuve & Larose.

BOURDIEU, PIERRE 1980. La "jeunesse" n'est qu'un mot. In: P. Bourdieu (ed.) Questions de Sociologie Paris: Minuit, 143–154.

BOURDIEU, PIERRE 1980. Questions de Sociologie Paris: Minuit.

BRAKE, MIKE 1980. Sociology of Youth Culture and Youth Subcultures: Sex, Drugs and Rock 'n' Roll?, London: Routledge.

BRAKE, MIKE 1981. Soziologie der jugendlichen Subkulturen: Eine Einführung, Frankfurt a.M./New York: Campus.

BRAKE, MIKE 1985. Comparative Youth Culture: The Sociology of Youth Cultures and Youth Subcultures in America, Britain and Canada, London: Routledge.

BREYVOGEL, WILFRIED (ed.) 1983. Autonomie und Widerstand: Zur Theorie und Geschichte des Jugendprotestes, Essen: Rigidon.

BROOKER, PETER 1999. Cultural Theory: A Glossary, London: Arnold.

BROWN, KATHERINE E. 2010. Contesting the Securitization of British Muslims: Citizenship and Resistance. In: P. Morey & A. Yaqin (eds.) Muslims in the Frame. Special Issue of Interventions: International Journal of Postcolonial Studies, 12 (2). London: Routledge, 171–182.

BRUBAKER, ROGERS & FREDERICK COOPER 2000. Beyond "Identity". Theory and Society, 29 (1), 1-47.

BRUNO, PIERRE 2000. Existe-t-il une culture adolescente?, Paris: In Press.

BUCHOLTZ, MARY 2002. Youth and Cultural Practice. Annual Review of Anthropology, 31, 525–552.

BUIJS, FRANK J. 1998. Een Moskee in de Wijk. De Vestiging van de Kocatepemoskee in Rotterdam-Zuid, Amsterdam: Het Spinhuis.

BUIJS, FRANK J. & JAN RATH 2002. Muslims in Europe: The State of Research. Available at: http://dare.uva.nl/document/144737 [accessed 07/06/2011].

BUSHILL-MATTHEWS, LUCY 2008. Welcome to Islam: A Convert's Tale, London: Continuum.

CALDWELL, JOHN C., PAT CALDWELL, BRUCE K. CALDWELL & INDRANI PIERIS 1998 (June). The Construction of Adolescence in a Changing World: Implications for Sexuality, Reproduction, and Marriage. Studies in Family Planning, 29 (2), 137–153.

CESARI, JOCELYNE 1994. Etre musulman en France. Associations, militants et mosquées, Paris: Karthala.

CESARI, JOCELYNE 1998a. Musulmans et républicains. Les jeunes, l'islam et la France, Paris: Complexe.

CESARI, JOCELYNE 1998b. Islam in France: Social Challenge or Challenge of Secularism? In: S. Vertovec & A. Rogers (eds.) Muslim European Youth: Reproducing Ethnicity, Religion, Culture. Aldershot: Ashgate, 25–38.

CESARI, JOCELYNE 1999 (March). Pluralism in the Context of Globalization: European Muslim Youth. ISIM Newsletter, 2, 25.

CESARI, JOCELYNE 2004. When Islam and Democracy Meet: Muslims in Europe and in the United States, New York/Basingstoke: Palgrave Macmillan.

CHAMBERS, IAIN 1985. Urban Rhythms: Pop Music and Popular Culture, London: Macmillan.

CLARKE, GARY 1990. Defending Ski-Jumpers: A Critique of Theories of Youth Subcultures. In: S. Frith & A. Goodwin (eds.) On Record: Rock, Pop and the Written Word. London: Routledge, 68–80.

CLARKE, JOHN 1993 [1976]. The Skinheads and the Magical Recovery of Community. In: S. Hall & T. Jefferson (eds.) Resistance through Rituals: Youth Subcultures in Post-War Britain. London: Routledge, 99–102.

CLARKE, JOHN 1993 [1976]. Style. In: S. Hall & T. Jefferson (eds.) Resistance through Rituals: Youth Subcultures in Post-War Britain. London: Routledge, 175–191.

CLARKE, JOHN, STUART HALL, TONY JEFFERSON & BRIAN ROBERTS 1993 [1976]. Subcultures, Cultures and Class: A Theoretical Overview. In: S. Hall & T. Jefferson (eds.) Resistance through Rituals: Youth Subcultures in Post-War Britain. London: Routledge, 9–74.

COLLINS-MAYO, SYLVIA & TOM BEAUDOIN 2010. Religion, Pop Culture and "Virtual Faith". In: S. Collins-Mayo & P. Dandelion (eds.) Religion and Youth. Farnham: Ashgate, 17–23.

COLLINS-MAYO, SYLVIA & PINK DANDELION (eds.) 2010. Religion and Youth, Farnham: Ashgate.

COPPES, ROSAN 1994. Niet zomaar een stukje stof. Hoofddoekjes-affaires in Frankrijk, Nederland en Groot-Brittannië. Sociologische Gids, 94 (2), 130–143.

CORRIGAN, PAUL 1993 [1976]. Doing Nothing. In: S. Hall & T. Jefferson (eds.) Resistance through Rituals: Youth Subcultures in Post-War Britain. London: Routledge, 103–105.

COUNCIL OF EUROPE 2004. Islamophobia and its Consequences on Young People, Strasbourg: Directorate of Youth and Sport of the Council of Europe.

CRESSEY, GILL 2006. Diaspora Youth and Ancestral Homeland: British Pakistani/Kashmiri Youth Visiting Kin in Pakistan and Kashmir, Leiden: Brill.

CURTIS, RIC & TRAVIS WENDEL 2000. Toward the Development of a Typology of Illegal Drug Markets. Crime Prevention Studies, 11, 121–152.

DAVIES, CHARLOTTE AULL 2008. Reflexive Ethnography: A Guide to Researching Selves and Others, Abingdon: Routledge.

DEPPERMANN, ARNULF 2008. Gespräche analysieren. Eine Einführung, Wiesbaden: VS.

DER SPIEGEL 14/03/2011. Tödliche Welt, by Matthias Bartsch and Holger Stark. Issue 11/2011, 44–45.

DER TAGESSPIEGEL 03/10/2010. Wulff: Islam gehört zu Deutschland, by Matthias Schlegel. Available at: http://www.tagesspiegel.de/politik/wulff-islam-gehoert-zu-deutschland/1948760.html [accessed 06/09/2011].

DEUTSCHE ISLAM KONFERENZ 2008. Geschichte der Muslime in Deutschland. Available at: http://www.deutsche-islam-konferenz.de/cln_101/nn_186

4666/SubSites/DIK/DE/Magazin/ZahlenDatenFakten/GeschichteIslam/gesch
ichteislam-node.html?__nnn=true [accessed 06/09/2011].

DEUTSCHLANDRADIO 16/06/2011. Musik als Propagandamittel. Wie Radi-
kalislamisten ihre Botschaften an Jugendliche bringen. Interview mit Jochen
Müller, by Katrin Heise. Available at: http://www.dradio.de/dkultur/sendung
en/thema/1483016 [accessed 05/07/2011].

DIE ZEIT 14/05/2010. Glaubensbekenntnis auf dem Rücken, by Cigdem Akyol.
Available at: http://www.zeit.de/gesellschaft/zeitgeschehen/2010-05/pop-
islam [accessed 05/07/2011].

DIE ZEIT 14/07/2009. Trauer um Ägypterin: Weiße Rosen für Marwa. Available at: http://www.zeit.de/online/2009/29/sherbini-trauer [accessed 06/09/
2011].

DIETZ, GERHARD-UHLAND, EDUARD MATT, KARL SCHUMANN &
LYDIA SEUS 1997. "Lehre tut viel...": Berufsbildung, Lebensplanung und
Delinquenz bei Arbeiterjugendlichen, Münster: Votum.

DREHER, TANJA & CHRISTINA HO (eds.) 2009. Beyond the Hijab Debates:
New Conversations on Gender, Race and Religion, Newcastle: Cambridge
Scholars.

EL HAMEL, CHOUKI 2002. Muslim Diaspora in Western Europe: The Islamic
Headscarf (Hijab), the Media and Muslims' Integration in France. Citizenship Studies, 6 (3), 293–308.

ESCUDIER, ALEXANDRE, BRIGITTE SAUZAY & RUDOLF VON THAD-
DEN (eds.) 2003. Der Islam in Europa. Der Umgang mit dem Islam in
Frankreich und Deutschland, Göttingen: Wallstein.

ESPOSITO, JOHN L. & IBRAHIM KALIN 2011. Islamophobia: The Challenge
of Pluralism in the 21st Century, New York: Oxford University Press.

ESTERBERG, KRISTIN 2002. Qualitative Methods in Social Research, New
York: McGraw-Hill.

EURO-ISLAM 05/02/2010. Is is Possible to Criticize Islam? Summary of a
Heated Debate in Germany. Available at: http://www.euro-islam.info/2010/0
2/05/is-is-possible-to-criticize-islam-summary-of-a-heated-debate-in-germa
ny [accessed 05/02/2010].

EURO-ISLAM 13/09/2009. UK Troubled by Right-Wing Anti-Islam Rallies.
Available at: http://www.euro-islam.info/2009/09/13/uk-troubled-by-right-
wing-anti-islam-rallies [accessed 13/09/2009].

EURO-ISLAM 30/01/2010. German Education of Islamic Schoolteachers and
Imams Remains Source of Conflict. Available at: http://www.euro-
islam.info/2010/01/30/german-education-of-islamic-schoolteachers-and-
imams-remains-source-of-conflict [accessed 30/01/2010].

FAURE, SYLVIA & MARIE-CARMEN GARCIA 2005. Culture hip-hop, jeunes des cités et politiques publiques, Paris: La Dispute.

FEATHERSTONE, MIKE, SCOTT LASH & ROLAND ROBERTSON (eds.) 1993. Global Modernities, London: Sage.

FETZER, JOEL S. & J. CHRISTOPHER SOPER 2005. Muslims and the State in Britain, France, and Germany, Cambridge: Cambridge University Press.

FLICK, UWE 2002. An Introduction to Qualitative Research, London: Sage.

FLICK, UWE, ERNEST VON KARDOFF & INES STEINKE (eds.) 2004. A Companion to Qualitative Research, London: Sage.

FORNÄS, JOHAN & GÖRAN BOLIN (eds.) 1995. Youth Culture in Late Modernity, London: Sage.

FOWLER, DAVID 2008. Youth Culture in Modern Britain, c. 1920–c. 1970: From Ivory Tower to Global Movement – A New History, Basingstoke: Palgrave Macmillan.

FRANKFURTER RUNDSCHAU 04/01/2011. Marketing für Mohammed, by Angela Breitkopf. Available at: http://www.fr-online.de/panorama/marketing -fuer-mohammed/-/1472782/5062136/-/index.html [accessed 05/07/2011].

FRIEDEBURG, LUDWIG VON (ed.) 1965. Jugend in der modernen Gesellschaft, Köln: Kiepenheuer & Witsch.

FRIEDMAN, JONATHAN 1997. Global Crises, the Struggle for Cultural Identity and Intellectual Porkbarrelling: Cosmopolitans versus Locals, Ethnics and Nationals in an Era of De-Hegemonisation. In: P. Werbner & T. Modood (eds.) Debating Cultural Hybridity: Multi-Cultural Identities and the Politics of Anti-Racism. London: Sage, 70–89.

FRITH, SIMON & ANDREW GOODWIN (eds.) 1990. On Record: Rock, Pop and the Written Word, London: Routledge.

GALLUP 2009. The Gallup Coexist Index 2009: A Global Study of Interfaith Relations. With an In-Depth Analysis of Muslim Integration in France, Germany, and the United Kingdom. Available at: http://www.abudhabigallup center.com/144842/REPORT-Gallup-Coexist-Index-2009.aspx [accessed 09/05/2009].

GARDELL, MATTIAS 1996. Countdown to Armageddon: Louis Farrakhan and the Nation of Islam, London: Hurst & Co.

GARFINKEL, HAROLD 1967. Studies in Ethnomethodology, Englewood Cliffs, NJ: Prentice Hall.

GASPARD, FRANÇOISE & FARHAD KHOSROKHAVAR 1995. Le Foulard et la République, Paris: La Découverte.

GAZZAH, MIRIAM 2009. European Muslim Youth: Towards a Cool Islam? In: J. S. Nielsen, S. Akgönül, A. Alibašić, B. Maréchal & C. Moe (eds.) Yearbook of Muslims in Europe 1. Leiden Brill.

GEERTZ, CLIFFORD 1973. The Interpretation of Cultures, London: Hutchinson.

GEMIE, SHARIF 2010. French Muslims: New Voices in Contemporary France, Cardiff: University of Wales Press.

GERHOLM, TOMAS & YNGVE GEORG LITHMAN (eds.) 1988. New Islamic Presence in Western Europe, London/New York: Mansell.

GERLACH, JULIA 2006. Zwischen Pop und Dschihad. Muslimische Jugendliche in Deutschland, Berlin: Links.

GERLACH, JULIA 2010. Pop-Islam revisited: Wohin entwickelt sich die transnationale Jugendbewegung der "neuen Prediger" in Europa und in der Arabischen Welt? In: C. Hunner-Kreisel & S. Andresen (eds.) Kindheit und Jugend in muslimischen Lebenswelten. Wiesbaden: VS, 109–124.

GILLIAT, SOPHIE 1997. Muslim Youth Organizations in Britain: A Descriptive Analysis. American Journal of Islamic Social Sciences, 14 (1), 99–111.

GILLIAT-RAY, SOPHIE 2010. Muslims in Britain: An Introduction, Cambridge: Cambridge University Press.

GILROY, PAUL 1993. The Black Atlantic: Modernity and Double Consciousness, London: Verso.

GILROY, PAUL 1995. There Ain't No Black in the Union Jack, London: Routledge.

GLASER, BARNEY & ANSELM STRAUSS 1967. The Discovery of Grounded Theory: Strategies for Qualitative Research, London: Weidenfeld and Nicolson.

GLASERSFELD, ERNST VON 1995. Radical Constructivism: A Way of Knowing and Learning, London: Falmer.

GOLD, RAYMOND 1958 (March). Roles in Sociological Field Observations. Social Forces, 36 (3), 217–223.

GUPTA, AKHIL & JAMES FERGUSON 1997. Discipline and Practice: "The Field" as Site, Method, and Location in Anthropology. In: A. Gupta & J. Ferguson (eds.) Anthropological Locations: Boundaries and Grounds of a Field Science. Berkeley, CA: University of California Press, 1–46.

GUPTA, AKHIL & JAMES FERGUSON (eds.) 1997. Anthropological Locations: Boundaries and Grounds of a Field Science, Berkeley, CA: University of California Press.

HADDAD, YVONNE YAZBECK & JANE I. SMITH (eds.) 2002. Muslim Minorities in the West: Visible and Invisible, Lanham: AltaMira Press.

HAENNI, PATRICK 2005. L'islam de marché. L'autre révolution conservatrice, Paris: Seuil.

HAENNI, PATRICK & HUSAM TAMMAM. 2003. Ganz entspannt shoppen im al-Salam Center. Ägyptens neue Prediger und der hedonistische Islam. Le Monde diplomatique (issue 7155), 12/09/2003.

HALL, STUART 1990. Cultural Identity and Diaspora. In: J. Rutherford (ed.) Identity: Community, Culture, Difference. London: Lawrence & Wishart, 222–237.

HALL, STUART 1996. Introduction: Who Needs "Identity"? In: S. Hall & P. Du Gay (eds.) Cultural Identity. London: Sage, 1–17.

HALL, STUART & PAUL DU GAY (eds.) 1996. Questions of Cultural Identity, London: Sage.

HALL, STUART & TONY JEFFERSON (eds.) 1993 [1976]. Resistance through Rituals: Youth Subcultures in Post-War Britain, London: Routledge.

HAMMERSLEY, MARTYN & PAUL ATKINSON 2007. Ethnography: Principles in Practice, Abington: Routledge.

HANNERZ, ULF 1992. Cultural Complexity: Studies in the Social Organisation of Meaning, New York: Columbia University Press.

HANNERZ, ULF 1997. Flows, Boundaries and Hybrids: Keywords in Transnational Anthropology. Available at: http://www.transcomm.ox.ac.uk/working%20papers/hannerz.pdf [accessed 26/08/2008].

HARTWIG, HELMUT 1980. Jugendkultur: Ästhetische Praxis in der Pubertät, Reinbek bei Hamburg: Rowohlt.

HAUG, SONJA, STEPHANIE MÜSSIG & ANJA STICHS 2009. Muslim Life in Germany: A Study Conducted on Behalf of the German Conference on Islam, released by the Bundesamt für Migration und Flüchtlinge (BAMF). Available at: http://www.deutsche-islam-konferenz.de/cln_101/SharedDocs/Anlagen/DE/DIK/Downloads/WissenschaftPublikationen/MLD-Vollversion-eng-dik,templateId=raw,property=publicationFile.pdf/MLD-Vollversion-eng-dik.pdf [accessed 16/02/2010].

HÄUSLER, ALEXANDER (ed.) 2008. Rechtspopulismus als „Bürgerbewegung": Kampagnen gegen Islam und Moscheebau und kommunale Gegenstrategien, Wiesbaden: VS.

HAUT CONSEIL À L'INTÉGRATION 2000. L'islam dans la République. Available at: http://lesrapports.ladocumentationfrancaise.fr/BRP/014000017/0000.pdf [accessed 06/09/2011].

HEBDIGE, DICK 1993. Subculture: The Meaning of Style, London: Routledge.

HEBDIGE, DICK 1993 [1976]. The Meaning of Mod. In: S. Hall & T. Jefferson (eds.) Resistance through Rituals: Youth Subcultures in Post-War Britain. London: Routledge, 87–98.

HELFFERICH, CORNELIA 2004. Die Qualität qualitativer Daten: Manual für die Durchführung qualitativer Interviews, Wiesbaden: VS.

HELFFERICH, CORNELIA, HEIKE KLINDWORTH & JAN KRUSE 2005. Männer Leben: Studie zu Lebensläufen und Familienplanung – Vertiefungsbericht. Bundeszentrale für gesundheitliche Aufklärung, Köln (Herausgeberin) [Online]. Available at: http://www.bzga.de/pdf.php?id=30a4b5778b d22b776e8a58342d557ead [accessed 02/05/2011].

HERDING, MARUTA 2007. Segregation und städtischer Konflikt. Die französischen Vorstadtunruhen von 2005, Master's degree thesis, Universität Freiburg.

HERTZ, ELLEN 1998. The Trading Crowd: An Ethnography of the Shanghai Stock Market, Cambridge: Cambridge University Press.

HESMONDHALGH, DAVID 2007. Recent Concepts in Youth Cultural Studies: Critical Reflections from the Sociology of Music. In: P. Hodkinson & W. Deicke (eds.) Youth Cultures: Scenes, Subcultures and Tribes. London/New York: Routledge, 37–50.

HESMONDHALGH, DAVID & CASPAR MELVILLE 2001. Urban Breakbeat Culture: Repercussions of Hip-Hop in the United Kingdom. In: T. Mitchell (ed.) Global Noise: Rap and Hip-Hop Outside the USA. Middletown, CT: Wesleyan University Press, 86–110.

HITZLER, RONALD 2002 (May). Sinnrekonstruktion: Zum Stand der Diskussion (in) der deutschsprachigen interpretativen Soziologie [The Reconstruction of Meaning: The State of the Art in German Interpretive Sociology]. Forum: Qualitative Social Research [Online], 3 (2), Article 7. Available at: http://www.qualitative-research.net/index.php/fqs/article/view/867/1885 [accessed 20/04/2011].

HITZLER, RONALD, ANNE HONER & MICHAELA PFADENHAUER (eds.) 2008. Posttraditionale Gemeinschaften: Theoretische und ethnografische Erkundungen, Wiesbaden: VS.

HITZLER, RONALD & ARNE NIEDERBACHER 2010. Leben in Szenen: Formen juveniler Vergemeinschaftung heute, Wiesbaden: VS.

HITZLER, RONALD & MICHAELA PFADENHAUER 1998. Let Your Body Take Control: Zur ethnographischen Kulturanalyse der Techno-Szene. In: R. Bohnsack & W. Marotzki (eds.) Biographieforschung und Kulturanalyse: Transdisziplinäre Zugänge qualitativer Forschung. Opladen: Leske + Budrich, 75–92.

HODKINSON, PAUL 2007. Youth Cultures: A Critical Outline of Key Debates. In: P. Hodkinson & W. Deicke (eds.) Youth Cultures: Scenes, Subcultures and Tribes. London/New York: Routledge, 2–21.

HODKINSON, PAUL & WOLFGANG DEICKE (eds.) 2007. Youth Cultures: Scenes, Subcultures and Tribes, London/New York: Routledge.

HUNNER-KREISEL, CHRISTINE & SABINE ANDRESEN (eds.) 2010. Kindheit und Jugend in muslimischen Lebenswelten, Wiesbaden: VS.

HUNTER, SHIREEN (ed.) 2002. Islam, Europe's Second Religion: The New Social, Cultural and Political Landscape, Westport, CT: Greenwood Press.

HUSAIN, ED 2007. The Islamist: Why I Joined Radical Islam in Britain, What I Saw Inside and Why I Left, London: Penguin.

HUTNYK, JOHN 1997. Adorno at Womad: South Asian Crossovers and the Limits of Hybridity-Talk. In: P. Werbner & T. Modood (eds.) Debating Cultural Hybridity: Multi-Cultural Identities and the Politics of Anti-Racism. London: Sage, 106–136.

IFOP 2009. Enquête sur l'implantation et l'évolution de l'Islam de France (Analyse: 1989–2009). Available at: http://www.ifop.fr/media/pressdocument/48-1-document_file.pdf [accessed 06/09/2011].

INGLEHART, RONALD & PIPPA NORRIS 2003. The True Clash of Civilisations. Foreign Policy, 135, 62–70.

ISLAM, YUSUF [no date]. Music, Faith or a Question of Da'wah? Available at: http://www.muslimhiphop.com/misc/docs/music_question_faith.pdf [accessed 24/06/2010].

ISLAMISCHE ZEITUNG 21/05/2008. "Rapmusik kann nur eine Alternative anbieten". Interview mit Ammar114. Islamische Zeitung [Online]. Available at: http://www.islamische-zeitung.de/?id=10335 [accessed 22/09/2008].

JACOBSON, JESSICA 1998. Islam in Transition: Religion and Identity Among British Pakistani Youth, London: Routledge.

JEFFERSON, TONY 1993 [1976]. Cultural Responses of the Teds: The Defence of Space and Status. In: S. Hall & T. Jefferson (eds.) Resistance through Rituals: Youth Subcultures in Post-War Britain. London: Routledge, 81–86.

JENKINS, RICHARD 1983. Lads, Citizens and Ordinary Kids: Working Class Youth Lifestyles in Belfast, London: Routledge & Kegan Paul.

JONKER, GERDIEN & VALÉRIE AMIRAUX (eds.) 2006. Politics of Visibility: Young Muslims in European Public Spaces, Bielefeld: transcript.

JUGENDWERK DER DEUTSCHEN SHELL (ed.) 1997. Jugend '97. Zukunftsperspektiven, Gesellschaftliches Engagement, Politische Orientierungen (12. Shell Jugendstudie), Opladen: Leske + Budrich.

JUNG, THOMAS & STEFAN MÜLLER-DOOHM (eds.) 1993. „Wirklichkeit" im Deutungsprozess: Verstehen und Methoden in den Kultur- und Sozialwissenschaften, Frankfurt a.m.: Suhrkamp.

JÜTTERMANN, GERD (ed.) 1985. Qualitative Forschung in der Psychologie. Grundfragen, Verfahrensweisen, Anwendungsfelder, Weinheim: Beltz.

KABIR, NAHID AFROSE 2010. Young British Muslims: Identity, Culture, Politics and the Media, Edinburgh: Edinburgh University Press.

KAHANE, REUVEN 1997. The Origins of Postmodern Youth: Informal Youth Movements in a Comparative Perspective, Berlin: de Gruyter.

KARLSSON MINGANTI, PIA 2010. Islamic Revival and Young Women's Negotiations on Gender and Racism. In: S. Collins-Mayo & P. Dandelion (eds.) Religion and Youth. Farnham: Ashgate, 115–121.

KAUR KALHON, RAMINDER & VIRINDER KALRA 1996. New Paths for South Asian Identity and Creativity. In: S. Sharma, J. Hutnyk & A. Sharma (eds.) Dis-Orienting Rhythms: The Politics of the New Asian Dance Music. London: Zed.

KEATON, TRICA DANIELLE 2006. Muslim Girls and the Other France: Race, Identity Politics and Social Exclusion, Bloomington: Indiana University Press.

KELLE, UDO & SUSANN KLUGE 1999. Vom Einzelfall zum Typus: Fallvergleich und Fallkontrastierung in der qualitativen Sozialforschung, Opladen: Leske + Budrich.

KHOSROKHAVAR, FAHRAD 1998. L'islam des jeunes, Paris: Flammarion.

KLUGE, SUSANN 1999. Empirisch begründete Typenbildung: Zur Konstruktion von Typen und Typologien in der qualitativen Sozialforschung, Opladen: Leske + Budrich.

KOOB, DIRK 2007 (January). Loriot als Symbolischer Interaktionist. Oder: Warum man selbst in der Badewanne gelegentlich soziale Ordnung aushandeln muss. Forum: Qualitative Social Research [Online], 8 (1), Article 27. Available at: http://www.qualitative-research.net/index.php/fqs/article/view/221/487 [accessed 20/04/2011].

KOOPMANS, RUUD, PAUL STATHAM, MARCO GIUGNI & FLORENCE PASSY 2005. Contested Citizenship: Immigration and Cultural Diversity in Europe, Minneapolis, MN: University of Minnesota Press.

KREIENBRINK, AXEL & MARK BODENSTEIN (eds.) 2010. Muslim Organisations and the State – European Perspectives. Released by the Bundesamt für Migration und Flüchtlinge (BAMF). Available at: http://www.deutsche-islam-konferenz.de/SharedDocs/Anlagen/DE/DIK/Downloads/Wissenschaft

Publikationen/muslime-organisationen-eng,templateId=raw,property=
publicationFile.pdf/muslime-organisationen-eng.pdf [accessed 06/09/2011].

KRUSE, JAN 2004. Arbeit und Ambivalenz: Die Professionalisierung Sozialer und Informatisierter Arbeit, Bielefeld: transcript.

KRUSE, JAN 2009 (October). Reader „Einführung in die Qualitative Interview-forschung". Available at: http://www.soziologie.uni-freiburg.de/kruse.

KRUSE, JAN, STEPHANIE BETHMANN, DEBORA NIERMANN & CHRISTIAN SCHMIEDER (eds.) 2012. Qualitative Interviewforschung in und mit fremden Sprachen: Eine Einführung in Theorie und Praxis, Weinheim/Basel: Beltz Juventa.

KUORTTI, JOEL & JOPI NYMAN (eds.) 2007a. Reconstructing Hybridity: Post-Colonial Studies in Transition, Amsterdam: Rodopi.

KUORTTI, JOEL & JOPI NYMAN 2007b. Introduction: Hybridity Today. In: J. Kuortti & J. Nyman (eds.) Reconstructing Hybridity: Post-Colonial Studies in Transition. Amsterdam: Rodopi, 1–18.

L'EXPRESS 07/06/2004, updated 09/03/2007. Les rappeurs d'Allah. Available at: http://www.lexpress.fr/outils/imprimer.asp?id=489437 [accessed 27/08/2010].

LAHIRE, BERNARD 2006. La culture des individus: Dissonances culturelles et distinction de soi, Paris: La Découverte.

LE COURRIER DE L'ATLAS 16/03/2009. Les drôles de dames version maghrébine, by Nadia Hathroubi-Safsaf. No. 24.

LE MONDE 26/01/2010. Voile islamique: chronologie d'une polémique. Available at: http://www.lemonde.fr/web/module_chrono/0,11-0@2-3224,32-1296722,0.html [accessed 06/09/2011].

LE MONDE DIPLOMATIQUE 09/2008. Rap domestiqué, rap révolté, by Jacques Denis. Available at: http://www.monde-diplomatique.fr/2008/09/DENIS/16290 [accessed 27/08/2011].

LEPOUTRE, DAVID 2001. Cœur de banlieue: Codes, rites et langages, Paris: Odile Jacob.

LEWIS, PHILIP 1994. Islamic Britain: Religion, Politics and Identity Among British Muslims, London/New York: I.B. Tauris.

LIBÉRATION 04/01/2011. L'islamophobie est à la source du nouveau populisme de droite, by Enzo Traverso. Available at: http://www.liberation.fr/livres/01012311407-l-islamophobie-est-a-la-source-du-nouveau-populisme-de-droite [accessed 06/09/2011].

LIECHTY, MARK 1995. Media, Markets and Modernisation: Youth Identities and the Experience of Modernity in Kathmandu, Nepal. In: V. Amit-Talai &

H. Wulff (eds.) Youth Cultures: A Cross Cultural Perspective. London: Routledge, 166–201.

LINDNER, ROLF 1981. Nachwort: Jugendkultur und Subkultur als soziologische Konzepte. In: M. Brake (ed.) Soziologie der jugendlichen Subkulturen: Eine Einführung. Frankfurt a.m./New York: Campus, 173–193.

LIPSITZ, GEORGE 2005. Midnight's Children: Youth Culture in the Age of Globalization. In: S. Maira & E. Soep (eds.) Youthscapes: The Popular, The National, The Global. Philadelphia, PA: University of Pennsylvania Press, vii–xiv.

LOFLAND, JOHN 1971. Analyzing Social Settings: A Guide to Qualitative Observation and Analysis, Belmont, CA: Wadsworth.

LÜBCKE, CLAUDIA 2007. Jugendkulturen junger Muslime in Deutschland. In: H.-J. v. Wensierski & C. Lübcke (eds.) Junge Muslime in Deutschland. Lebenslagen, Aufwachsprozesse und Jugendkulturen. Opladen: Barbara Budrich, 285–318.

LUKOSE, RITTY 2005 (June). Consuming Globalization: Youth and Gender in Kerala, India. Journal of Social History, 38 (4), 915–935.

MAIRA, SUNAINA 2002. Desis in the House: Indian American Youth Culture in New York City, Philadelphia, PA: Temple University Press.

MAIRA, SUNAINA & ELISABETH SOEP (eds.) 2005a. Youthscapes: The Popular, The National, The Global, Philadelphia, PA: University of Pennsylvania Press.

MAIRA, SUNAINA & ELISABETH SOEP 2005b. Introduction. In: S. Maira & E. Soep (eds.) Youthscapes: The Popular, The National, The Global. Philadelphia, PA: University of Pennsylvania Press, xv–xxxv.

MALIK, ABD AL 2007. Qu'Allah bénisse la France !, Paris: Albin Michel.

MANDAVILLE, PETER 2001. Reimagining Islam in Diaspora: The Politics of Mediated Community. International Communication Gazette, 63 (2–3), 169–186.

MANDAVILLE, PETER 2002. Muslim Youth in Europe. In: S. Hunter (ed.) Islam, Europe's Second Religion: The New Social, Cultural and Political Landscape. Westport, CT: Greenwood Press.

MANDAVILLE, PETER 2003. Towards a Critical Islam: European Muslims and the Changing Boundaries of Transnational Religious Discourse. In: S. Allievi & J. S. Nielsen (eds.) Muslim Networks and Transnational Communities in and across Europe. Leiden: Brill, 127–145.

MANDAVILLE, PETER 2009a. Hip-Hop, Nasheeds, and "Cool" Sheikhs: Popular Culture and Muslim Youth in the United Kingdom. In: C. Timmerman, J. Leman, H. Roos & B. Segaert (eds.) In-Between Spaces: Christian and

Muslim Minorities in Transition in Europe and in the Middle East. Brussels: Peter Lang, 149–168.

MANDAVILLE, PETER 2009b (Summer). Hip-Hop and Urban Islam in Europe. Global Studies Review [Online], 5 (2). Available at: http://www.globality-gmu.net/archives/1426 [accessed 21/06/2011].

MARÉCHAL, BRIGITTE (ed.) 2002. A Guidebook on Islam and Muslims in the Wide Contemporary Europe, Louvain-la-Neuve: Academia Bruylant.

MARÉCHAL, BRIGITTE, STEFANO ALLIEVI, FELICE DASSETTO & JØRGEN S. NIELSEN (eds.) 2003. Muslims in the Enlarged Europe: Religion and Society, Leiden: Brill.

MAUGER, GÉRARD 2009. La sociologie de la délinquence juvénile, Paris: La Découverte.

MAYRING, PHILIPP 2000 (June). Qualitative Content Analysis. Forum: Qualitative Social Research [Online], 1 (2), Article 20. Available at: http://www.qualitative-research.net/index.php/fqs/article/view/1089/2386 [accessed 28/04/2011].

MAYRING, PHILIPP 2004. Qualitative Content Analysis. In: U. Flick, E. von Kardoff & I. Steinke (eds.) A Companion to Qualitative Research. London: Sage, 266–269.

MAYRING, PHILIPP 2010. Qualitative Inhaltsanalyse: Grundlagen und Techniken, Weinheim/Basel: Beltz.

MCGOLDRICK, DOMINIC 2006. Human Rights and Religion: The Islamic Headscarf Debate in Europe, Oxford/Portland, OR: Hart.

MCLOUGHLIN, SEÁN & TAHIR ABBAS 2010. United Kingdom. In: J. S. Nielsen, S. Akgönül, A. Alibašić, H. Goddard, B. Maréchal & C. Moe (eds.) Yearbook of Muslims in Europe 2. Leiden: Brill.

MCROBBIE, ANGELA 1990. Settling Accounts with Subcultures: A Feminist Critique. In: S. Frith & A. Goodwin (eds.) On Record: Rock, Pop and the Written Word. London: Routledge, 55–67.

MCROBBIE, ANGELA & JENNY GARBER 1993 [1976]. Girls and Subcultures: An Exploration. In: S. Hall & T. Jefferson (eds.) Resistance through Rituals: Youth Subcultures in Post-War Britain. London: Routledge, 209–222.

MEAD, GEORGE HERBERT 1934. Mind, Self & Society from the Standpoint of a Social Behaviorist, Chicago, IL: University of Chicago Press.

MILON, ALAIN 2000. L'étranger dans la ville: Du rap au graff mural, Paris: Presses Universitaires de France.

MITCHELL, TONY (ed.) 2001. Global Noise: Rap and Hip-Hop Outside the USA, Middletown, CT: Wesleyan University Press.

MODOOD, TARIQ, ANNA TRIANDAFYLLIDOU & RICARD ZAPATA-BARRERO (eds.) 2006. Multiculturalism, Muslims and Citizenship: A European Approach, Abingdon: Routledge.

MÖLLER, KURT 2010. Hybrid-Kulturen – Wie „Jugendliche mit Migrationshintergrund" postmigrantisch werden. In: Projektgruppe JugendArt (ed.) KanakCultures. Kultur und Kreativität junger MigrantInnen. Berlin: Archiv der Jugendkulturen, 9–21.

MOREY, PETER 2010. Terrorvision: Race, Nation and Muslimness in Fox's 24. In: P. Morey & A. Yaqin (eds.) Muslims in the Frame. Special Issue of Interventions: International Journal of Postcolonial Studies, 12 (2). London: Routledge, 251–264.

MOREY, PETER & AMINA YAQIN (eds.) 2010. Muslims in the Frame. Special Issue of Interventions: International Journal of Postcolonial Studies, 12 (2), London: Routledge.

MOREY, PETER & AMINA YAQIN 2011. Framing Muslims: Stereotyping and Representation after 9/11, Cambridge, MA: Harvard University Press.

MÜLLER, JOCHEN, GÖTZ NORDBRUCH & BERKE TATAROGLU 2008. Jugendkulturen zwischen Islam und Islamismus: Lifestyle, Medien, Musik (Themenheft), Berlin: Schule ohne Rassismus – Schule mit Courage (Bundeskoordination).

MURTHY, DHIRAJ 2007. A South Asian American Diasporic Aesthetic Community? Ethnicity and New York City's "Asian Electronic Music Scene". Ethnicities, 7 (2), 225–247.

N-TV 07/04/2007. "Kopftuch ist Freiheit". Sahira Awad rappt für Toleranz, by Aygül Cizmecioglu. Available at: http://www.n-tv.de/788147.html [accessed 05/07/2001].

NAYAK, ANOOP 2003. Race, Place and Globalization: Youth Cultures in a Changing World, Oxford: Berg.

NEDERVEEN PIETERSE, JAN 1993. Globalization as Hybridization. In: M. Featherstone, S. Lash & R. Robertson (eds.) Global Modernities. London: Sage, 45–68.

NIELSEN, JØRGEN S. 1995. Muslims in Western Europe, Edinburgh: Edinburgh University Press.

NIELSEN, JØRGEN S., SAMIM AKGÖNÜL, AHMED ALIBAŠIĆ, HUGH GODDARD, BRIGITTE MARÉCHAL & CHRISTIAN MOE 2010. Yearbook of Muslims in Europe 2, Leiden: Brill.

NIELSEN, JØRGEN S., SAMIM AKGÖNÜL, AHMED ALIBAŠIĆ, BRIGITTE MARÉCHAL & CHRISTIAN MOE 2009. Yearbook of Muslims in Europe 1, Leiden: Brill.

NIEUWKERK, KARIN VAN (ed.) 2006. Women Embracing Islam: Gender and Conversion in the West, Austin: University of Texas Press.

NONNEMAN, GERD, TIM NIBLOCK & BOGDAN SZAJKOWSKI (eds.) 1997. Muslim Communities in the New Europe, Reading: Ithaca Press.

NORDBRUCH, GÖTZ 2009 (September). "I love my Prophet" – Zwischen Lifestyle, Glauben und Mission. Islamische Jugendkulturen in Deutschland. Unsere Jugend, 13 (9), 296–303.

NORDBRUCH, GÖTZ. 2010. Islamische Jugendkulturen in Deutschland. Das Parlament (no. 27), 05/07/2010.

NORRIS, H.T. 1993. Islam in the Balkans: Religion and Society between Europe and the Arab World, Columbia, SC: University of South Carolina Press.

OEVERMANN, ULRICH 1981. Fallrekonstruktionen und Strukturgeneralisierung als Beitrag der objektiven Hermeneutik zur soziologisch-strukturtheoretischen Analyse (unveröffentlichtes Manuskript). Available at: http://www.agoh.de/cms/de/downloads/uebersicht/func-download/39/chk, d12259db6d283e98b496b5753101cc9e/no_html,1 [accessed 14/04/2011].

OEVERMANN, ULRICH 1993. Die objektive Hermeneutik als unverzichtbare methodologische Grundlage für die Analyse von Subjektivität. Zugleich eine Kritik der Tiefenhermeneutik. In: T. Jung & S. Müller-Doohm (eds.) „Wirklichkeit" im Deutungsprozess: Verstehen und Methoden in den Kultur- und Sozialwissenschaften. Frankfurt a.M.: Suhrkamp, 106–189.

OFFICE FOR NATIONAL STATISTICS 2004. Focus on Religion: 2004 Summary Report. Available at: http://www.ons.gov.uk/ons/rel/ethnicity/focus-on-religion/2004-edition/focus-on-religion-summary-report.pdf [accessed 06/09/2011].

ÖZTÜRK, HALIT 2007. Wege zur Integration. Lebenswelten muslimischer Jugendlicher in Deutschland, Bielefeld: transcript.

PARSONS, TALCOTT 1942 (October). Age and Sex in the Social Structure of the United States. American Sociological Review, 7 (5), 604–616.

PECQUEUX, ANTHONY 2007. Voix du rap: Essai de sociologie de l'action musicale, Paris: L'Harmattan.

PENN, ROGER & PAUL LAMBERT 2009. Children of International Migrants in Europe: Comparative Perspectives, Basingstoke: Palgrave Macmillan.

PENNAY, MARK 2001. Rap in Germany: The Birth of a Genre. In: T. Mitchell (ed.) Global Noise: Rap and Hip-Hop Outside the USA. Middletown, CT: Wesleyan University Press, 111–133.

PÉTONNET, COLETTE 1982. L'Observation flottante. L'exemple d'un cimetière parisien. L'Homme, 22 (4: Etudes d'anthropologie urbaine), 37–47.

PEUKERT, DETLEV 1983. Die „Wilden Cliquen" in den zwanziger Jahren. In: W. Breyvogel (ed.) Autonomie und Widerstand: Zur Theorie und Geschichte des Jugendprotestes. Essen: Rigidon.

PEW RESEARCH CENTER 2006. The Great Divide: How Westerners and Muslims View Each Other. Available at: http://pewglobal.org/files/pdf/253. pdf [accessed 19/07/2007].

POPOVIC, ALEXANDRE 1994. Cultures Musulmanes Balkaniques, Istanbul: Isis.

PRABHU, ANJALI 2007. Hybridity: Limits, Transformations, Prospects, Albany, NY: State University of New York Press.

PRÉVOS, ANDRÉ 2001. Postcolonial Popular Music in France: Rap Music and Hip-Hop Culture in the 1980s and 1990s. In: T. Mitchell (ed.) Global Noise: Rap and Hip-Hop Outside the USA. Middletown, CT: Wesleyan University Press, 39–56.

PROJEKTGRUPPE JUGENDART 2010a. KanakCultures. Kultur und Kreativität junger MigrantInnen, Berlin: Archiv der Jugendkulturen.

PROJEKTGRUPPE JUGENDART 2010b. Auf Entdeckungstour in der islamischen Jugendkultur. In: Projektgruppe JugendArt (ed.) KanakCultures. Kultur und Kreativität junger MigrantInnen. Berlin: Archiv der Jugendkulturen, 64–77.

PRZYBORSKI, AGLAJA & MONIKA WOHLRAB-SAHR 2010. Qualitative Sozialforschung: Ein Arbeitsbuch, München: Oldenbourg.

QANTARA 04/12/2008. "Islam verbietet Gewalt". Interview mit Rapper Ammar114, by Nimet Seker. Available at: http://de.qantara.de/Islam-verbietet-Gewalt/4815c4898i1p429 [accessed 05/07/2011].

RABINOW, PAUL 1977. Reflections on Fieldwork in Morocco, Berkeley, CA: University of California Press.

RAMADAN, TARIQ 2002. Europeanization of Islam or Islamization of Europe? In: S. Hunter (ed.) Islam, Europe's Second Religion: The New Social, Cultural and Political Landscape. Westport, CT: Greenwood Press, 207–218.

RAMADAN, TARIQ 2003. To Be a European Muslim, Markfield: The Islamic Foundation.

RATH, JAN, RINUS PENNINX, KEES GROENENDIJK & ASTRID MEYER 2001. Western Europe and its Islam: The Social Reaction to the Institutionalization of a "New" Religion in the Netherlands, Belgium and the United Kingdom, Leiden: Brill.

REDDIE, RICHARD S. 2009. Black Muslims in Britain: Why Are a Growing Number of Young Black People Converting to Islam?, Oxford: Lion.

REIMER, BO 1995. Youth and Modern Lifestyles. In: J. Fornäs & G. Bolin (eds.) Youth Culture in Late Modernity. London: Sage, 120–144.

REUTER, EDWARD B. 1936 (July). Sociological Research in Adolescence. American Journal of Sociology, 42 (1), 81–94.

ROBBERS, GERHARD 2009. Germany. In: J. S. Nielsen, S. Akgönül, A. Alibašić, B. Maréchal & C. Moe (eds.) Yearbook of Muslims in Europe 1. Leiden: Brill, 142–150.

ROHE, MATHIAS 2010. Germany. In: J. S. Nielsen, S. Akgönül, A. Alibašić, H. Goddard, B. Maréchal & C. Moe (eds.) Yearbook of Muslims in Europe 2. Leiden: Brill, 217–232.

ROY, OLIVIER 2004. Globalised Islam: The Search for a New Ummah, London: Hurst & Co.

ROY, OLIVIER 2006. Der islamische Weg nach Westen. Globalisierung, Entwurzelung und Radikalisierung, München: Pantheon.

ROY, OLIVIER 2007. Islam in Europe: Clash of Religions or Convergence of Religiosities? Available at: http://eurozine.com/pdf/2007-05-03-roy-en.pdf [accessed 07/04/2008].

ROY, OLIVIER 2010. Holy Ignorance: When Religion and Culture Part Ways, London: Hurst & Co.

RUNNYMEDE TRUST 1997. Islamophobia: A Challenge for Us All, London: Runnymede Trust, Commission on British Muslims and Islamophobia.

RUTHERFORD, JONATHAN (ed.) 1990. Identity: Community, Culture, Difference, London: Lawrence & Wishart.

SACKMANN, ROSEMARIE, BERNHARD PETERS & THOMAS FAIST 2003. Identity and Integration: Migrants in Western Europe, Aldershot: Ashgate.

SALHI, KAMAL (ed.) 2012 (forthcoming). Music, Culture and Identity in the Muslim World: Performance, Politics and Piety, London: Routledge.

SANDT, FRED-OLE 1996. Religiosität von Jugendlichen in der multikulturellen Gesellschaft: Eine qualitative Untersuchung zu atheistischen, christlichen, spiritualistischen und muslimischen Orientierungen, Münster: Waxmann.

SAPHIRNEWS 16/07/2003. Le rap musulman débarque, by Lazrak Jihen. Available at: http://www.saphirnews.com/Le-rap-musulman-debarque_a470.html [accessed 27/08/2010].

SAPHIRNEWS 20/05/2008. Le tee-shirt fait le musulman, by Assmaâ Rakho Mom. Available at: http://www.saphirnews.com/Le-tee-shirt-fait-le-musulman_a8973.html [accessed 05/07/2011].

SARRAZIN, THILO 2010. Deutschland schafft sich ab: Wie wir unser Land aufs Spiel setzen, München: Deutsche Verlangs-Anstalt.

SAVAGE, JON 2007. Teenage: The Creation of Youth 1875–1945, London: Chatto & Windus.

SCHERR, ALBERT 2009. Jugendsoziologie. Einführung in Grundlagen und Theorien, Wiesbaden: VS.

SCHIFFAUER, WERNER 2010. Nach dem Islamismus: Die Islamische Gemeinschaft Milli Görüş. Eine Ethnographie, Berlin: Suhrkamp.

SCHNEIDERS, THORSTEN GERALD (ed.) 2010. Islamfeindlichkeit: Wenn die Grenzen der Kritik verschwimmen, Wiesbaden: VS.

SÉNAT 2004. Loi n° 2004-228 du 15 mars 2004 (encadrant, en application du principe de laïcité, le port de signes ou de tenues manifestant une appartenance religieuse dans les écoles, collèges et lycées publics). Available at: http://legifrance.gouv.fr/affichTexte.do;jsessionid=7539A146FB5E52BCD4 6C4169BE5D5D16.tpdjo12v_1?cidTexte=JORFTEXT000000417977&categ orieLien=id [accessed 06/09/2011].

SHAHID, WASEF ABDELRAHMAN & P. S. VAN KONINGSVELD 1996. Political Participation and Identities of Muslims in Non-Muslim States, Leuven: Peeters.

SHARMA, SANJAY, JOHN HUTNYK & ASHWANI SHARMA (eds.) 1996. Dis-Orienting Rhythms: The Politics of the New Asian Dance Music, London: Zed.

SHELL DEUTSCHLAND HOLDING (ed.) 2006. Jugend 2006. Eine pragmatische Generation unter Druck (15. Shell Jugendstudie), Bonn: Bundeszentrale für politische Bildung.

SKELTON, TRACEY & GILL VALENTINE (eds.) 1998. Cool Places: Geographies of Youth Cultures, London.

SMITH, FIONA M. 1998. Between East and West: Sites of Resistance in East German Youth Cultures. In: T. Skelton & G. Valentine (eds.) Cool Places: Geographies of Youth Cultures. London: Routledge, 290–305.

SOYSAL, LEVENT 2001 (March). Diversity of Experience, Experience of Diversity: Turkish Migrant Youth Culture in Berlin. Cultural Dynamics, 13 (1), 5–28.

STRATTON, ALLEGRA 2006. Muhajababes: Meet the Middle East's Next Generation, London: Constable.

STRAUSS, ANSELM & JULIET CORBIN 1990. Basics of Qualitative Research: Grounded Theory Procedures and Techniques, Newbury Park, CA: Sage.

SÜDDEUTSCHE ZEITUNG MAGAZIN 04/2010. Mode-Prophet. Interviews mit Menschen, die wir gut finden, by Christoph Cadenbach. Available at: http://sz-magazin.sueddeutsche.de/texte/anzeigen/32490 [accessed 05/07/2011].

SWEDENBURG, TED 2001. Islamic Hip-Hop versus Islamophobia: Aki Nawaz, Natacha Atlas, Akhenaton. In: T. Mitchell (ed.) Global Noise: Rap and Hip-Hop Outside the USA. Middletown, CT: Wesleyean University Press, 57–85.

TACEY, DAVID 2003. The Spirituality Revolution: The Emergence of Contemporary Spirituality, Pymble, NSW: HarperCollins.

TARLO, EMMA 2010a. Visibly Muslim: Fashion, Politics, Faith, Oxford/New York: Berg.

TARLO, EMMA 2010b. Hijab Online: The Fashioning of Cyber Islamic Commerce. In: P. Morey & A. Yaqin (eds.) Muslims in the Frame. Special Issue of Interventions: International Journal of Postcolonial Studies, 12 (2). London: Routledge, 209–225.

TARLO, EMMA & ANNELIES MOORS (eds.) 2007 (June/September). Muslim Fashions. Special Double Issue of Fashion Theory: The Journal of Dress, Body & Culture, 11 (2/3), London: Berg.

TAYLOR, JENNIFER MAYTORENA 2009. New Muslim Cool [Film], United States.

TENBRUCK, FRIEDRICH H. 1965. Moderne Jugend als soziale Gruppe. In: L. v. Friedeburg (ed.) Jugend in der modernen Gesellschaft. Köln: Kiepenheuer & Witsch.

THE GERMAN TIMES 10/2010. Pop-Islam, made in Germany, by Karin Schädler. Available at: http://www.german-times.com/index.php?option= com_content&task=view&id=36833&Itemid=179 [accessed 05/07/2011].

THE GUARDIAN 20/01/2011. Lady Warsi Claims Islamophobia is Now Socially Acceptable in Britain, by David Batty. Available at: http://www.guardian.co.uk/uk/2011/jan/20/lady-warsi-islamophobia-muslims-prejudice [accessed 06/09/2011].

THE GUARDIAN 21/05/2009. Muslim fashion: "Anyone can wear these clothes". Video coverage on Elenany fashion, by Riazat Butt and Hildegunn Soldal. Available at: http://www.guardian.co.uk/lifeandstyle/video/2009/may /21/muslim-fashion-elenany [accessed 05/07/2011].

THE INDEPENDENT 31/03/2010. The Big Question: Are Efforts to Tackle Home-Grown Muslim Extremism Backfiring?, by Jerome Taylor. Available at: http://www.independent.co.uk/news/uk/home-news/the-big-question-are-efforts-to-tackle-homegrown-muslim-extremism-backfiring-1931455.html [accessed 06/09/2011].

THE REVIVAL 08/04/2008. Single, Muslim and Pregnant, by Alveena Salim. Available at: http://www.therevival.co.uk/single-muslim-and-pregnant [accessed 05/07/2011].

THE TIMES 30/01/2009. Muslim population "rising 10 times faster than rest of society", by Richard Kerbaj. Available at: http://www.timesonline.co.uk/tol/news/uk/article5621482.ece [accessed 06/09/2011].

THERBORN, GÖRAN 1995. Routes to/through Modernity. In: M. Featherstone (ed.) Global Modernities. London: Sage, 124–139.

THERBORN, GÖRAN 2004. Between Sex and Power: Family in the World, 1900–2000, Abingdon: Routledge.

THERBORN, GÖRAN 2011. The World: A Beginner's Guide, Cambridge: Polity.

TIESLER, NINA CLARA 2006. Muslime in Europa: Religion und Identitätspolitiken unter veränderten gesellschaftlichen Verhältnissen, Berlin: Lit Verlag.

TIETZE, NIKOLA 2001. Islamische Identitäten: Formen muslimischer Religiosität junger Männer in Deutschland und Frankreich, Hamburg: Hamburger Edition.

TIME MAGAZINE 06/11/2005. How much more French can I be?, by Médine. Available at: http://www.time.com/time/magazine/article/0,9171,1126720,00.html [accessed 27/08/2011].

TIME MAGAZINE 12/02/2010. Why France's National Identity Debate Backfired, by Bruce Crumley. Available at: http://www.time.com/time/world/article/0,8599,1963945,00.html [accessed 06/09/2011].

TIMMERMAN, CHRISTIANE, JOHAN LEMAN, HANNELORE ROOS & BARBARA SEGAERT (eds.) 2009. In-Between Spaces: Christian and Muslim Minorities in Transition in Europe and in the Middle East, Brussels: Peter Lang.

UFUQ 28/10/2008. Muslim-Shirts: Mit Botschaft und gutem Gewissen. Available at: http://www.ufuq.de/newsblog/243-muslim-shirts-mit-botschaft-und-gutem-gewissen [accessed 05/07/2011].

UFUQ 2011 (February). Jugendkultur, Religion und Demokratie. Politische Bildung mit jungen Muslimen (Newsletter no. 19). Available at: http://www.bpb.de/files/GS8C07.pdf [accessed 01/03/2011].

UNESCO 2005. International Flows of Selected Cultural Goods and Services, 1994–2003: Defining and Capturing the Flows of Global Cultural Trade, Montreal: UNESCO Institute for Statistics.

VERTOVEC, STEVEN 1998. Young Muslims in Keighley, West Yorkshire: Cultural Identity, Context and "Community". In: S. Vertovec & A. Rogers (eds.) Muslim European Youth: Reproducing Ethnicity, Religion, Culture. Aldershot: Ashgate, 87–102.

VERTOVEC, STEVEN & ALISDAIR ROGERS (eds.) 1998. Muslim European Youth: Reproducing Ethnicity, Religion, Culture, Aldershot: Ashgate.

WARRAQ, IBN 2003. Leaving Islam: Apostates Speak Out, Amherst, NY: Prometheus Books.

WATZLAWICK, PAUL (ed.) 1984. The Invented Reality: How Do We Know What We Believe We Know? Contributions to Constructivism, London: Norton.

WEBER, MAX 1990 [1922]. Wirtschaft und Gesellschaft. Grundriß der verstehenden Soziologie, besorgt von Johannes Winckelmann, Tübingen: Mohr.

WELT AM SONNTAG 29/08/2010. Streetwear für Allah, by Katharina Bons. Available at: http://www.welt.de/die-welt/regionales/koeln/article9263908/Streetwear-fuer-Allah.html [accessed 05/07/2011].

WENSIERSKI, HANS-JÜRGEN VON 2007. Die islamisch-selektive Modernisierung – Zur Struktur der Jugendphase junger Muslime in Deutschland. In: H.-J. v. Wensierski & C. Lübcke (eds.) Junge Muslime in Deutschland. Lebenslagen, Aufwachsprozesse und Jugendkulturen. Opladen: Barbara Budrich, 55–82.

WENSIERSKI, HANS-JÜRGEN VON & CLAUDIA LÜBCKE (eds.) 2007. Junge Muslime in Deutschland. Lebenslagen, Aufwachsprozesse und Jugendkulturen, Opladen: Barbara Budrich.

WERBNER, PNINA 1997. Introduction: The Dialectics of Cultural Hybridity. In: P. Werbner & T. Modood (eds.) Debating Cultural Hybridity: Multi-Cultural Identities and the Politics of Anti-Racism. London: Zed, 1–26.

WERBNER, PNINA 2002. Imagined Diasporas Among Manchester Muslims: The Public Performance of Pakistani Transnational Identity Politics, Abingdon: James Currey.

WERBNER, PNINA & TARIQ MODOOD (eds.) 1997. Debating Cultural Hybridity: Multi-Cultural Identities and the Politics of Anti-Racism, London: Zed.

WERNET, ANDREAS 2009. Einführung in die Interpretationstechnik der Objektiven Hermeneutik, Wiesbaden: VS.

WHYTE, WILLIAM FOOTE 1943. Street Corner Society: The Social Structure of an Italian Slum, Chicago, IL: University of Chicago Press.

WINTER, BRONWYN 2008. Hijab and the Republic: Uncovering the French Headscarf Debate, Syracuse, NY: Syracuse University Press.

WISE, MACGREGOR J. 2008. Cultural Globalization: A User's Guide, Carlton: Blackwell.

WISSENSCHAFTSRAT (GERMAN COUNCIL OF SCIENCE AND HUMANITIES) 2010. Recommendations on the Advancement of Theologies and Sciences concerned with Religions at German Universities. Available at: http://www.wissenschaftsrat.de/download/archiv/9678-10_engl.pdf [accessed 06/09/2011].

WITZEL, ANDREAS 1985. Das problemzentrierte Interview. In: G. Jüttermann (ed.) Qualitative Forschung in der Psychologie. Grundfragen, Verfahrensweisen, Anwendungsfelder. Weinheim: Beltz, 227–256.

WITZEL, ANDREAS 2000 (January). The Problem-Centered Interview [26 paragraphs]. Forum: Qualitative Social Research [Online], 1 (1), Article 22. Available at: http://www.qualitative-research.net/index.php/fqs/article/view/1132/2522 [accessed 15/04/2001].

WOHLRAB-SAHR, MONIKA 1999. Konversion zum Islam in Deutschland und den USA, Frankfurt a.m./New York: Campus.

WOODHEAD, LINDA 2010. Epilogue. In: S. Collins-Mayo & P. Dandelion (eds.) Religion and Youth. Farnham: Ashgate, 239–241.

YAQIN, AMINA 2010. Inside the Harem, Outside the Nation: Framing Muslims in Radio Journalism. In: P. Morey & A. Yaqin (eds.) Muslims in the Frame. Special Issue of Interventions: International Journal of Postcolonial Studies, 12 (2). London: Routledge, 226–238.

YOUNG, ROBERT J. C. 1995. Colonial Desire: Hybridity in Theory, Culture and Race, London: Routledge.

ZAMAN, SAMINAZ 2008. From Imam to Cyber-Mufti: Consuming Identity in Muslim America. The Muslim World, 98 (4), 465–474.

ZENTRUM FÜR TÜRKEISTUDIEN 2009. Türkischstämmige Migranten in Nordrhein-Westfalen und Deutschland: Lebenssituation und Integrationsstand. Available at: http://www.mgffi.nrw.de/presse/pressemitteilungen/pm2009/pm090817a/Bericht_NRW_2008_end.pdf [accessed 24/06/2010].

ZICK, ANDREAS, BEATE KÜPPER & ANDREAS HÖVERMANN 2011. Intolerance, Prejudice and Discrimination: A European Report (on behalf of the Friedrich-Ebert-Stiftung). Available at: http://www.fes.de/cgi-bin/gbv.cgi?id=07908&ty=pdf [accessed 30/08/2011].

ZWILLING, ANNE-LAURE 2010. France. In: J. S. Nielsen, S. Akgönül, A. Alibašić, H. Goddard, B. Maréchal & C. Moe (eds.) Yearbook of Muslims in Europe 2. Leiden: Brill, 183–201.

WEBSITES

A PART ÇA TOUT VA BIEN: http://www.apartcatoutvabien.com [accessed 05/07/2011], http://comediemuslim.apartcatoutvabien.com [accessed 30/07/2013].

AEROSOL ARABIC: http://www.aerosolarabic.com/v2/index.php [accessed 05/07/2011].

AHIIDA: http://www.ahiida.com [accessed 05/07/2011].

AMMAR114: http://www.ammar114.de [accessed 01/10/2008].

BUNDESVERFASSUNGSGERICHT: http://www.bverfg.de/entscheidungen/rs 20030924_2bvr143602.html [accessed 27/10/2010].

COMUNI-T: http://www.comuni-t.com/shop/index.php [accessed 05/07/2011].

DAWAH WEAR: http://www.dawahwear.com [accessed 27/08/2010].

DEUTSCHE ISLAM KONFERENZ: http://www.deutsche-islam-konferenz.de [accessed 06/09/2011].

ELENANY FASHION: http://elenany.co.uk, http://elenany.co.uk/page/model [accessed 05/07/2011].

EMEL – The Muslim Lifestyle Magazine: http://www.emel.com [accessed 05/07/2011].

FANPOP: http://www.fanpop.com/clubs/superman/images/546265/title/super man-clark-kent-fanart.

GAZELLE MEDIA: http://www.gazellemedia.co.uk [accessed 05/07/2011].

HIJAB STYLE BLOG – The UK's first style guide for Muslim women: http://www.hijabstyle.co.uk [accessed 05/07/2011].

ISLAM EXPO 2008: http://www.islamexpo.com/attractions.php?id=1&art=18 [accessed 05/07/2011].

ISLAM SCHOOL WELKOUM: http://www.islamschoolwelkoum.com [accessed 05/07/2011].

LE SAVOIR EST UNE ARME: http://www.le-savoir-est-une-arme.com [accessed 05/07/2011].

LE SILENCE DES MOSQUÉES: http://www.myspace.com/silencedes mosquees, http://www.silencedesmosquees.com [accessed 27/08/2010].

MUSLIM CAFÉ: http://www.muslimcafe.tv [accessed 14/09/2008], http://www. gazellemedia.co.uk/projects/view/muslimcafe-tv [accessed 05/07/2011].

MUSLIME WORDPRESS: http://muslime.wordpress.com/2007/12/26/zeig-mir-deinen-style-styleislamcom [accessed 07/04/2008].

MUSLIM HIP-HOP: http://www.muslimhiphop.com/index.php?p=What_is_MH H/Music_in_Islam [accessed 05/07/2011].

MUSLIM SHIRT: http://www.muslim-shirt.de [accessed 09/12/2008].

MUSLIM YOUTH HELPLINE: http://www.myh.org.uk [accessed 05/07/2011].

MUSLIMISCHE JUGEND IN DEUTSCHLAND: http://www.mjd-net.de [accessed 25/03/2009].

MUSLIMYOUTHNET: http://www.muslimyouth.net, http://www.muslimyouth. net/campaigns [accessed 05/07/2011].

MUXLIM – Enhancing the Muslim Lifestyle: http://muxlim.com [accessed 05/07/2011].

ORIENTAL COMIC: http://www.orientalcomic.fr [accessed 05/07/2011].

PEARLS OF ISLAM: http://www.myspace.com/pearlsofislam [accessed 01/03/2010].

POETIC PILGRIMAGE: http://www.myspace.com/poeticpilgrimage [accessed 27/08/2010], http://www.euterpemedia.de/Poetic-Pilgrimage-Freedom-Times [accessed 30/07/2013].

PROUD TO BE A BRITISH MUSLIM CAMPAIGN: http://www.islamispeace. org.uk/itmc.php?id_top=24 [accessed 05/07/2011].

RÉALITÉ ANONYME: http://www.myspace.com/realiteanonyme, http://realite-anonyme-13.skyrock.com [accessed 27/08/2010].

SADAKA CHARITY FESTIVAL: http://www.sadaka-benefiz.de/index.php?pid =programm [accessed 01/03/2010].

SAMIA ET LES 40 COMIQUES, http://www.samiaetles40comiques.com [accessed 05/07/2011].

SAPHIRNEWS – quotidien musulman d'actualité: http://www.saphirnews.com [accessed 05/07/2011].

SAYFOUDIN114: http://www.sayfoudin114.de [accessed 05/07/2011].

STYLEISLAM: http://styleislam.com, http://blog.styleislam.com/styleislam-in-medina [accessed 05/07/2011].

TAWHEED IS UNITY: http://www.tawheedisunity.com, http://www.myspace. com/tawheedisunity [accessed 05/07/2011].

THE BRITISH PRIME MINISTER'S OFFICE: http://www.number10.gov.uk/ news/pms-speech-at-munich-security-conference [accessed 30/08/2011].

UFUQ.DE – Jugendkultur, Medien & politische Bildung in der Einwanderungs-gesellschaft: http://www.ufuq.de [accessed 02/10/2008].

ÜNICITÉ: http://www.unicitewear.com [accessed 30/03/2009].

URBAN UMMAH: http://www.urbanummah.com [accessed 05/07/2011].

WAYMO JUGENDPLATTFORM: http://waymo.de, http://waymo.de/rules [accessed 05/07/2011].

WEBSITE SONG "[FÜNF:32]": http://www.fuenf32.de [accessed 27/08/2010].

ZAYNAB: http://www.zaynab-styliste.com [accessed 05/07/2011].